D1562212

A Philosophical Disease

Reflective Bioethics

Series Editors:

Hilde Lindemann Nelson and James Lindemann Nelson

Bioethics,
Culture
and Identity

A Philosophical
Disease

Carl Elliott

Routledge
New York
London

Published in 1999 by
Routledge
29 West 35th Street
New York, NY 10001

Published in Great Britain by
Routledge
11 New Fetter Lane
London EC4P 4EE

Copyright © 1999 by Routledge
Text design by Debora Hilu

Printed in the United States of America on acid-free paper.

All rights reserved. No part of this book may be reprinted or reproduced or utilized
in any form or by any electronic, mechanical, or other means, now known or here-
after invented, including photocopying and recording or in any information storage
or retrieval system, without permission in writing from the publishers.

Library of Congress Cataloging-in-Publication Data

Elliott, Carl.
    A philosophical disease : bioethics, culture and identity / by Carl Elliott.
        p.   cm.
    ISBN 0-415-91939-8. — ISBN 0-415-91940-1 (pbk.)
    1. Medical ethics—Philosophy.   2. Psychiatric ethics—Philosophy.
3. Wittgenstein, Ludwig, 1889–1951. I. Title.
R725.5.E44   1999
174'.2—DC21   98-7053
                                                                  CIP

For Ina, Crawford and Martha

The philosopher is the man who must cure himself of many sicknesses of the understanding before he can arrive at the notion of the sound understanding.

If in the midst of life we are in death, so in sanity we are surrounded by madness.

——Ludwig Wittgenstein

CONTENTS

ACKNOWLEDGMENTS

This is not a book about Wittgenstein, but many of its central ideas come from Wittgenstein's later work. My interest in Wittgenstein began in 1989, when I was a Fellow at the Center for Clinical Medical Ethics at the University of Chicago. During that year I took part in a seminar taught by Stephen Toulmin, who had been a student of Wittgenstein's at Cambridge in the 1940s, and whose influential book with Allan Janik, *Wittgenstein's Vienna*, I read in Chicago for the first time. At the time I was sharing an apartment with my brother Britt, who knew quite a bit more about Wittgenstein than I did and who pointed me toward the work of his former teacher at Furman University, James Edwards, particularly Jim's extraordinary interpretation of Wittgenstein's ethics, *Ethics Without Philosophy: Wittgenstein and the Moral Life*. A postdoctoral fellowship the next year at the University of Otago's Bioethics Research Center in New Zealand allowed me to develop my interest in Wittgenstein and bioethics further while working with Grant Gillett, who was extremely generous with his time and his ideas. Those who are familiar with the work of Stephen, Jim and Grant will realize the extent to which I am indebted to each of them.

Much of this book was developed in conversation with my brothers Hal and Britt—Britt on Wittgenstein and cultural identity, and Hal on psychiatry and medical practice.

Jim and Hilde Lindemann Nelson, the Reflective Bioethics series editors for Routledge, have been extraordinarily supportive for many years in ways too many to number here. I am grateful to Hilde for her quick, helpful comments on the manuscript as my final deadline was approaching. Tod Chambers and John Lantos also graciously agreed to read and comment on several chapters of the manuscript at the last minute. Robert Crouch deserves special thanks for his able research assistance at McGill from 1994 to 1996, especially for directing me to important work on Deaf culture.

Thanks to Robin Downie, for helping me to cultivate my growing interest in fiction with the Literature and Medicine Group at Glasgow University; to Kathryn Hunter, for allowing me to sit in on her narrative seminar at Northwestern University in 1989 to 1990; to Solomon Benatar, for hosting me in September, 1992, at the University of Cape Town; to the graduate students in my Bioethics at the Margins seminar at McGill University, for their enthusiastic discussion of Wittgenstein and Walker Percy; to Bob Hutcheon, Laura Arbour, Frank Carnevale and the staff of 9D at the Montreal Children's Hospital, for many hours of case discussions; to Louis Charland at McGill, for allowing me to read several of his works in progress on competence and emotion theory; to Ken DeVille at East Carolina University, for his helpful suggestions on authenticity and American culture; to John Heil at Davidson College, for lending me his copy of M.O'C. Drury's *The Danger of Words* when it was still out of print; to Jim Edwards, for allowing me to read the manuscript for *The Plain Sense of Things* before it went to press; to Erik Parens, for including me in the Hastings Center project he directed on enhancement technologies; to Alice Dreger, for sharing with me her work on intersexuality; to Charles Weijer, for his comments on an earlier version of Chapter 5; and to my fellow expatriate Trudo Lemmens, for many long talks at Thompson House about culture and identity.

Several chapters in this book include parts of essays that have been previously published. I am grateful to the following organizations for permission to reprint my work here: *Medical Humanities Review* for parts of "A Quest Without a Grail," *Medical Humanities Review* 11:2 (Fall 1997), pp. 108–111; the American Medical Association for "Caring About Risks: Are Severely Depressed Patients Competent to Consent to Research?" *Archives of General Psychiatry* 54 (1997), pp.

113–116; the BMJ Publishing Group for parts of "Doing Harm: Living Organ Donors, Clinical Research and The Tenth Man," *Journal of Medical Ethics* 21 (1995), pp. 91–96; the Johns Hopkins University Press for "Puppetmasters and Personality Disorders: Wittgenstein on Mechanism and Responsibility," *Philosophy, Psychiatry and Psychology* 1:2 (1994), pp. 91–100; Blackwell Publishers for parts of "Constraints and Heroes," *Bioethics* 6:1 (1992), pp. 1–11; the University of Chicago Press for parts of "On Psychiatry and Souls: Walker Percy and the Ontological Lapsometer," *Perspectives in Biology and Medicine* 35:2 (1992), pp. 236–248; and to Kluwer Academic Publishers for parts of "On Being Unprincipled," *Theoretical Medicine and Bioethics* 19:2 (1998), pp. 153–159 and "Hedgehogs and Hermaphrodites: Toward a More Anthropological Bioethics," Ronald Carson and Chester Burns, eds. *Philosophy of Medicine and Bioethics: A Twenty Year Retrospective and Critical Appraisal* (Dordrecht: Kluwer, Philosophy and Medicine 50), pp. 197–211. Parts of Chapters 2 and 8 appeared in *The Hastings Center Report* as, respectively, "Why Can't We Go On as Three?" *The Hastings Center Report* 28:3 (1998), pp. 14–17, and "Where Ethics Comes From and What to Do About It," *The Hastings Center Report* 22:4 (1992), pp. 28–35.

The book would not have been written without the financial help of a grant from Fonds pour la Formation de Chercheurs et l'Aide a la Recherche in Quebec, which supported my work from 1994 to 1997. I am also grateful for the support I received for this work from the institutions where various parts of it were written: the University of Natal Medical School in Durban, South Africa; the Bioethics Research Centre at the University of Otago in Dunedin, New Zealand; the Department of Medical Humanities at East Carolina University; the Biomedical Ethics Unit at McGill University; the Montreal Children's Hospital in Montreal; and my current academic home, the Center for Bioethics at the University of Minnesota. My thanks to Jeff Kahn for making the Center for Bioethics such a congenial place to work.

Introduction: Writing Morality

"You can't hear God speak to someone else, you can hear him only if you are being addressed."–That is a grammatical remark.
——Ludwig Wittgenstein

I

For me, the high point of Jean Jacques Rousseau's *Confessions* comes at the start of Book Three, when Rousseau gives an account of what he calls his "extravagant behavior." By extravagant behavior Rousseau means, apparently, that he is a flasher. Or as he rather poetically puts it, "I haunted dark alleys and lonely spots where I could expose myself to women from afar off in the condition in which I should have liked to be in their company." Rousseau goes on to tell of an encounter with a group of young girls in a courtyard to whom he had, in a state of nature, displayed himself, and then fled. Pursued and eventually caught by a large man with a mustache and a group of angry, broomstick-wielding women, Rousseau pleads that he is a mentally deranged stranger of noble birth who has run away from home to escape an abusive father. It is only then—in pity, one suspects, as much as in forgiveness—that the angry crowd agrees to let him go unpunished.

It is not the most flattering self-description, and this is exactly what makes the story so remarkable. Rousseau's intention in the *Confessions* was to give his readers as honest an account of himself as possible, "a portrait in every way true to nature" that revealed even his most humiliating and disgraceful behavior. "Let them groan at my depravities," says Rousseau, "and blush for my misdeeds." For however shameful those misdeeds happened to be, thought Rousseau, at least they were honestly recorded. *The Confessions* are not exactly philosophy, but they are a philosopher's attempt to come to grips with the tenuous connection between life and art, between events as they are lived and events as they are told. It is the unique way that Rousseau tries to bridge this gap between art and life that makes *The Confessions* so unsettling, and often so darkly comic. I doubt that many of us would be so willing to put our private flaws on such public display. But Rousseau also realizes that art has a life of its own, and that by recording his own life he will change the memory of it, perhaps even win sympathy for his more outrageous actions. This strategy also carries risks, of course, particularly for those of us who cannot hope to match Rousseau's literary gifts. We know that not all art is good art, and the danger of bad art is that it will distort or cheapen an experience that it is meant to make sense of and represent.

Art and life, observer and participant, detachment and involvement: these are the tensions that drive the work of the memoirist, the ethnographer, the psychiatrist, and, I want to argue, the bioethicist. How to write in a way that matches up to the reality of moral experience? How, even, to think about the moral life in a fashion that both represents it adequately and somehow makes sense of it? I do not think that this task sufficiently intimidates most of us who write about bioethics. For the most part we go about the job unself-consciously. But as Rousseau realized, we are often tempted to write about life in a way that is convenient for our purposes, rather than in a way that matches up to life in all its comedy and ugliness and disarray. The danger for bioethics, as for moral philosophy as a whole, is that of widening the gap between art and life still further, of inventing creatures who live only in the pages of philosophy textbooks and medical journals, and whose world bears little resemblance to the world that we actually inhabit.

"All human beings carry about a set of words," writes Richard Rorty, "which they employ to justify their actions, their beliefs, and their lives."[1] We use these words to denounce our enemies, honor those we admire, express our self-doubts, tell our stories. These words Rorty calls a "final vocabulary." They are final in the sense that if doubt is cast upon their worth, they cannot themselves be justified without resorting to circular argument. These words are as far as we can go with language, and so at this point justifications come to an end. As Wittgenstein puts it, "[i]f I have exhausted the justifications I have reached bedrock, and my spade is turned. Then I am inclined to say: 'This is simply what I do.'"[2]

For some years the vocabulary of bioethics has consisted of thin descriptors such as "autonomous," "harmful," and "just," as well as a thicker, more specialized vocabulary of words such as "personhood," "brain-dead" and "minimal risk." This moral vocabulary, cobbled together with the tools found in hospitals, courts and the academy, is not final in the ultimate sense that Rorty describes; most of us who have put this vocabulary to work have done so in a relatively circumscribed realm, alongside our own personal, overlapping but distinct moral vocabularies. But it has approached finality by giving us the basic language that we have used to express and frame our ethical problems in the medical domain, and which we have fallen back on when called upon to justify our decisions and our actions.

Critics have started to challenge this vocabulary, first in a quiet and respectful manner, then with a certain disgruntled pleasure. Like snipers hidden in the underbrush, critics have been firing away at the language of rights, the methods of law, the rhetoric of individualism, the worship of rationality, the ideology of patriarchy. The most congenial target has been the most visible one: the principles-based approach to bioethics that was introduced by Tom Beauchamp and James Childress in their book, *The Principles of Biomedical Ethics*, and which suggested four principles of autonomy, beneficence, nonmaleficence and justice as guides to decision-making in bioethics. But the attack on the principles-based approach to bioethics is symptomatic of a much deeper and broader worry about philosophy. This is a worry not simply about the principles of bioethics, but about philosophical *theorizing*—that is, about the usefulness of any type of systematic philosophical theory. For bioethics, this translates (for example) into a suspicion of statements such as that which Beauchamp and

Childress make in the first edition of their book, describing how a piece of conceptual work in ethics should look: "(J)udgments about what ought to be done in particular situations are justified by moral rules, which in turn are grounded in principles and ultimately in ethical theories."[3]

II

"A philosopher's treatment of a question is like the treatment of an illness," writes Wittgenstein in the *Philosophical Investigations*.[4] Wittgenstein saw the questions that trouble many philosophers as symptoms of philosophical confusion, which he likens to a kind of spiritual illness. The grammar and structure of our language tempt us to ask certain kinds of philosophical questions, or to ask them in certain ways (How do I know that other people really have minds? That the world exists? That I am really in pain?); and when we ask and try to answer these questions, we are led into confusion. We stumble around in the dark, blind and disoriented, because we do not have a clear view of our language. For Wittgenstein, philosophical problems have the form: I don't know my way around.

Wittgenstein often used images of sickness and therapy to describe philosophy. Part of his aim in using these images is to describe the confusion that results from trying to sort out philosophical problems, but the images also have another aspect to them. By comparing the activity of philosophy to the treatment of an illness, Wittgenstein is trying to convey the sense that many philosophical problems are in fact *false* problems—that if we were not led into confusion by our language and the conceptual pictures it suggests to us, these problems might not even arise.

Yet it is important to realize that for Wittgenstein, philosophical confusion is not something that afflicts only philosophers, or people who ask nonsensical questions that should not be asked. It can afflict *anyone*. We are all susceptible, because we are led to certain ways of thinking about philosophical questions by the structure of our language and of our form of life. Treating this confusion may be a matter of gaining a synoptic overview of the language, sorting out sense from nonsense.[5] But some problems run deeper than this. As Wittgenstein writes, "The sickness of a time is cured by an alteration in the mode of life of human beings, and it was possible for the sickness of philosophical problems to get cured only through a changed mode of thought and of life, not through a medicine invented by an individual."[6]

Wittgenstein is not arguing against *all* of philosophy, nor is he suggesting that all philosophical questions are symptoms of intellectual illness. He is directing his remarks against a particular conception of philosophy, the roots of which run very deep in the history of philosophy but which is identified most prominently with the modern tradition. This is the traditional conception of philosophy as "explanation," or as James Edwards puts it, of philosophy as "queen of the sciences."[7] According to the traditional conception, the aim of philosophy is to provide us with general explanations of the way things are, and ultimate justifications for our ethical and epistemological practices; as Wilfrid Sellars says, to "understand how things in the broadest sense of the term hang together in the broadest sense of the term."[8] Wittgenstein rejects this view of philosophy unequivocally. "We must do away with all explanation, and description alone must take its place."[9] Philosophical theory, including moral theory, must be done away with.[10] Philosophy cannot give a foundation for our use of language; it must leave everything as it is.[11]

What Wittgenstein is rejecting here is (among other things) the philosopher's appetite for generality. On the traditional conception, philosophers explain particular phenomena or facts by showing how they fit into more general theoretical constructions. As in science, the particular is explained by the general; the task of the philosopher is to construct larger, more general philosophical theories in order to explain what we think and experience in particular cases.[12] "Philosophers constantly see the method of science before their eyes, and are irresistibly tempted to ask and answer questions in the way science does. This tendency is the real source of metaphysics, and leads the philosopher into complete darkness."[13]

Wittgenstein saw his own later work as something very different from philosophy as traditionally conceived. "I am not interested in

constructing a building, so much as in having a perspicuous view of
the foundations of possible buildings."[14] Indeed, the *Philosophical
Investigations* are the very antithesis of philosophical system-building.
Composed in seemingly obscure aphorisms, obsessively attentive to
the particularities of language, filled with striking metaphors and fanciful thought experiments, always resistant to generalities, devoid of
philosophical theses: Wittgenstein sometimes spoke as if this were
not philosophy at all, but the heir to philosophy. His aim was not to
devise or refine a system of rules for using language properly or
improperly, but to investigate the way language is actually used.[15] Of
the tension between actual language and the "crystalline purity of
logic" Wittgenstein writes, "We have got onto slippery ice where there
is no friction and so in a certain sense the conditions are ideal, but
also, just because of that, we are unable to walk. We want to walk: so
we need *friction*. Back to the rough ground!"[16]

Wittgenstein did not hold out much optimism about the reception
his later work was likely to receive. "It is not impossible that it should
fall to the lot of this work, in its poverty and in the darkness of this
time, that it should bring light into one brain or another—but of
course, it is not likely."[17] That many philosophers would resist
Wittgenstein's work is not surprising; it is, in many ways, a profoundly destructive project, one which leaves those who take it seriously wondering what, if anything, is left for philosophers to do. To
eavesdrop on many conversations about the state of contemporary
philosophy is like listening to a group of disaster victims remember-
ing the calamity that made them homeless, still wondering where to
go next. The picture that comes to my mind is a ruined faculty
lounge, kudzu vines climbing through the windows, furniture stained
by mildew and swamp water. The philosophers who haven't dis-
persed have the dazed look of trauma victims, muttering about private languages as they wander through the wreckage. A few world-
weary survivors sit hunched over the bar like Humphrey Bogart, iron-
ically surveying the ruins over a half-empty bottle of Jack Daniels.
Some are thinking about appointments in the literature department.
One or two talk wistfully about the old days. Others want to rebuild
the lounge in the classical Greek style. Most would rather pour them-

selves another glass of whiskey and heckle the metaphysicians.

If, as Rorty himself puts it, the Platonic conception of philosophy has outlived its usefulness, some philosophical soul-searching is clearly in order. Perhaps we are right to be asking ourselves what we should be doing as we wander through the post-Enlightenment wreckage. Yet oddly, even the philosophers who ask themselves this question seldom come up with the answer: "practical philosophy." With the notable exception of Stephen Toulmin, even philosophers who take Wittgenstein seriously have resisted the notion that a proper job of postmodern philosophy is to deal with practical questions— such as the problems of medical practice.[18] Even philosophers such as Hilary Putnam and Richard Rorty, who see the pragmatism of James and Dewey as an antidote to Wittgenstein's worries, have little to say about practical philosophy. For the most part, philosophers seem to see the problems presented by medicine and biology either as boring diversions that are hardly free of the problems that cause conventional philosophers to despair, or as something altogether different from philosophy—perhaps better than philosophy, but more likely worse, and in any case a road that will lead them far away from what they have been trained as philosophers to do.

III

"As long as there has been such a subject as philosophy," writes Bernard Williams, "there have been people who have hated or despised it."[19] People who hate philosophy hate it because they think it is useless, and they think it is useless because they do not understand it. So thinks Williams, at any rate. I suspect otherwise. I think that many people who believe that philosophy is useless simply do not see the connection between doing philosophy and living a life. (And if they do see the connection, they may suspect that the effect of philosophy is not entirely healthy. After all, Rousseau was a flasher, Heidegger was a Nazi, Schlick was murdered by one of his own philosophy students.) People who hate philosophy usually argue that it is preoccupied with irrelevant subjects, and that even when everyone agrees that the subjects are pressing and important, philosophers write about these subjects in prose that is sterile, technical, and altogether detached from the world's richness and complexity.

If philosophical bioethics has managed to escape the first of these charges (it might even be seen as a response to it), it has not always escaped the second. Clinicians consistently argue that they cannot see how philosophy is clinically useful, largely because the manner in which philosophers write and speak about medicine is driven less by a concern for practical usefulness than by what is philosophically (not clinically) interesting. And they may be right. As a rule, philosophers are about as concerned with the usefulness of what they do as abstract mathematicians and performance artists, and this attitude can carry over to the way philosophers write about real-life problems. Yet if the occupational hazard of philosophy is uselessness, that of medicine is an unthinking pragmatism. When bioethics is driven solely by clinical concerns, usually those of the hospital, it runs the danger of getting stuck in a permanent feedback loop in which the same issues are discussed again and again: informed consent, termination of life-sustaining treatment, patient confidentiality, brain death, surrogate decision-making and, most recently, the concept of medical futility. Constrained by the demand for immediately useful answers, clinical ethics (at its worst, at any rate) comes dangerously close to being a purely technical enterprise carried out in isolation from any kind of deep reflection about the examined life, the way lives ought to be lived and the way they ought to end.

The problem may lie in the struggle between academe and professionalism, or perhaps between the speculative and the pragmatic, or even between art and life. Either way, it translates into a difficulty bioethics has in striking a balance between intellectual depth and practical utility. There is nothing especially interesting about a pair of suture scissors, but they are worth having in an emergency room; and there is nothing especially useful about metaphysics, although it is diverting to think about if you have drunk too much coffee. The dilemma for bioethics is how to steer a course between the two extremes—how to think both reflectively and usefully, in a way that pays sufficient attention to conceptual issues to be both thoughtful and intellectually mature, and that pays sufficient attention to practical issues to be more than just an intellectual diversion.

For all their differences, however, what both the clinic and philosophy classrooms share is an aspiration towards dispassionate objectivity. The rational deliberators in John Rawls's *Theory of Justice* and the population of white American males with cardiovascular disease in the *New England Journal of Medicine* may not have much in common, but they are all anonymous, stripped of what makes them distinct as human beings, and seen from a standpoint of impartial detachment. Whether it was inherited from medicine or philosophy or both, this standpoint of impersonal detachment has given rise to a certain way of thinking and writing about bioethical problems.

Take, for example, the following case study.

> A child is born prematurely and suffers anoxic brain damage. He is currently on a ventilator and if he survives he will always be profoundly mentally retarded. Should treatment be discontinued?

I want to describe this brief case study and the problem it presents as general, impersonal and factual. The case is *general* in that it is not about any particular child, say, a child named Jean-Pierre whose parents have just moved to Quebec from Haiti and who had been trying to have a child for six years; whose father repairs shoes at a small shop on Monkland Avenue and whose mother is devoutly Catholic. It is instead about any child in the relatively general circumstances it describes. The case is *impersonal* in its presentation: it places the reader not within the case but outside it as an objective, impartial observer. That is, it is not a case in which you, the reader, are involved, nor is it one in which I, the narrator, am involved, nor for that matter is it one in which any agent whatsoever is involved. Agency is completely absent from this case; we are not asked what we should do, or indeed what any agent should do, but rather what should happen— what event should occur. And finally, this is a case that emphasizes the *factual*. The relevant information is deemed to be the empirical, medical facts of the case, and by implication, how they will affect the child's quality of life.

Thin cases like this have come under a fair amount of criticism in bioethics, of course. One common thread that winds its way through this criticism, as well as through criticism of philosophy as a whole, is a suspicion of universality. By this I mean that many writers in philosophy (and many outside philosophy) have attacked the notion that philosophers can justify a set of ethical and epistemological practices that transcend the varied forms of life in which human practices and languages are embedded. Some philosophers may still dream of discovering a set of universal ethical standards that all rational human beings must accept as binding, but that dream is starting to look rather unlikely. This antifoundationalist critique has given rise to a well-known emphasis on ethical pluralism, but it has also brought about a renewed emphasis on describing and thinking about ethical problems in the light of locally contingent frameworks of understanding. "Like sailing, gardening, politics and poetry," says Clifford Geertz, "law and ethnography are crafts of place: they work by light of local knowledge."[20] If not quite as much a craft of place as gardening or law, ethics too must steer by local guideposts, at least to a far greater extent than many modern philosophers have acknowledged.

Now this renewed attention to the local contains a number of different strands. One that has become familiar in bioethics, if not always in philosophy as a whole, is the importance of moral particularity. It is only a fairly recent development, of course, that moral philosophers thought it their business to ask and answer questions about particular cases in ethics, rather than about general ideas, concepts, theories or rules. Even describing a particular case at all is a change from what one saw moral philosophers doing a few decades ago, and different from what one sees many doing now.[21] But particularity is important also for the case descriptions themselves. Many bioethicists are starting to take to heart the idea that we will never get straight about how to think about a given ethical problem until we get straight about the details of the case. Single-paragraph case descriptions are not enough, much less formulations such as *A* did *X* to *B*. Our moral intuitions start to kick in only when we know a lot more. We want to know medical details, diagnosis and prognosis; we want to know about the characters who are involved, their histories, their flaws and virtues, what their consciences are telling them; we want to know the dramas that have unfolded on the ward and at home. We want to know these things not simply because the most important thing about the case might turn out not to be the ethical issue at all, but something completely different; we want to know them because these details are important *morally*. If there is anything that practical ethics has taught us, it is that genuine moral experience is rich in detail, and it is often on these rich details that our minds are made up or changed. In the abstract it may be irrelevant to your point to know that the person you have been designating C is a scheming, duplicitous son-of-a-bitch who can't be trusted any further than he can be thrown; or that the real story behind a clinical scenario where A does X to B is that everyone on the ward is terrified of a lawsuit; but if you want to come to a genuine conclusion rather than to explore a conceptual point, these features make all the difference.

What sets clinical ethicists as a species apart from moral philosophers is this insistence on dealing with real cases, and not hypothetical ones. Part of this insistence comes from the (justifiable) suspicion that philosophers sometimes make up cases in order to persuade. Thomson's well-known thought experiment is a case in point, in which a famous violinist is kidnapped and strapped to a table in order to save the life of a stranger.[22] The case is largely meant to make a point about abortion—namely, that just as a woman cannot be justifiably strapped to a table for nine months for the sake of a stranger, so a woman cannot be forced to undergo an unwanted pregnancy for the sake of a fetus. Clearly Thomson's case is less a starting point for moral reflection than a sharp-edged tool for moral argument. Other philosophers use hypothetical cases as a kind of check for ethical theory: as a way of confirming whether the conclusions to which their theory has led them accord with common moral intuitions. (Even G.E. Moore, hardly a practical philosopher, claimed that casuistry is the goal of ethical investigation.) But in clinical ethics there are no kidnapped violinists, no fat men in caves, no South American villagers forcing you into moral dilemmas. Clinical ethicists disdain these kinds of hypothetical examples because they do not seem to advance one's thinking about real moral experience, which, pragmatists that they are, clinical ethicists take as the litmus test for the worth of an intellectual exercise.

Yet this is not the only reason for talking about real cases rather than philosopher's cases. If they are used exclusively, philosopher's cases teach us to look for certain things to the exclusion of others. They teach us to look for conceptual points and forget about practical details. They teach us to look for only one conceptual point, while real cases often contain many. Perhaps most crucially, they fail to teach us how to pick out the morally relevant details from a case. If the entire reason a case has been made up is to make a moral point—to show us why a woman has the right to control her own body—then the morally relevant details are already glaringly obvious. Picking them out is like shooting ducks on the water. Whereas the real work of bioethics, more often than not, is in listening, reading, and watching carefully in order to judge what is important and what is not.

But it is a mistake to think that in order to fulfill this role, cases must be true. They simply must be complex enough and sufficiently well told to match up to life. Novels, plays and films can be as good as or better than real cases, for the mere reason that novelists, playwrights and filmmakers are better at telling stories than philosophers, lawyers and doctors. The important distinction here is not between the true and the artificial, but between descriptions devised to demonstrate a principle and descriptions that demonstrate the richness and disarray of human life.

In bioethics the term "thick description," invented by Ryle and made famous by Clifford Geertz, often stands in for this point, that cases must be described in very rich detail in order for us to make sensible ethical decisions.[23] But what Ryle and Geertz had in mind was something a bit different and far more complicated; that is, the interpretive nature of describing human behavior and of reading such descriptions. For example, Ryle made the point, familiar now to all philosophers of action, that all actions are actions under a description. What is perfectly accurately described as "throwing a ball" can equally accurately be described, under a given set of circumstances, as "shooting a free throw" or "missing the backboard" or "making a fool of yourself." The context of the action makes all the difference.

Some actions are even more complicated still, because of their symbolic significance. As Ryle notes, there is a world of difference between a wink and an involuntary twitch of the eye. A twitch becomes a wink only by virtue of layers of code and understood meanings about what such a twitch means.

We often take these layers of understood meanings for granted. To see this point, consider (to take Ryle's example) not just a schoolboy winking, but a second schoolboy mocking the first one's wink; an exaggerated lifting of the eyebrow, eyelid closed and opened again in a long, drawn-out parody of a wink. Then imagine again that this imitation wink is misunderstood: that a third schoolboy mistakes the fake wink for a real one. Ryle's point is that what might simply be a twitch of the eye is transformed and retransformed again and again by virtue of these tacit, hidden yet commonly understood layers of meaning.

And naturally, it is only in the context of these elaborate and often hidden layers of meaning that we can truly get at what we need to get at morally. The difference between a wink and a twitch may make all the difference. These differences are not things that can be determined in the abstract, nor in general. They depend on local frameworks of understanding. Descriptions of an action as, say, "adulterous" depend on a background of locally contingent institutions such as marriage and on common understandings about the meaning of certain actions within the context of that institution. Thus how we (thickly) describe a case such as the one briefly outlined above will depend on a web of interlocking, locally contingent understandings about (for example) authority, kinship, healing, personhood and death.

IV

A certain way of writing about bioethics plays naturally into a certain way of thinking about it. The way of thinking that my written case plays into is that of an *observer.* An observer is not personally engaged in the case, has no stake in it herself, but rather watches the case from the outside and makes a judgment as a detached spectator.[24] This perspective comes naturally to the philosopher, and indeed to the judge, both of whom consider cases and make their judgments from a stand-point of impartiality. And of course, this detached, observational style of writing is typical of legal and philosophical literature. But detached observation is not, of course, the natural perspective of the doctor or the nurse, whose involvement with patients may be intensely personal. It seems slightly odd, then, that this impersonal style represents the dominant way of writing about ethics in the medical literature, which generally represents ethics cases in the *faux* objective, passive-voiced style of the medical case presentation (for example, "Baby X is a 27-week-old premature infant who was admitted to the NICU after suffering an anoxic insult during delivery to a 29-year-old G3 P2 mother"). This makes for an odd match between medical experience and reading about medical experience—a gap between the personal, even intimate, relationships between doctors, nurses and families as they gather around the bed of a dying child, and the detached, clinical prose in which that encounter is described.

But if medicine supplies the setting for this impersonal style, then law supplies the script. I am certainly not the first one to remark that the law is the *lingua franca* of bioethics. The language in which bioethics is discussed revolves around largely quasi-legal notions such as consent, competence, rights to refuse treatment, to have an abortion and so on. Many writers have targeted the language of rights and autonomy for special criticism, suggesting that we need to develop an alternative vocabulary. This is an understandable suggestion, but I also think that the law's influence on bioethics has been much deeper and more subtle. It has given us a picture of morality as somehow like the law in *structure*—for example, as a set of rules that govern interactions between strangers. This picture of morality may work adequately as long as we are in fact talking about interactions between strangers, especially between strangers whose relationship is adversarial. But it overlooks many kinds of questions that are crucial to morality, and it distorts many others. "What shall it profit a man if he gains the whole world but loses his own soul?" asks Jesus in the Gospel of Matthew. Like questions of honor or integrity, this is a quintessentially moral question, one that is crucial to the actions of doctors and nurses in the clinic, but it is a question that the law cannot even begin to address.

Nor do legal concepts always fit ethical problems comfortably. The quasi-legal question "What rights does an institution have to regulate the sexual behavior of an adult?" may sound like a reasonable way of introducing an ethical issue if the institution in question is a psychiatric hospital and the point at issue is its responsibilities in regard to sexually active, mentally ill patients. But it would sound rather awkward if the institution in question were a family and the question concerned a 17-year-old daughter and her boyfriend. Legal language rings false here at least partly because relationships within families are not impersonal, and family members do not ordinarily think of one another from a perspective of impartial detachment.[25] Indeed, for Tolstoy, as Stephen Toulmin points out, authentically *moral* relations exist only between intimates.[26] Tolstoy had deep reservations about the possibility of living a moral life in the modern city, where life consists largely of encounters between strangers. Interactions between strangers did not count as moral for Tolstoy; for him, the scope of morality extended only to one's family, friends and neighbors, the persons with whom one lived, worked and associated. Thus in *Anna Karenina*, when moral pressures become too much for her to stand, Anna boards a train and leaves the world of intimates for the world of strangers. Tolstoy's view of morality exaggerates the importance of intimacy but, as Toulmin points out, its exaggerations provide a striking counterpoint to the view implicit in the way we have become accustomed to writing and talking in bioethics, where relationships between strangers are in some ways the paradigm for our moral language.

The impersonality of conventional bioethics writing also emerges in its (implicit) view of moral agency. In medical case histories, for instance, agency is often hidden by the passive voice. Patients are brought to the hospital, an ultrasound is performed, a cholecystectomy is carried out—all without any mention of the agent behind the actions. So when a case history such as the one above concludes with an ethical question, it is no surprise that it is phrased, "Should treatment be discontinued?" This is a curiously disembodied picture of moral action—or rather, not so much a picture of moral action as a picture that contains no actions, only events. But a picture of morality that contains only events is, in some sense, not a picture of morality at all, because actions, not events, carry moral import. We cannot judge the morality of hurricanes or unexpected wins at the lottery because they are not actions; no agent brings them about. Actions are things that people do and for which they are (sometimes) morally responsible.

Asking agentless moral questions alters the issues at stake in several ways. It ignores the question of who ought to be performing the action, which will naturally affect how we answer it. We may well give a different answer to the question "Should the child's doctor stop treatment?" than we would to the question "Should the parents authorize stopping treatment?", especially if we knew that the parents and the doctor disagreed about what to do. Perhaps even more perniciously, agentless ethical questions distort in subtle ways the manner in which we think about the issue in question. Ethical questions ordinarily present themselves as questions about what you ought to do, or about what someone else ought to do—but not about which event would be best. And these two things may be very different. Merely because I think a child with profound neurological damage might be better off dead does not mean I think it would be ethically acceptable to kill her.

In his early "Lecture on Ethics," Wittgenstein struggles to put into words what he means by the term "ethics."[27] He begins by saying that it is the inquiry into what is good or what is valuable, a fairly conventional definition, but then he goes on to say that by ethics he also means the inquiry into the meaning of life, or into the right way of living, or into what makes life worth living. For Wittgenstein, ethics was not merely a question of good or bad conduct, or even good or bad character; it was an inquiry into the sense of life. And this, for Wittgenstein, was a matter of incomparable importance. Later in the lecture he puts it this way: "I can only express my feeling by the metaphor, that, if a man could write a book on ethics which was really a book on ethics, this book would, with an explosion, destroy all the other books in the world."[28]

Wittgenstein's striking metaphor gestures at something important. Wittgenstein is not simply making the familiar point that ethical imperatives carry an authority that overrides other considerations.

For the early Wittgenstein, ethics was something *beyond words*. To speak about ethical matters was to try to say what cannot be said. Wittgenstein was struggling towards understanding (within the rigid confines of his early metaphysics) the relationship between ethics and those considerations that are sometimes called transcendent or spiritual. He was trying to connect ethics with questions about meaning and ultimate ends, and about the struggle to make sense of life.

Bioethics generally, if implicitly, assumes its subject matter to be questions of conduct and (sometimes) character, or even more narrowly, questions about the obligations human beings have toward one another. It does not conventionally consider questions about the sense or meaning of life, and it considers only in very awkward constructions (such as "quality of life") those questions about what makes life worth living. These are ultimate questions about the framework against which our judgments of value get their sense, but they are for the most part absent, or at least hidden, in mainstream bioethics. In the case study I related earlier, the question that is asked concerns the conditions under which it would be acceptable for doctors or parents to stop treating a neurologically damaged child. The relevant information for such a decision is the medical condition of the child, primarily the quality of life that could be expected for the child in light of his neurological damage. But on the view of ethics that Wittgenstein tries to express, the issue becomes broader, and also much deeper. The question of what to do is tied to the transcendent in that it is tied to questions about what counts as a meaningful life. Is a profoundly neurologically damaged but pain-free life meaningful? What counts as a meaningful life? If such a life is not meaningful, what efforts should parents make to preserve it?

Evaluations like these—a variety of what Charles Taylor would call "strong evaluations"—are made against a background understanding about the sense of life and how lives are situated in the world.[29] In North America we often simply assume a certain background understanding of such things, which is why we can talk about, for example, "quality of life" with at least a minimal amount of coherence. But it is important to realize that the way in which questions about meaning and purpose are answered will depend on understandings which may vary from one time and place to another. It is unclear whether we late-twentieth-century North Americans have an uncontroversial answer to the question "What counts as a meaningful life?" and so we may have no clear answer to the question of whether a human being who will never be capable of any higher thought or any relationship with another person can live a meaningful life. But this does not mean that these questions are equally unclear for all cultures and all times, or even that these are questions that it would occur to people of all cultures and times to ask.

Stanley Hauerwas has written that when he asks people how they would like to die, they inevitably give an answer such as "quickly and painlessly" or "in my sleep." But this kind of answer, Hauerwas points out, would have certainly struck a medieval European as irrational or even immoral. What the medieval European feared most was a sudden death that struck before one had the chance to make proper spiritual preparations. To die without preparation might mean spiritual damnation. The differences between our attitudes toward death and those of medieval Europe come about because of our dramatically different background understandings about the sense and purpose of life. We fear cancer, says Hauerwas, because it represents a lingering death; but would it have presented the same kind of threat to a medieval European? Hauerwas says: "The medieval person could look forward to dying in war, since there was time prior to battle to prepare for potential death. We prefer to die in unanticipated automobile accidents."[30]

Moral theologians debate how a reasonable moral conversation can take place if those who are conversing each use a vocabulary built on different metaphysical foundations: Orthodox Jews and Pentecostal Holiness fundamentalists, Muslims and Catholics, Jehovah's Witnesses and atheists. One solution is to use a largely secular vocabulary based loosely on ideals of tolerance and democratic liberalism. This may be the best that bioethics can do, but it is important to realize that what we gain by using such a vocabulary comes at a price. The price is that by talking exclusively in the language of secular liberalism, we may start to think that way as well; by agreeing that we cannot impose on others our assumptions about meaning and ultimate purposes, we run the risk of failing to think about them at all. The result, if we are not careful, is a moral vocabulary that is altogether flatter: more pragmatic but more mundane, functional but incapable of conveying a sense of deep significance.

IV

One way to make sense of a human life is to place it in a larger context. Richard Rorty suggests that we usually do this in one of two ways. One is to describe ourselves in relation to a nonhuman reality, such as the God and heaven of Christianity, or the Truth of philosophers and scientists. These kinds of descriptions exemplify a desire for objectivity. The other way is to situate our lives in relation to a community, either a historical community or an imagined one. Rorty says that these kinds of stories exemplify a desire for solidarity. Insofar as a person seeks solidarity, she does not ask how her community or its practices stand in relation to anything outside that community. Insofar as she seeks objectivity, she distances herself from other human beings, in that her standing in relation to them will matter less to her than her standing in relation to a reality that can be described apart from its connection to any particular human beings.[31]

One way to think about the aims of this book would be to ask what happens to human beings—their self-conceptions, their connections to other human beings, their relationship to the institutions of health care—when they move from the search for objectivity to the search for solidarity. Another way would be to ask how we can think philosophically about morality and medicine while striving to protect ourselves against the sicknesses that Wittgenstein warned against. I want to think about how the institutions of medical life, including clinical ethics, work in the absence of commonly agreed-upon ends. I am interested in the way conceptions of disability and difference can vary from one culture and historical period to the next, how those conceptions connect one person to another, and how they influence a person's conception of herself. I want to think about how the mechanistic assumptions of biomedicine influence the way we think about human agency, the self, and what Wittgenstein calls "an attitude towards a soul." And I want to explore how to think sensibly and clearly about bioethics in the absence of ethical theory. Is it possible to think philosophically about the sense of life, and how it is situated in relation to other lives and to the institutions of medicine, once we have given up on ultimate explanations?

In *Contingency, Irony and Solidarity*, Rorty makes a distinction between metaphysicians and ironists. An ironist, says Rorty, is a person who has deep reservations and doubts about his own final vocabulary, having been impressed by other vocabularies, yet who realizes that arguments phrased in his own vocabulary can neither sanction nor do away with these doubts. An ironist does not believe that the words he uses are any closer to reality than others, nor does he see the search for new words as an effort to get closer to reality. New words are simply new words, no more, no less. Ironists have given up trying to formulate criteria for choosing between vocabularies, and this puts them in the precarious position of never being able to take themselves quite seriously. As Rorty says, ironists are always "aware that the terms in which they describe themselves are subject to change, always aware of the contingency and fragility of their final vocabularies, and thus of their selves."[32]

Metaphysicians, on the other hand, have not given up on criteria for choosing between vocabularies. For the metaphysician, the choice between vocabularies depends on which vocabulary brings us closer to reality, or truth, or rationality, or human nature, or God. Because the metaphysician believes that we have much of the correct vocabulary already, he believes our major philosophical task to be defining these words, refining the intuitions that give these words their context and forming the whole into a philosophical system. The watchword of the metaphysician is common sense. Common sense allows the metaphysician to use his own vocabulary unself-consciously and without irony, and it tells him his vocabulary is sufficient to describe the lives and actions of those who use other final vocabularies.

Bioethics, it seems to me, is snared somewhere between irony and metaphysics, between the unself-conscious use of a vocabulary we have inherited and the realization that it is only one possible vocabulary among many, and perhaps even inadequate to its task. Some metaphysicians cling to bioethical principles as a way of transcending different, local vocabularies. Raanan Gillon writes that the principles-based approach to bioethics, which he endorses, "claims that whatever your personal philosophy, politics, religion, moral theory or life stance, you will find no difficulty in committing yourself to four *prima facie* moral principles plus a concern for their scope of application."[33] Other metaphysicians, such as Danner Clouser and Bernard Gert, are not principlists but remain devout theoreticians. They denounce the principles-based approach for being insufficiently systematic: specifically, "the 'principles' as dealt with by principlism are not systematically related to each other by any underlying unified theory." [34] What most metaphysicians share is a concentration on the thinner, more flexible words in our moral vocabulary, such as "autonomous," "just" and "principle." The thinner the word, the more contexts in which it can be used, the larger the number of people who will use it, and the more useful it will be.[35]

An ironist would point out that in actual practice, it is often the thicker, more specialized terms that do most of the work—terms like "clinical equipoise," "best interests" and "competent," which take their meanings from the local, particular language games in which they are rooted. An ironist would defend the use of this vocabulary not on the grounds that people from all cultures, political systems and theological stances could agree to use it in similar ways, but on the grounds that it works for us, here and now, in this situation. More likely than not, an ironist would be suspicious of efforts to construct overarching metavocabularies that transcend these thick, locally contingent vocabularies.

My sympathies lie more with the ironists than with the metaphysicians, but I don't think that irony and solidarity are enough. As Wittgenstein once remarked to his friend M.O'C. Drury, "I am not a religious man but I cannot help but see everything from a religious point of view." Which is to say that while not all human lives are religious lives, all human lives are situated within broader structures of meaning within which they can be said to have (or lack) sense or purpose.[36] These structures tell us when, as a result of having lived in a certain way or having carried out certain actions, we are better or lesser beings. These frameworks cannot be reduced to community and the search for solidarity, nor can they necessarily be seen as any sort of objective reality. They are given to us (we do not choose them) by the form of life in which we find ourselves. The difficulty for us is to articulate those structures, and to diagnose our particular predicament, in the absence of any universal solutions.

Chapter 1

Notes of a Philosophical Scut Monkey: The Bureaucracy of Medical Ethics

We don't drive the trucks, we only load them.
——Nick Pavona, M.D., *The Scut Monkey's Handbook*

I

I come from a family of doctors and South Carolinians. My father has been practicing family medicine in Clover, South Carolina, for close to forty years. My great-great-uncle Ernest Walker, also a South Carolinian, graduated from the Medical College of Bellevue Hospital at the turn of the century, trained as a surgeon and spent several decades ministering to the sinners of New York City before rejoining the saved back in Rock Hill. My father graduated from the Medical University of South Carolina in 1956; I graduated in '87; my brother Hal in '89. South Carolina is a God-fearing part of the country, and in our family that meant the Presbyterian Church, the game of basketball and the practice of medicine, in roughly that order. My brothers and I grew up with the kind of reflected, small-town fame that comes from being the sons of doctors or ministers. Patients turned up on our doorstep at all

hours of the night. In the '60s my father drove a Corvair with a medical bag and a three-iron in the trunk, the medical bag for dealing with
patients and the three-iron for dealing with their dogs.

At some point, though, medicine in our family started to change.
The first sign of trouble came when I started medical school in 1983.
To say I didn't take to it would be an understatement. The Medical
University of South Carolina seemed to me like a cross between military training and a correctional institution, except that the military
would have been less hierarchical, and in a correctional institution
the teaching would have been better. The president of the university
was an ex-dentist who had served in Ronald Reagan's cabinet, and
this set the tone for the university's intellectual and political life:
white, wealthy, Republican, anti-intellectual, deeply impressed with
the hazing model of medical education, and even more impressed
with the pursuit of happiness through third-party payment.

The next warning sign came from my father. After twenty-five
years of solo family practice, he started moonlighting at a walk-in
medical center a few towns over. The reason was money. Our county
was growing, and more doctors were setting up practice, but at one
point my father found himself the only one who would see patients
on Medicaid. The others would see only patients who were insured
or could pay cash. The well-off patients started to gravitate toward the
for-profit walk-in clinics, which were open on weekends and
evenings, and the poorer patients, out of necessity more than anything else, gravitated toward my father. My brothers and I admired
him for it, but admiration doesn't pay the bills, and so he started to
work two days a week at the doc-in-the-box, where one day's salary
exceeded a week's income at his own practice. I don't think it was as
bad as he had expected. The hours were long, but the patients were
wealthier and better-educated, and if they didn't have health insurance or a credit card, a very efficient office manager would politely
send them away. Sometimes, in fact, she would send them to my
father's own office.

Things got worse for us in 1985 when my brother Hal started medical school, and disliked it, if this is possible, even more than I did. He
refused to call the professors "teachers," saying this would imply an

incorrect impression of what they did, and instead called them "disseminators and withholders of information." This caused more than a little tension when we went home, because my father had loved medical school. When we were children he had entertained us with stories of medical fraternities, eccentric professors, and irreverent student hijinks. No hijinks for us. We muttered profanity under our breath and called the American Medical Association "the Great Satan."

I had started doing clinical rotations on the wards, which meant learning how to do scut work. Scut, as any medical student quickly realizes, is all-consuming and all-important, transcending grades, the pursuit of knowledge, the care of patients. Much of it is simply an introduction to the mechanical skills necessary to the practice of medicine, such as drawing blood, starting IV lines, performing a routine history and physical exam, inserting a nasogastric tube, writing progress notes in the patient's chart. But at least as much scut work is necessary only because of the fragmented, specialized and bureaucratic nature of hospital medicine: chasing down lab values, asking patients to sign informed consent forms, finding the radiologist to see what she thought of a chest X ray, tracking down old medical charts from patients' previous hospital visits, finding out what kind of insurance (if any) they have. Scut is best learned at county and VA hospitals, where patients are used to a lot worse than being poked and stuck by inexperienced and unsupervised medical students. The common element of all scut work is that it is necessary, even vital, to the care of patients, but involves no real power, no serious thought, and no genuine decision-making. Scut work is how clinical clerks justify their existence on the wards. But I hated scut, and so my existence became a problem.

Towards the end of my third year of medical school, I told my parents that I was thinking of not registering for the residency match, and that I was planning to go to graduate school in philosophy instead. Fallen Catholics must go through a similar experience when they leave the church. My choice did seem to make things a little easier for Hal two years later when he told our parents he was planning to go into psychiatry. Compared to my decision, what might have been cause for serious worry became an occasion for relief.

My father's practice continued to change. For the first time in his life he was sued for malpractice. He was accused of missing a fracture on an x-ray, by a patient he had seen only once at the walk-in clinic. My father won the suit—the so-called "fracture" he had missed turned out to be a nonpathological anomaly the patient had had for his entire life, bilaterally—but the case took over a year to resolve. Shortly thereafter he was reported to the Drug Enforcement Agency by a pharmacist for allegedly overprescribing Percocet, a controlled pain-reliever. He was not the only one so investigated. The DEA had revoked several other local doctors' licenses to prescribe controlled substances for similar reasons, which made the investigation of my father all the more intimidating. Like the malpractice suit, the investigation eventually came to nothing. The DEA dropped the investigation before it even started when they discovered that my father was prescribing the pain medication for an AIDS patient in the last stages of his illness.

My father doesn't seem at all bitter about any of these experiences. If I ever ask him whether he regrets going into medicine, he just shakes his head and says, Well, I don't know what else I would have done.

II

Do we still need doctors? The question that John Lantos asks in his book of the same name is not as strange as it looks.[1] His question is not whether we still get sick, or whether we need health care, but whether we really need that care to be provided by doctors. Hospital medicine is already conducted by teams of specialized professionals, most of whom are not doctors: nurses, nutritionists, speech pathologists, occupational therapists, social workers, clinical psychologists, physical therapists, pastoral counsellors, music therapists and respiratory therapists. Outside the hospital, patients get their health care from psychoanalysts, homeopaths, personal fitness trainers, chiropractors, naturopaths, acupuncturists, aromatherapists and massage therapists (to name only a few practitioners on what could be a very long list). Even allopathic medicine itself is becoming increasingly fragmented and narrow, at least in the United States. It has become the domain of specialists and subspecialists, many of whom (such as pathologists and radiologists) rarely see a living patient, and even more of whom (such as neonatologists and anesthesiologists) spend most of their time mastering the skills necessary to operate complicated machinery. A world without doctors might not be such a strange place, or at least any stranger than the strange world we live in now, because the kind of practice undertaken by so many of today's doctors is so different from what used to be known as doctoring that we may as well call it by a different name.

So-called "traditional" doctors like my father are already pretty hard to find. Objective, scientific medicine has rendered the special, personal bond between doctor and patient far less important than it might have been in the past. Solo practitioners have been largely absorbed into group medical practices, which treat doctors as interchangeable one for the other. Rigid, evidence-based practice standards are enforced by the threat of malpractice litigation. The machinery of capitalism has given us doctors who advertise their services in magazines, newspapers and on roadside billboards. Cosmetic surgeons troll for patients on the Internet. Doctors must answer to the directors of large, for-profit health delivery organizations, and to their bottom lines. All this has meant that the so-called "traditional" doctor—defined as a solo, fee-for-service, generalist practitioner who is skilled not just at curing illness but at caring for people, who is familiar with families for generations, and who is answerable to no one but his patients and his colleagues—is about as close to extinction as the snail darter.

What would a world without doctors be like? Lantos says it would simply be a world where a certain set of roles, duties and privileges that we have come to associate with doctors are done away with or conceptualized differently. Health care need not be provided by doctors, and just as the figure of the doctor is not the same as it was fifty years ago, in the future it need not be the same as it is now. As Lantos puts it, "Imagining such a world of health care without doctors should be no more of a challenge than imagining a world in which we have shoes but no cobblers, trains but no engineers, farms but no farmers, or drive-through banks with nothing but automatic teller machines. Something is lost but something is gained."[2]

The standard history of bioethics, as written by bioethicists, is that the field developed in response to ethical problems created by new technological developments, such as intensive care units and organ transplantation, and is now responding to new developments in institutional structures, such as managed care. What Lantos sees more clearly than most is that new institutional structures or new medical technologies are not the whole story here, or even the most important one. The ethical issues facing doctors and patients are the result of an ethos, a *Weltanschauung*, a vast, relentlessly progressive, political and economic machine. The task at hand is not akin to solving a puzzle. It is closer to comprehending a cosmology, in which the endless debates of today's bioethicists will eventually come to seem as arcane as the debates of medieval theologians. Doctors and patients seem to be caught in the grip of forces that, like a patient in endless psychoanalysis, they only half-understand. The new medicine, says Lantos, "is a profession driven by science, technology, reductionist ethics and entitlement economics," a profession that is both "rigorously scientific and dogmatically close-minded."[3] It has created a medical creature that no longer much resembles the doctor of myth and popular fantasy, but which carries the same name. It is a creature as technically skilled as any doctor has ever been, but unwilling to consider questions about its larger purpose and moral significance. Lantos calls medicine "an inexorably progressive enterprise without direction, a quest without a grail."[4]

How has American medicine come to such a pass? For writers like Alasdair MacIntyre and Stanley Hauerwas, the root of the problem lies in the notions of practice and authority.[5] Hauerwas and MacIntyre argue that all rational practices require some kind of authority, by which they mean authority about what it is to perform a practice well and (consequently) what the proper ends of a practice are. A practice can't flourish unless we recognize some figure of authority as possessing judgment better than ours, even if we disagree with that judgment. But the practice of medicine has no such authority anymore, or at least any commonly agreed-upon authority. This is because we have no common agreement about the ends of medicine, which in turn is the result of our having no common agreement about the ends and significance of human life.

The contemporary doctor and the contemporary patient approach one another as strangers. As MacIntyre notes, when strangers encounter one another, they ordinarily do so with the hesitation and wariness proper to encounters with strangers, because they do not quite know what to expect of the encounter.[6] The remedy for encounters with strangers is to supply some sort of bureaucratic structure to insure that one's expectations will be met. Contemporary American medicine is organized according to such bureaucratic structures, and the contemporary American doctor is becoming a reluctant bureaucrat.

The bureaucratic structures of medicine are necessary to enforce the customs and constraints that govern it in the absence of any commonly agreed authority. Like any bureaucracy, medicine needs rules to govern how the system will operate, interpreters to explain the rules, and clerks to manage day-to-day life within those rules. In a medical world characterized by a studied indifference to deeper moral questions, what is needed are moral rules, with a set of clerks and interpreters to negotiate the kinds of questions that medicine has been unwilling or unable to consider. Hence clinical ethicists, the scut monkeys of the medical bureaucracy.

Many doctors will bristle at this conclusion, and probably a few clinical ethicists as well. I suspect most doctors do not realize quite how bureaucratic the medical encounter can be until they are patients themselves. But it is evident to anyone who has visited a hospital emergency room, which is no less bureaucratic than a visit to the Department of Motor Vehicles or an interrogation by an officer of the Immigration and Naturalization Service.

As Alasdair MacIntyre pointed out almost twenty years ago, the medical encounter has many of the critical marks of a bureaucratic encounter (all of which, incidentally, predate the arrival of managed care). For example, it is an encounter mediated by the machinery and rituals of a bureaucracy: forms, applications, written records, secretaries, receptionists, waiting rooms, and so on. The patient does not see the doctor without having to pass through these mediating devices. (The same can also be said of the patient's encounter with the clinical ethicist.) Many right-minded doctors and ethicists have pointed out how alienating this can be for the patient, but what they often fail to realize is how the machinery of bureaucracy heightens the sense of powerlessness and dependency the patient feels. Because it is one of the characteristics of a bureaucracy that the bureaucrat feels at home in the bureaucracy, while the client of the bureaucracy feels lost.

The bureaucratic medical encounter reinforces this sense of powerlessness and dependency in many different ways. Who the patient is becomes first and foremost what the medical record *says* she is, for example, in the same way that the applicant for citizenship or a bank loan becomes what her records and application forms say she is. Patients are expected to wait in line to see the doctor, in the same way that they wait in line to take their driving license examination or to apply for unemployment benefits. The wait tells them that the bureaucrat's time is valuable while theirs is not (or at best, that it is less valuable than the bureaucrat's). And as with encounters with bureaucrats who, by virtue of their position, mediate access to information and services that the client needs, patients are expected to behave in certain ways commensurate with their dependency on the doctor-bureaucrat's superior skills and knowledge. If they do not behave correctly, they are labelled noncompliant.

Finally, and perhaps most critically, medicine is bureaucratic in its impersonality. It is impersonal in that what is important in the relationship is the role that is played and not the individual who is playing it. What is important about my visit to a gastroenterologist is not the *individual* who is my gastroenterologist but the fact that he *is* a gastroenterologist. If he is not available, another gastroenterologist can replace him. If another gastroenterologist replaces him, he can learn what is necessary for my care from my records. The crucial thing for a client or customer who encounters a bureaucracy is not the individual she encounters but the fact that the individual possesses a certain kind of authority, whether it is the authority of the surgeon, the agent of the Internal Revenue Service, or the technician staffing the help line at Microsoft.

If American doctors see medicine as a bureaucracy, they generally see it as something new, the result of managed care and corporate medicine. And to be fair, some areas of medicine have been more successful at resisting bureaucratization than others. If the most bureaucratic encounter is the urban hospital emergency room or the walk-in clinic, perhaps the least bureaucratic is the encounter with a psychiatrist, with whom a personal relationship is often critical for successful treatment, and many of whom have avoided the trappings of bureaucracy, such as group practices and long waiting periods before appointments. Even medical specialists in many small towns have remained insulated from the bureaucracy and impersonality that characterizes virtually every teaching hospital and academic health center. Yet many of these same doctors are becoming frustrated by the bureaucratic changes brought on by managed care, and all the more so because they see the changes as having occurred without their consent and almost without their knowledge. What has changed recently is not the bureaucratization of medicine, however. What has changed is that doctors are no longer in charge. They are becoming functionaries in the bureaucracy, mere middle-management figures, while they still aspire to be (and continue to think of themselves) as the men on top.

It isn't hard to see why the encounter between doctor and patient is so often a disappointment for patients. They want to be treated as individuals, and well-intentioned doctors often do their best, but the fundamentally bureaucratic structures of medicine make even the most well-intentioned efforts seem artificial, like a personalized form letter. This disappointment is complicated still further by the fact that, like most bureaucracies, medicine is governed by internal practices and informal rules that discourage the admission of mistakes to those outside the bureaucracy. So medicine discourages strict truthfulness to patients about medical mistakes. (The reason is often said to be the fear of a malpractice suit, and to some degree this is true, but medical culture discourages truthfulness about errors even when no such risk exists, because it also discourages doctors from admitting their errors to their colleagues.) The result is a pose of infallibility that no one could possibly live up to. The disappointment of

patients is all the more acute because the backdrop to the bureaucracy of medicine is an idealized, personal, truthful, doctor-patient relationship, which contemporary medicine inevitably fails to meet.

The answer to these problems, of course, is supposed to be medical ethics. But medical ethicists are really just bit players in a much
larger drama, scut boys in the vast medical-bureaucratic system. For
Hauerwas, the problems of the bureaucracy of medicine stem from a
larger problem with liberalism. The problem with liberalism is that it
protects privacy rather than practices. Practices contain (ideally)
some conception of an end, or a goal, and consequently some idea of
virtue—what it means to do a practice well, in proper alignment to a
proper goal. Protection of privacy, on the other hand, the liberal ideal,
simply leaves the matter of "ends" to individuals. This leaves us with
individually defined practices, or practices whose ends are up for
grabs, and consequently no common agreement on what it is to perform that practice well, except in cases when the ends are agreed
upon.

In the case of medicine, we only have agreement on what it means
to do the practice well when we have agreement on the ends of medicine; and the only commonly agreed-upon ends of medical practice
are the cure of illness and the prolongation of human life. (Hauerwas,
in fact, includes only the second of these.) This leaves medicine with
a few problems. First, it is left with the question of how to rank a plurality of ends. If we have no common agreement on what the ends of
medicine are, only a variety of ends which are contested by individual practitioners and individual patients, then we have the problem
of how to rank those ends, especially when confronted with patients
where the dilemma is which end to pursue: curing illness, prolong-
ing life, relieving pain, preventing addiction, preserving the life of a
fetus, reversing infertility, improving physical appearance, producing
psychic well-being and so on.

Second, medicine is left in a vacuum when it comes to patients
whose lives cannot be prolonged or whose illnesses cannot be cured,
such as people who are disabled or who are in chronic pain. The result,
at least for some doctors, is a sensation of futility and aimlessness. More
and more illnesses can be cured, yet as Lantos points out, "the net

amount of disease and suffering does not seem to decrease. The more people who are alive at any time, the more people who are dying."[7]

Ideally, for Hauerwas, the state would protect practices with agreed-upon ends, virtues and authorities. But what we have instead is a liberal state that is dedicated to the protection of individuals to pursue their own ends, under their own authority, with their own self-defined virtues. So what is really a debate about the proper ends of medicine is turned into a debate over patient autonomy: Whose life is it anyway? Whose ends count? Any authority that is granted a doctor over a patient is based not on the doctor's moral authority within a given practice but instead on his technical expertise, which is ultimately a hollow justification for any real authority.

So medical care, which might have been (and sometimes still is) an exemplar of the kind of practice that Hauerwas admires, is instead reduced to yet another bureaucracy in the liberal state. And medical ethicists are the practice's maintenance engineers, medicine's moralizing scut monkeys, who outline and argue for certain limitations on medical practice. For Hauerwas, this is a poor substitute for what medical practice could be. As he puts it, "Accordingly, we have been turned into a community called medical ethicists, who now threaten to destroy what we are allowed to observe because our theories are not rich enough for us to understand why we should care for those we cannot cure."[8]

III

It is sometimes said that clinical ethics is a response to the moral problems created by the new institutional structures of medicine. The irony of this formulation, if it is true, is that as clinical ethics has developed as a field, it has increasingly become a part of the bureaucratic structures whose problems it was intended to correct. Clinical ethicists have hospital offices and secretaries, carry pagers, respond to consultation requests, write notes on medical charts, staff ethics committees and Institutional Review Boards. It is now commonplace for clinical ethicists to refer to themselves as professionals, and this is understandable. Clinical ethicists want—need, in fact—to be health care insiders, for otherwise they would not have access to the kinds of confidences, privileges and information necessary to do their job well. Yet by embracing and joining the medical bureaucracy, clinical ethicists court the problems of a bureaucracy, including its moral problems.

Consider an increasingly common situation. Let's say that you are a clinical ethicist working for a university ethics center, and you get a telephone call from a hospital administrator in another state or province. He wants an ethics consultation from you. It concerns a child in a persistent vegetative state, a family who insists that she be treated aggressively and a medical team who wants treatment stopped. The hospital does not have a clinical ethicist, nor does it have an ethics committee. The hospital offers to fly you in for a day, give you whatever support you need, arrange interviews with family members and give you access to all medical records. They want an honest opinion, and say they will abide by your recommendation. They offer you a $3,000 consultation fee.

Is there anything morally objectionable about this? Many people working in bioethics—perhaps most of them—would say no. Doctors and administrators often find themselves genuinely puzzled by situations like this and sincerely want advice. Clinical ethicists have the training and expertise to help them navigate their way through these dilemmas. The fee? Fee-for-service medicine is well established in this country. Academics accept honoraria for lectures, including lectures on bioethics. Attorneys are paid well for their opinions, and expert witnesses are paid to testify in court. Why should ethics consultation be any different? It would be inconsistent (perhaps even unfair to underpaid ethicists) to ban fee-for-service ethics consultation.

When I have asked colleagues whom I respect about such a case, very few express any concerns. The concerns they do express relate to administrative matters, such as the ability of an outside consultant to gather all the necessary information for an adequate consultation in such a short time, or the size of the fee. Some wonder about what the hospital expects in return. Do they want clarification of issues or a recommendation for action? If the latter, does anything ride on the content of the recommendation—money, future consults, political goodwill? Most people will concede the potential for bias, even if they do not consider this a serious problem. But as long there is a clear understanding of what is being agreed to, and the consultant is free to offer an honest and uncoerced recommendation, most see no reason to worry.

But the question of what is expected of an ethics consultant is a critical one, even for consultants who do not work on a fee-for-service basis. What is the purpose of an ethics consultation? It sounds like an easy question, but the answer is far from clear. Is the purpose to help solve moral problems? To resolve conflicts? To help health care workers behave more ethically? To improve the care of patients? To educate health care workers? To clarify moral issues? To clarify them for whom? Doctors? Other health care workers? Hospital administrators? Patients? How do you tell if the goal has been met? What if the goals conflict? If the ends of medicine are contested, as MacIntyre and Hauerwas suggest, all the more so for the ends of ethics consultation.

Every year or so I go to a conference at the University of Chicago's Maclean Center for Clinical Medical Ethics, where I once spent a year as a Fellow. At most of these conferences I will hear several presentations by former Fellows who have set up clinical ethics consultation services at their own hospitals. They enthusiastically present statistics indicating the number of consultations they have done over the past year, which often number in the hundreds and are growing year to year. The question nobody in the audience ever asks is whether more consultations is a good thing or not. The clinical ethicist inevitably presents the data as if it indicates that she is doing a good job, because she is being consulted more and more often. More consultation requests indicate success. But it is equally arguable that the consultant who is consulted more and more often must be doing a bad job, even if health care workers asking for the consultations find them helpful, because otherwise why would those people calling for consultations need help? If a doctor is pleased with an ethics consultation and asks for another one the next time she encounters a similar dilemma, then it could well be argued that this indicates an abject failure. Why shouldn't the goal of ethics consultation be to get doctors to make their own moral decisions? Should the goal of ethics consultation be to get doctors to share their moral agency with someone else?

The cynical answer is that clinical ethicists have a professional interest in not working themselves out of jobs. But this makes it sound as if ethicists are creating problems where before there were none. The truth is that the moral problems clinical ethicists deal with are sometimes genuine, that the help they give is often genuinely useful and that their advice is often sought after and valued by conscientious health care workers. Like psychotherapists, clinical ethicists are responding to the needs of people who are troubled. Yet also like psychotherapists, clinical ethicists appropriate just a little of a person's sovereignty over herself by agreeing to take for themselves a small portion of the person's moral agency.

And they do it for a price, of course. In some cases this may be a salary, but some ethicists work on fee-for-service arrangements. Is anything morally worrying about an ethics consultant profiting financially and professionally from the act of advising others about their moral problems? Those who see bioethics as a profession like medicine or the law may see no problem with financial compensation. But professional ethicists (if the adjective does in fact apply) must face the problems that other professionals face, such as conflict of interest, and then some additional ones. For example, in a fee-for-service arrangement, who picks and pays for the ethicist? If the dispute has arisen between a hospital and a patient's family, the appearance of impartiality (still less the reality of it) becomes pretty hard to maintain when the hospital has chosen the ethicist, flown him in, paid for his lodging and then sent him away with a hefty fee. How would we reassure a family that the consultation was impartial if the consultant—chosen and paid for by the hospital—has recommended against what they sincerely believe is morally right?

At issue here is both the money and the choice of ethicist. If the ethicist is profiting in some way from the consultation, the possibility arises that profit will influence the outcome of the consultation—

perhaps even unconsciously, not unlike the way that, as pharmaceutical companies have found, gifts to doctors influence their prescribing patterns. But there is also the issue of who chooses the ethicist and why. Bioethics thrives on controversy and there is generally no shortage of ethicists who will support any number of moral stances on a complex issue. Surely shrewd administrators will do their homework and choose ethicists they can bet will support the position they prefer. Perhaps, then, to be fair, families should be permitted (or encouraged) to choose and hire their own ethicists. But is this really a healthy development for medicine: each side in an ethical dispute hiring its own moral litigator?

In some ways, of course, there is little new here. Many hospitals, medical schools and even some managed care organizations have ethics consultants on staff who are either paid directly by the organization itself or through some kind of other indirect financial arrangement, such as annual contributions to an ethics center. Yet this should not put us entirely at ease. I am not sure that these more conventional arrangements are as innocent as they seem. Even if an ethicist's fee (or salary) is not directly contingent on a particular consultation, subtler long-term pressures come into play, such as political inclusion in hospital affairs, or academic advancement, or, more directly, the willingness of a hospital to continue to contribute to the salary of an ethicist who is consistently critical of its policies.

Which brings up a second, more elusive concern. Is moral advice something that should be bought and sold? By this I mean something apart from the question of where the money comes from, but rather the question of whether a price should be put on the consultation at all. Does the attachment of money to moral counsel change the nature of the act? If it does, then is this a change with which we should be comfortable?

The idea that some monetary exchanges should not be permitted is nothing new, of course. We do not permit the sale of votes, children or Nobel prizes. We block some exchanges because they would violate standards of justice, such as buying your way into political office or out of the military draft, but some we block because we feel the exchange of money would alter the meaning of the good that is being exchanged. Buying sex and having sex are not the same thing, for example; and for a man to offer a woman money for sex is (unless she is in the business) often regarded as an insult. Likewise, Europeans laugh at rich Americans who try to buy aristocratic titles. To think noble birth is something that can be bought betrays a misunderstanding of the nature of European aristocracy.

Does the exchange of money alter the nature of an ethics consultation? I am inclined to answer yes. At the very least, it changes it from the kind of advice one might seek from a wise, trusted friend in other circumstances, to a service of the sort offered within the structures of a bureaucracy. At most it turns moral counsel into a commodity that can be bought, sold, priced, marked down, haggled over or withheld if the price isn't right. Which is not to say that such exchanges should be blocked, of course. But it does suggest that clinical ethics should stop for a moment and consider how these kinds of exchanges will eventually shape the nature of the field.

Shortly before he died in 1997, Benjamin Freedman, a philosopher and clinical ethicist at McGill University, published a paper titled "Where Are the Heroes of Bioethics?"[9] The point of that paper was to ask why, when bioethics offers so many opportunities to stand up against injustice and cruelty, is it so rare to hear of a bioethicist who has suffered some kind of professional setback for having done the right thing? Other professions have their heroes, but in his entire career working in bioethics, wrote Freedman, he had never heard of a bioethicist who had, for example, lost her job as a result of having taken a principled stand. This fact might be understandable in fields that offer little opportunity for heroism—as Freedman said, firefighters have more chances at heroism than shoe salesmen—but it seems remarkable for clinical ethics. Clinical ethicists are routinely placed in situations where actions they feel are morally wrong are being taken, and where protesting those actions could damage their careers in different ways. One would think that professional setbacks would be commonplace. If they are as rare as Freedman thought, what does this say about the field? It has become a cliché to point out that ethicists don't necessarily behave more ethically than other people, but what if we behave worse? It would be disturbing to conclude that ethicists are more self-serving, or greedier, or more narcissistic than other academics; and it would be especially disturbing to conclude that our special flaw is a kind of moral spinelessness.

Clinical ethicists are generally expected to give some kind of moral counsel to others. But we have not generally worried too much about the ways in which the institutional structures of bioethics can influence the kinds of moral judgments we make. It is a strange oversight. We pay plenty of attention to the way that the judgment of politicians and judges and police officers can be influenced by the ways in which they are paid, for example, or the settings in which they work; we even spend a lot of time thinking about the way doctors can be corrupted—by gifts from drug companies or involvement in for-profit research, or even by managed care organizations. But we don't pay much attention to the way that bioethicists can be corrupted or even unduly influenced. (Maybe this is because we think that bioethicists have no power anyway, and that may be right.) Yet all the while we work in settings where we are expected to render impartial moral judgments about the hospitals that pay our salaries; we sit on ethics committees and Institutional Review Boards (IRBs) with our administrative superiors; we do fee-for-service ethics consults for institutions that we have a financial interest in keeping happy; we seek out financial support from drug companies and other corporations whose practices we're expected to write about and comment on to the media; we find ourselves in moral conflicts with clinicians who will one day be evaluating our tenure applications. It would be remarkable if these situations *didn't* affect our moral judgment, but still we act as if our integrity is enough to protect us and that we are innocent of any undue influence.

Several years ago I was a member of two Institutional Review Boards, one at a children's hospital where I had a 40% time appointment, and the other at a psychiatric hospital where I had no affiliation whatsoever. Shortly after I joined the psychiatric hospital IRB the board started approving profitable protocols that I thought were clearly harmful to patients, and which were in fact prohibited by university guidelines. They were industry-sponsored clinical trials testing new antipsychotic and antidepressant medications, and they involved randomizing patients with acute schizophrenia and major depression to arms of the trial where they would receive no active medication, only placebo. Because I was not affiliated with the hospital, it was not risky for me to try to block these protocols from being carried out, even though many of them were being done by the chief of psychiatry, the chair of the IRB and other senior psychiatrists in the hospital. (This was not heroism, I hasten to say; I had nothing to lose. In fact it was motivated more by malice than by goodwill.) This would have been infinitely more difficult to do if it had happened at the children's hospital, not only because the chief of pediatrics there was my administrative superior, but because I would have been alienating people many of whom were, after all, my friends.

Both medicine and bioethics have responded to situations like this by relying on the integrity of their practitioners. But there is a problem with the idea of integrity. Integrity involves, among other things, the notion of being true to your own ideals or moral convictions, of not allowing coercion or temptation to lead you away from what you believe is right. It is a matter of being true to yourself. The problem is that you change; or rather, you are changed, by what you do, where you live, whom you associate with and so on. So your ideals and convictions change. And integrity then becomes a matter of being true to *those* convictions and ideals. The problem comes if you and your convictions are changed in the wrong ways; if you—as a result of what you do and where you work and whom you associate with and so on—become the kind of person who no longer perceives the moral world in the way you once did. The problem then is not betraying your ideals but being true to the wrong ones, and wrong ones that you can no longer even see as wrong. The world looks different to you now. And if this is the case, we have a somewhat different question, not a question of integrity, but a question that involves stepping back from the practices and institutional structures of bioethics and asking whether they are changing us in ways that we can be proud of.

IV

Like John Lantos, Bruce Charlton believes that medicine is in mortal danger, but he has a very different diagnosis of the illness.[10] In a brilliantly blunt polemic against everything from alternative medicine to medical commercialism to health promotion, Charlton warns doctors of the grave threat posed to medicine by postmodernism. We live between two worlds, he writes: that of modernity, which is centered around ideas of progress, of the rational pursuit of truth and overarching master visions of the world; and that of postmodernity, where rationality is revealed as subjectivity, where truth is constructed rather than discovered and where aesthetics have replaced objectivity. For postmodernism there is no purpose or progress, merely change; no argument, merely conversation. While the broader culture has embraced a glamorous, relativistic, ironic pose, medicine still clings to notions of progress, purpose and objectivity. And rightly so. Charlton sees medicine as an island of modernity in a sea of postmodernity, a fortress under siege by the postmodern onslaught. "The post-modernist trend poses a serious threat to medicine as we know it, portending an erosion of diagnostic and therapeutic objectivity, and dissolution of the profession itself."[11]

How would postmodern medicine look? Alternative therapies would abound. They would be marketed aggressively. Medicine would discard science as too narrow for the varieties of human pleasure. It would abandon rationality in favor of fashion and design. Health care would be negotiated between individuals. "You could select the doctor (or 'healer') with the ethical or spiritual outlook that suited you."[12] Professional ethics would dissolve into commercialism. Concepts of illness and health would blur together. Charlton writes, "Sickness is modern; health is postmodern! Negative sickness and positive health would become part of the same equation, so that anything that makes you feel good would be on a par with treatment for illness or disease."[13]

In fact, postmodern medicine would look something like American medicine, writes Charlton from across the Atlantic. And this, for him, is deeply worrying. The only solution is to retrench into medical professionalism. Chin up, steel yourself and resist the post-modern seductress. "It is a frighteningly easy matter to break down the accumulated morality and objective wisdom of medical practice," he writes.[14] And once the morality and objective wisdom that doctors have accumulated are gone, they could be recovered only very slowly and with a lot of pain. The course, advises Charlton, is clear: "We should reform, refortify and safeguard traditional standards of medical professionalism," preserving this one last outpost of modernity as a "port and haven in a post-modern storm."[15]

Medicine is in a fix, that's for sure, and perhaps American medicine is in a fix worse than most. But I doubt that the blame can be realistically placed on postmodernism. Charlton fires his gun so rapidly in so many directions and at so many different assailants that it is hard to know when he has hit one and when he has missed. It is tempting just to get out of the way. But when you are observing anyone who fires his gun with such fervor, it is a good idea to ask what he is afraid of. Writers who attack postmodernism are usually afraid of relativism or even nihilism; the fear is that if our practices cannot be given an ultimate and universal justification, then they cannot be justified at all. But I suspect that postmodernism and relativism have been attacked just a little too often. As MacIntyre has remarked, it is a sure sign that an idea has a grain of truth to it when it needs to be refuted again and again.[16]

It is a mistake to confuse a postmodern critique of the idea of scientific truth with an attack on medicine. Medicine is not a science. In fact, medicine is a perfect representative of the kind of pragmatism that many postmodernists embrace. Success in medicine is measured not by whether a proposition is true or false, but by what works: whether a given action helps a patient. Even in the so-called "scientific" area of medicine, clinical research, the gold standard is the randomized controlled trial, which compares one course of treatment to another or to a placebo. The question is not "How does this new treatment work?" but "Is this new treatment better than standard therapy?" For the most part, doctors are not scientists; they are pragmatists.

This confusion between what is true and what works is evident in an illustration Charlton picks to illustrate how postmodernism would endanger medicine. A "postmodern attitude" towards building a bridge or an airplane is inappropriate, says Charlton; "We would be well-advised to pick the most truthful engineering technique, rather than the trendiest or most profitable." But engineering techniques are not true or false (truth is a property of sentences) any more than medical techniques are. The measure here, for medicine as for engineering, is not what is true but what works. In fact, much medical treatment has become standard therapy without much idea at all *why* it works, only *that* it works.

In no area of medicine is the triumph of pragmatism more evident than in psychiatry, one of Charlton's own disciplines. In psychiatry you can find a stunningly varied array of theories, not just in the old debates between psychodynamic and biological theories, but in the philosophies of mind that motivate them. You would expect chaos, yet psychiatrists do their work quite well—spectacularly well, to judge by their progress in treating schizophrenia, bipolar disorder and depression over the past half-century. Why isn't there chaos? Because what counts in psychiatry is not so much whether a particular theory is true or false as whether it helps patients. Psychiatrists feel free to pick and choose bits and pieces from a variety of theories (and label themselves "eclectic").

Even if postmodernism were a threat to the notion of scientific truth (and I doubt that it is), it is hard to see how that threat would portend the dissolution of medical morality. Science is not a necessary part of professional morality. Science is not connected to the ministry, for example, and it was not even very closely connected to the medical profession until fairly recently. Nor is it clear how medical morality in itself can protect medicine from the dangers of the market, as Charlton suggests. U.S. medicine's professional organizations have been among the most powerful and consistent backers of fee-for-service medicine. The American Medical Association has opposed virtually every governmental effort this century to provide greater access to medical care, including Medicaid and Medicare.[17]

Charlton treats postmodernism as if it were a deranged and dangerous idea invented by French philosophers that is being smuggled across the channel to corrupt right-thinking doctors. But if a philosophical idea has any real power, it is because it responds to needs and pressures that people feel themselves. If doctors respond to the idea that medicine serves a plurality of goods rather than one single good, it is probably because they have seen that the good for each of their patients with a single illness is nevertheless not always the same. If they respond to the idea that concepts of illness are variable and blurred at the margins, it is probably because they have seen concepts of illness change over time, or because they have treated patients of different cultural heritages whose concepts of illness are very different from their own. If they respond to the idea that health care needs to be negotiated between individual doctors and patients, it is probably because they have found that their own notions of what is good for their patients do not always correspond to what their patients believe is good for themselves.

It would be heartening if philosophical ideas did have the kind of power that Charlton attributes to postmodernism. Then it might be possible to take clinical ethics more seriously as the solution to what ails American medicine. American bioethicists tend to cast the institutions and influence of bioethics as the primary engine of moral progress in medicine. I am more cynical, I suppose. In America we build shrines to technology in urban ghettos; we deify medical specialists; we sue them mercilessly when they fail us; we bewitch ourselves with magical instruments of diagnosis and therapy; we devise an ingeniously brutal and degrading way to train our doctors and charge them upwards of $100,000 for the privilege; we willfully ignore the poor, and pay our doctors the highest incomes of any doctors in the world—and then we try to correct the situation with an ethics consultation service and a few hours of humanities in the medical curriculum? The suggestion might be funny if it were not made with such sincerity.

Perhaps Hauerwas and MacIntyre are right. Perhaps the problem with American medicine is that its ends are unclear or contested. Yet I suspect that the real issue may not be a debate about what the ends of medicine are, but about what determines the direction of medicine in the absence of ends. This is not a question about where the truck is going, nor even about who is driving it. In a country where the mechanics of capitalism determine the direction and shape of life, the question is about who is paying the driver. In the absence of an agreed-upon destination, the trucks go mainly where the drivers are paid to go.

Chapter 2

You Are What You Are Afflicted By: Pathology, Authenticity and Identity

For the story of my life is always embedded in the stories of
those communities from which I derive my identity.
——Alasdair MacIntyre

Major Strasser: What is your nationality?
Rick: I'm a drunkard.

Casablanca

I

It is not uncommon these days for groups of human beings with a particular biological characteristic, often an illness or disability, to identify themselves as a culture or a community. In the same way that we hear of Jewish or Amish or African-American cultures and communities, we now hear about the AIDS community, the breast cancer community or the transgender community, or, say, about Deaf culture or gay culture. For biology to be connected with identity is nothing new, of course. It is at least partly a question of biology whether one is Afrikaner or Zulu, or for that matter, male or female. What seems to be new is the way the lines between identity and illness are being drawn. Some people insist that a particular biological characteristic is properly seen as pathology, while others insist that it is normal human variation. More crucially, many people contend that illness and disability (or alternately, what they insist is *not* illness or a disability) is essential to their sense of who they are. This makes the once-familiar lines between biology, identity and culture look rather tangled. "It has got to the point," writes Anthony Appiah, "that when you hear the word 'culture' you reach for your dictionary."[1]

What makes the border between pathology and ordinary human variation so difficult to distinguish is the way that the territory changes beneath our feet, often so slowly that at first we do not even notice it. Frequently, as Willard Gaylin points out, it is a new technology that changes the boundaries of illness.[2] Before various reproductive techniques such as artificial insemination were developed, infertility was simply a fact of nature; now that it can be treated, it is a medical problem. Before the invention of the lens, poor vision was simply a consequence of getting old. Now it is something to be treated by a medical specialist. And by virtue of knowledge, skill or, in some cases, mere happenstance, doctors have also come to treat a broad range of conditions that no one considers illnesses, that would more easily be called enhancements, but which no seems especially bothered by: minoxidil for baldness, estrogen for postmenopausal women, cosmetic surgery for people unhappy with their looks, acne treatment for self-conscious teenagers.

It is precisely when we move closer to aspects of identity that the line between pathology and normal variation becomes fuzziest—things like physical appearance, intelligence, sexual identity and personality. Psychiatry is a striking example. Before the development of psychotherapy, mental illness was limited to psychotic disorders; now it includes phobias, obsessions, compulsions, personality disorders and the like.[3] Today it is disarmingly easy to speak of any disagreeable personality trait as if it were an illness—and even some that are not so disagreeable. This is also true for genetic variation. We used to have a very rich vocabulary, albeit a somewhat backward one by today's standards, for all manner of genetic variation: one spoke of dwarves, lunatics, imbeciles, mongoloids—a vocabulary that has now been transformed into one of illness. A person with three copies of chromosome 21 is no longer a mongoloid; she has a genetic disease, Down syndrome. Whereas we used to think of her as a different type of human being, now we think of her as sick. And of course, we also slide easily in the other direction, from illness to identity. A person who is sexually attracted to others of his own sex is not considered mentally ill, as he once was. Homosexuality is simply part of a person's identity, a constituent of the way some people are.

What makes this an ethical issue is the question of whether a characteristic properly belongs to the medical domain. If it does, it will often be seen as something to be fixed. But if not, then the impulse to bring it to the attention of a doctor will scarcely arise.

II

Over the past ten years or so, bioethics has become increasingly preoccupied with what have come to be known as "enhancement technologies."[4] The term generally refers to the use of medical technologies not to cure or control illness and disability, but to enhance human capacities and characteristics. The debate first emerged with speculation that gene therapy might be used to alter a person's intelligence, personality or physical appearance, a prospect that some people found worrying. Thus the term "enhancement" was used to mark off the unacceptable uses of gene therapy from what was deemed to be their acceptable uses, which fall under the rubric of "treatment." Thus it was seen as morally acceptable to use gene therapy for, say, the treatment of adenosine deaminase deficiency, or cystic fibrosis, or other genetic illnesses, but unacceptable to use it for "cosmetic" purposes. The term "enhancement technology" now includes a much wider range of medications and interventions, such as the use of human growth hormones to boost height, the use of Prozac and other antidepressants for shyness, a compulsive personality or low self-esteem, the use of Ritalin to improve attention and concentration, cognitive enhancers to improve memory, cosmetic surgery to improve physical appearance, anabolic steroids to improve athletic performance and the use of beta-blockers for performance anxiety.

The term "enhancement technologies" suggests that the ethical issue at stake is self-improvement. And when bioethicists write about self-improvement, they generally concentrate on improvement and overlook the self. But perhaps this is a mistake. What is worrying about so-called "enhancement technologies" may not be the prospect of improvement but the more basic fact of altering oneself, of changing capacities and characteristics fundamental to one's identity.

I don't want to suggest that the distinction between treatment and enhancement is entirely misguided. It is a fluid distinction, but it gets at some important questions about justice. Does using steroids give an athlete an unfair competitive advantage? Should we strive towards giving everyone equal access to enhancement technologies just like conventional therapy, regardless of their ability to pay? Or should enhancements be regarded not as a right but as a luxury that people can buy as they wish and can afford? There are even more subtle pressures to worry about here. For example, does the use of enhancement technologies reinforce cultural pressures that we ought to be troubled by? Some people worry, for example, that cosmetic surgery reinforces a certain ideal of the female body type that women find oppressive. This is what Maggie Little calls "the ethics of complicity": the notion that by giving in to these pressures that you justifiably feel are oppressive, you are yourself reinforcing the very norms that produce them.[5]

But I also think these are relatively straightforward questions in comparison to the questions of identity, which seem to me much more profound. For example, it is certainly true that for a concert musician to use beta-blockers so that she can perform better is an enhancement. Her hands will shake less, her voice will not tremble, she won't sweat as much and so on. And this may give her advantages over other musicians. But this doesn't really seem to present a profound ethical problem to me. Much deeper questions seem to be at issue when we talk about changing a person's identity, the very core of what that person is. Making him smarter, giving him a different personality or even giving him a new face—these things cut much closer to the bone. And they cut close to the bone regardless of whether they are enhancements or cures, or even altering someone for the worse. They mean, in some sense, transforming him into a new person.

In his book *Listening to Prozac*, Peter Kramer worries about using Prozac for patients who do not meet clinical criteria for depression.[6] One of those worries is that, at least in some cases, Prozac seems to change some of his patients in rather dramatic ways. Shy people become more outgoing, uptight ones become more easy-going, people with poor self-esteem become more self-confident. What might have seemed to be an aspect of a patient's personality seems changeable with a drug. This is a disturbing possibility, or at least it seems so for some observers. If Prozac really does alter a person's personality in important ways, the notion of being a "new person" on Prozac would take on a more literal truth.

For example, Kramer writes about one patient who was not exactly clinically depressed but chronically sad and uncertain of herself. She has few friends, lots of obligations, poor self-esteem.[7] She takes Prozac and soon she is happier, more outgoing, more self-confident. She knows when and how to say no. Her life is much better. Kramer tapers her Prozac and then takes her off of it; in a few months, she comes back and says, "I am not myself." A remarkable statement: she has returned to the very state in which she has been for twenty or thirty years, her entire life apart from the past eight months, and she says she doesn't feel like herself. Instead, she says she feels like herself when she's on Prozac. What do we make of these kinds of remarks? It's clear that this patient changes quite a lot on Prozac. But is the appropriate language to use a transformation to a *new* self, or a restoration to a *true* self? Or something else? Kramer, in his more enthusiastic passages, seems to hint that at least in some cases Prozac restores a true or authentic self, a self that has been masked by pathology. The authentic self is the one that has the proper levels of serotonin in the brain.

But there are other cases in the book that seem to point in the opposite direction. Kramer tells of one patient, a college undergraduate, who is not a success on Prozac.[8] Before Prozac he is bitter, moody, rather angry and irritable in a way that he seems to have cultivated.

And unhappy. On Prozac, he becomes less bitter, less alienated, less disdainful; he loses his edge. And he doesn't like it. He feels phony, and so he goes off Prozac. For him, Prozac doesn't seem so much to restore an authentic self as to create a new one, and a new one that he thinks isn't his.

There is another very different area of medicine where you hear remarks similar to these, and that is transsexual surgery. People undergoing transsexual surgery often say, "I am really a woman trapped in a man's body," that the surgery will let them be who they really are. This explanation is not unlike what Arthur Frank in *The Wounded Storyteller* calls a "restitution narrative."[9] A restitution narrative has the basic form, "I was healthy, then I got sick, and then I was restored to health." These stories of transsexuals sound like such a restitution narrative, but the restitution is to something that never existed before, only wished for—not restoration back to health, but restoration to an ideal of health that had never before been realized. What interests me is not so much whether this narrative is true or not, whatever that would mean, or even the conditions under which it could be true or not, but how persuasive this sort of explanation is. Even people who are troubled by the idea of a person changing his or her sex find themselves swayed by this kind of story: "I really am a man trapped in a woman's body." That this possibility rings true to us is a testament to the depth of Cartesian dualism in our thought. The soul trapped in the wrong body. A ghost locked in the wrong machine. Which is not to say that I am skeptical about the explanation: transsexuals can be Cartesians too. Yet we could also just as usefully speak here not of authentic and inauthentic selves, or true or false selves, but of the way that the people in question have imagined themselves to be, the direction in which they envisioned the narrative of their lives as going.

In some ways these transformations of identity, for all their apparent novelty, are old problems: old in the sense that medicine is about illness, which can itself be profoundly transformative of human identity (Alzheimer's disease, stroke or schizophrenia), but also because bioethics has seen these types of issues before. I am thinking particularly about psychosurgery, once a widely used procedure that seemed to relieve a patient of symptoms of mental illness but also changed him into a different type of person. Yet these transformations are also an old problem in a more general way. In ordinary life we maintain the fiction that while circumstances change, character is constant—that whatever we do, our essential, core identity remains the same. That fiction has a lot of truth in it, of course, but it is also true that over time our characters can change dramatically. Anyone who has been to a high school reunion knows this. And we do have some control over the manner and direction in which we change, although often in an indirect way. I realize that I might have become quite a different person had I gone to war, gone to business school, or gone to prison. In some ways, changing our identities is merely an extension of what has always been a part of our moral lives.[10]

Kurt Vonnegut wrote a book about identity and authenticity in 1961 called *Mother Night*. It is about an American playwright called Howard W. Campbell living in Germany at the outbreak of World War II, who is recruited by American intelligence officers to become an American agent. So while working for the Allies, Campbell becomes a Nazi. And not just a Nazi: he becomes a Nazi propagandist, famous all over the world for his anti-Semitic German propaganda speeches on the radio, speeches in which he rants about Jewish conspiracies and President Franklin Delano Rosenfeld, as he calls him. His job for American intelligence is to deliver secret coded messages to the Allies in his propaganda speeches. While he is delivering these anti-Semitic rants, he will pause at various intervals and cough, or clear his throat, or stumble over a word—all of which signifies various coded messages that only Allied intelligence agents listening to the broadcast can understand. Not even Campbell himself understands the coded messages he is broadcasting.

Yet although he is working for the Allies, very few people in the world know it. Not even his wife, who is herself a sort of apolitical German. Campbell becomes a Nazi celebrity. Germans tell him enthusiastically that they would never have become Nazis if it weren't for his wonderful radio addresses. So when the war ends, he is captured and imprisoned as a Nazi. And although American intelligence eventually spirits him out of captivity, no one will say that he was really working for the Allies, and over the years all the people who knew that he was really an American agent start to die off. Eventually there is only one left. And so Campbell lives in obscurity in New York until it is discovered that there is an ex-Nazi living openly in the United States. So then, thirty years later, Campbell is a celebrity again; only this time he's reviled by the public, and his only friends are a small neo-Nazi organization called The White Christian Minutemen.

Who is the real Howard W. Campbell? Is he an American patriot or a Nazi propagandist? He tells himself that he's not really a Nazi, that deep down he never really bought into the Nazi ideology, but how is he distinguishable from a Nazi? He eventually even admits to himself that if Germany had won the war, he might well have stayed in Germany and lived a comfortable life there rather than turning himself in as an American spy. Even the things he "does" for the Allied cause he doesn't consciously "do"; he doesn't even understand the coded messages he is broadcasting. How is a fake Nazi different from the real thing? Vonnegut says the moral of his story is: we are what we pretend to be. So we have to be very careful about *what* we pretend to be.

Vonnegut's message is that it is wrongheaded to think that our inner selves exist in isolation from our outer selves; that if there is no difference between the behavior and speech of a Nazi and the behavior and speech of a man pretending to be a Nazi, then there is no difference between the two men. Obviously there is, of course; if we are truly what we pretend to be, then there would be no way to distinguish pretending from the real thing. Yet Vonnegut's broader point is worth considering: that the idea of a true, authentic self is itself a sort of self-creation.

I suspect that explanations using the language of authenticity often tell us less than they seem to tell us. They are a little like the line in *Casablanca* where Bogart is asked what kind of man Claude Rains is and he replies, "He's just like any other man, only more so." You can use the language of authenticity to suit your own purposes. If you think a given technology is a positive thing, you'll be more likely to describe it as restoring an authentic self that has been masked by pathology or the circumstances of a person's genetic inheritance; and if you think it is something we should worry about, you will be more likely to describe it as changing the self or altering who the person really is.

These descriptions correspond to two competing ideas in American life. One is the idea of self-creation as a positive ideal. America often likes to see itself as a place of new beginnings, a place where you can make of yourself whatever you want. Americans go off to college, move out West, joint the Navy, reinvent themselves. If you go to California or Montana you'll find it populated by people who have moved there from somewhere else to start over, ex-bankers who are working on horse ranches, lapsed Presbyterians who are now into channelling and crystals.

But there is also a strand in American thought that resists this ideal. This is the notion that we should aspire not to create a new life, but to find a more authentic life. We Americans talk about self-discovery, about finding ourselves, being true to who we really are. It is a kind of bad faith to pretend to be something that you're not, to try to forget your roots—to discard your Jewishness, for example, or to move to the city and forget the folks back on the farm. So much of American life is about this kind of struggle, between trying to reconcile yourself with who you are, on the one hand, and trying to change it on the other.

Enhancement technologies are no different. Some technologies seem like positive things precisely because they help you change yourself. What overweight person wouldn't welcome a risk-free technology to help him become thin? Yet some changes bother us precisely *because* they help us change ourselves. If it is worrying to you that a sixteen year-old girl wants breast augmentation surgery, or that an Asian-American girl wants surgery to have her eyes look more Western, think how much more worrying it would be if there were technologies to help African-Americans look whiter. I think we would have some of these worries even if the technologies were risk-free. The worry is not that people will get something they don't expect; it's a worry that they will get exactly what they want.

III

Common sense is the watchword of a good clinician. And common sense tells us that the world of human beings is divided into male and female, boys and girls, men and women. Or does it? Wittgenstein once wrote, "If you believe that our concepts are the right ones, the ones suited to intelligent human beings, that anyone with different ones would not realize something that we realize, then imagine certain general facts of nature different from the way they are, and conceptual structures different from our own will appear *natural* to you."[11] To see something of what Wittgenstein is getting at here, consider the following story.

In the 1970s Julliane Imperato-McGinley and colleagues published studies identifying a rare deficiency of testosterone metabolism, 5-alpha-reductase deficiency syndrome.[12] Children with this condition are genetically XY, but are born sexually ambiguous. In the rural Dominican Republic where the studies were conducted, these children are often raised as girls. Until puberty, that is. Because when the children reach puberty they undergo striking changes. Their voices deepen; their muscles develop; their testes descend; and what was thought to be a clitoris enlarges to become more like a penis. The child who was thought to be a girl, or sexually ambiguous, gradually becomes a boy. Dominican Republic villagers call these children *guevedoches*, or "penis at twelve."

How you see this case (as with any case) will depend on where you are standing. For the US researchers who published the study, it is a case of mistaken sexual identity: boys who were mistakenly raised as girls and whose true sexual identity is discovered only at puberty. According to Imperato-McGinley and colleagues, once it became clear that these children were actually male rather than female, they were able to change from being female to being male with relative ease. As the children went through puberty they gradually began to feel less like girls and more like boys; eventually, they came to see themselves as men. Of the 18 children followed in the study who were raised as girls, 17 changed to a male gender identity during puberty. Sixteen changed to a male gender role, working as farmers and doing other traditionally male work, and 15 of them went on to marry women. For those of us whose world is divided into men and women, like these US researchers, the relative ease of this female-to-male transformation looks like evidence that in matters of sexual identity, biology outweighs socialization. In the end, the children's male genes and hormones prevailed.

But this is not the only way to see this case. Gilbert Herdt has argued that what we see here is not so much a case of "mistaken" sex as a culture with a "third sex"; that the transition from female to male was unproblematic not because of male biology and a *laissez-faire* attitude toward sexual identity, as the US researchers assumed, but because the local Dominican Republic culture into which these children were born recognizes a third-sex category: *guevedoche*.[13] Not all cultures code for two sexes the way Western cultures do, and in the areas of the Dominican Republic where 5-alpha-reductase deficiency is common, "the villagers have more than a simple word for hermaphrodite; they have a triadic sexual code."[14] Thus the sexually ambiguous child is born not into a world divided into male and female, but into a world divided into male, female and *guevedoche*. Different concepts, different facts of nature.

In fact, we don't even need to postulate different facts of nature, only (as Wittgenstein would say) different forms of life. History and anthropology have shown us many examples of societies whose conceptions of sex and gender are vastly different from our own. One of the most well-known examples of a third sex/third gender are the *berdaches* of traditional North America societies.[15] *Berdaches* defy easy categorization in our terms—they are sometimes described as men who adopt the dress and gender roles of women—but it seems clear that at least some of them are intersexed, such as the *nadle* in Willard Hill's 1935 study, "The Status of The Hermaphrodite and Transvestite in Navaho Culture."[16] What is striking about the Navaho *nadle* is not simply the fact that the culture codes for and accepts a third-sex/third-gender category, but the status and prestige which the *nadle* are accorded. "You must respect a *nadle*," one Navaho elder tells Hill. "They are, somehow, sacred and holy." A family into which a *nadle* is born is considered very fortunate, because a *nadle* ensures wealth and success. They are made

heads of the family and are given control of family property. "They
know everything. They can do both the work of a man and a woman,"
another Navaho says. Still another: "If there were no *nadle*, the country
would change. They are responsible for all the wealth in the country. If
there were no more left, the horses, sheep and Navaho would all go.
They are leaders just like President Roosevelt."

The issue dividing us and the Navaho, as Clifford Geertz suggests
in one of his more dazzling turns, is one of commonsense judgments,
our untutored, no-nonsense, matter-of-fact attitudes towards the
world.[17] It isn't just that what the Navaho call *nadle* we call hermaphrodites or transvestites, or that what certain Dominican Republic villagers call *guevedoche* we call (some of us, anyway) 5-alpha-reductase
deficiency syndrome. The difference lies in our basic apprehensions
of the obvious, the way life is, once it is stripped of artifice and theory and intellectual pretensions: the things anyone knows (or at least
anyone with a lick of sense). Knowing that you shouldn't play with
fire, that sugar causes tooth decay, that (as all Southerners know) you
can't make good barbecue and comply with the health code: this is all
common sense. And so, argues Geertz, is the idea that human beings
come in two varieties. Or three, as the case may be, since according
to Geertz, common sense is itself a local cultural system.

For Geertz, intersexuality is so problematic for Americans because
it defies our common sense. To see Geertz's point, imagine yourself
the mother or father of an intersexed newborn; imagine further that
you must answer the questions of relatives and friends about the sex
of your child. It is one thing to say that it is not immediately clear
whether the child is a boy or a girl, as clinicians often recommend,
because of a medical condition. Such an admission would, for
Americans, be embarrassing enough. But it would be far preferable to
saying that your child is neither male nor female but a hermaphrodite. For most Americans, I suspect, this would be unthinkable. The
condition of having both male and female sexual organs is something
that cannot be openly admitted. Americans, as Geertz puts it, "apparently regard femaleness and maleness as exhausting the natural categories in which persons can conceivably come: What falls between is
a darkness, an offense against reason."[18]

How do Americans (and most other Westerners) deal with this "offense against reason"? In general, they have regarded it as a medical problem to be fixed with surgical and hormonal therapy. Intersexuality (or "ambiguous genitalia") is not an uncommon occurrence. One recent estimate is one in 1500 live births (although some estimates of its incidence run as high as 4% to 5% of live births).[19] The term intersexuality itself is usually used to designate a range of anatomical conditions in which feminine and masculine anatomical characteristics are mixed. "True hermaphrodites," or individuals who have both XX and XY chromosomes, and both ovaries and testes, are relatively rare. More common are so-called "pseudohermaphrodites"—individuals who are, for example, genetically XY but who have a feminized appearance because of androgen insensitivity ("male pseudohermaphrodites"), or who are XX but have a masculinized appearance because of virilizing hormones ("female pseudohermaphrodites"). Intersexed children are generally treated with some kind of normalizing surgery and hormonal therapy to make their genitalia and reproductive organs conform as closely as possible to those of what is regarded as a typical male or female. The theory motivating the treatment of intersexed children says that sexual identity is determined primarily not by biology, but by the way the child is reared. Therefore children need to be assigned to one sex or the other as early as possible, with his or her genitalia matching his or her assigned sex as closely as possible, in order to ensure that the child forms an unambiguous sexual identity.

The problem, as one standard endocrinology textbook puts it, is this: "Few people are sufficiently sophisticated to accept a sex of rearing discordant with their chromosomal or gonadal sex."[20] And as a result, many intersexed patients are never told their medical diagnosis. Many are deceived about the nature of their condition, at least partly because it is feared that the truth might be harmful to them. I say "partly" because there is also an internal therapeutic logic to this deception. Intersexuals are deceived not simply because they can't handle the truth, but because deception is thought to be a necessary part of the treatment. In order to *be* (for example) a female the child must really *believe* she is a female. If she doesn't unquestioningly believe she is a female she may not think of herself as female; and if she does not think of herself as female then she is not a female. (Or at least, not *simply* a female.) The same kind of logic goes for the practice of deceiving parents, and for undertaking the treatment as early as possible, before the child is able to give consent. Sexual identity is largely determined by anatomical appearance and socialization, the reasoning goes, so if parents do not unquestioningly believe that the child is female, their doubts will become apparent to the child. The child will then have doubts herself, and consequently her own identity will come into question. This logic is apparent in the instructions to endocrinologists such as these: "There should never be any doubt in the mind of parent or patient that a child is being reared in his or her own 'true sex.'. . ."[21]

True sex: this is a revealing phrase. Parents must believe that treatment is not *altering* their child's sexual identity, but is *restoring* the child's true sex, which has been masked by pathology. Parents must not have any question that the true sex of the child, underneath all the surface aberrations, is straightforwardly male or female. But since sex is, in fact, not so straightforward, and particularly since all manner of surgical and medical interventions must be undertaken over the course of the child's life, this deception can be difficult to maintain. The irony, as Alice Dreger has pointed out, is that the deception and secrecy that are intended to alleviate the child's feelings of freakishness may in the end only exacerbate them. Knowing that something is medically wrong with his or her body, yet not knowing what it is, the child's fears about an imagined condition may well be worse than the reality.[22]

A more difficult question is whether, and under what conditions, such "normalizing" procedures should be done. A growing number of adult intersexuals, under the auspices of groups such as the Intersex Society of North America, are protesting the kinds of procedures that were performed on them as children.[23] They argue that intersexuals are often left with genitalia that may (or may not) meet surgical criteria for a good cosmetic result, but which function very poorly—for example, a constructed vagina that doesn't lubricate, or a surgically reduced clitoris so insensitive as to prohibit orgasm. Many scholars from outside medicine have criticized what they see as sexist criteria governing the sex assignment decisions.[24] For example, Dreger argues that intersexed children are more often assigned as female rather than male because surgeons have much more demanding criteria for what counts as a functional penis than for a functional vagina. A functional penis must be large enough to be recognizable as a penis, must be adequately shaped and colored, must have the ability to become erect and flaccid at the appropriate times and must transmit semen and urine. But a functional vagina need only be a hole large enough to fit a penis.[25]

Even if they are not sexist, decisions about sex assignment often seem to be based on criteria that are, in comparison to the gravity of the decision and the invasiveness of the surgery, rather difficult to take seriously. (One endocrinology textbook says that the criteria for whether an intersexed child should be assigned male are (1) whether he will be able to have sex as a man and (2) whether he will be able to urinate standing up.)[26] Many standard texts say that a phallus is too small to be a penis, and therefore should be reconstructed into a clitoris, if its stretched length is less than 2.5 centimeters. A clitoris should be surgically reduced if it is longer than a centimeter. The justification for such surgery is made even more problematic by the fact that few long-term follow-up studies are available to tell us the results. One wants to know not just how the genitalia turn out cosmetically, but things such as: In what ways do the sexual identities of these patients develop? Under what circumstances, and after what procedures, do they come to think of themselves as men, or as women, or most crucially, as something else? What are their sex lives like? *Are they happy?*

Clitoral reduction, the surgical resection of part of the clitoris, often comes in for particular criticism. Dreger asks why clitoral reduction does not count as one of the procedures prohibited by recent federal legislation banning female genital mutilation. That legislation was intended to prohibit African traditionalists from performing "female circumcision" on girls under the age of 18. Female circumcision often involves the excision, reduction or infibulation of the clitoris; its defenders argue that it is an important part of traditional

African cultures. While Dreger does not defend African female circumcision, she points out that the notions motivating clitoral reduction of intersexed infants—that a clitoris has a proper size, and that a clitoris which is too big can be damaging to the psychosocial well-being of a child—are, like the African procedures, a product of local culture and custom. Only they are our customs, the dictates of common sense, and so we take them very seriously.

Yet at the same time it is hard to blame parents for consenting to surgery for their intersexed children, especially if the child's genitalia and secondary sexual characteristics are a more obvious mix of male and female anatomy. I suspect parents are often terrified at the prospect of their children being outcasts, of being seen as freaks of nature, of being desperately unhappy, of being completely bewildered about their place in the world, of never being able to attract a sexual partner, of being forced to live a life of secrecy and shame, of being tortured and bullied and ridiculed by other children while they are growing up. And who is to say that these fears are not justified? It would be a mistake to overlook the consequences of damaging and stigmatizing cultural pressures an intersexed child may face. We might think the Navaho in the 1930s were more enlightened than we are today, but we can't simply decide to see the world that way. We have the culture that we have, and we live in the present, not the past. Cultures change, of course, and it is more likely that ours will change if fewer surgeries are done and intersexuality is acknowledged openly. But few parents will willingly risk what they believe to be the well-being of their child in order to protest a cultural norm.

Cultural critics often describe physicians who perform intersex interventions as shoring up our categories of masculinity and femininity, or trying to protect the established cultural order from chaos, or framing intersexuality as something to be eradicated.[27] These descriptions are accurate in their own way, I suppose, but they misleadingly imply a kind of agency on the part of doctors, a conscious effort to fend off threats to a cultural order. One might say with equal accuracy that doctors are trapped by this order themselves, imprisoned in a cell with only one window on the world. The fact is, we treat these children the way we do because this is how we see the world. And it isn't just the way doctors see the world; it is the way parents see the world, and most importantly, it is the way that the children themselves are taught to see the world. It is the fact that they do not fit into this way of seeing the world that causes the problems.

IV

In the collection of fragments by Wittgenstein known as *Zettel*, there appears the following cryptic question: "What would a society all of deaf men be like? Or a society of the 'feeble-minded'? *An important question!* What then of a society that never played many of our customary language games?"[28] In the context of the passages that are placed next to this one, Wittgenstein seems to be asking a question here about what elsewhere he calls *Lebensformen*, or forms of life.[29] What forms would a society take, for example, if none of its members could hear? What sort of language would its members develop? What concepts would they use, and what kinds of lives would they lead?

Though Wittgenstein may not have known it, the answers to these questions are available to us. Deaf people have associated with one another, communicated with one another and been educated with one another for centuries. It is not hyperbole to speak of Deaf culture; indeed, culture is exactly what Deaf people speak of themselves: not merely a sense of identification with others who share a similar physical condition (like, say, the intersex community) but a social heritage and way of living that is transmitted over generations. The Deaf world has its own unique values, traditions, rituals, institutions and stories, as well as its own manual languages. Like members of a hearing culture, writes Harlan Lane, "deaf children growing up in the deaf community learn in manual language from older deaf children and adults what it means to be a deaf person, the lives that deaf people have lived before them and therefore the possible lives for them to lead, the wisdom of the minority, peculiar to its situation and accumulated across the centuries."[30] If, as Clifford Geertz puts it, "man is an animal suspended in webs of significance that he himself has spun," then Deaf men and women are suspended in webs as intricate and fragile as any other.

Deaf people are commonly thought of as handicapped, not only by doctors but by hearing people in general. Deafness is a medical problem, a deficit, something to be overcome through remedial education and medical technology. Deaf people are said to be imprisoned in silence, cut off from the world.[31] Yet the self-perception of the Deaf community is strikingly different. That self-perception is something closer to an ethnic or cultural identity, a condition to be proud of rather than to overcome. On this view, Deafness is not merely a physiological condition. Members of the Deaf community sometimes capitalize the word "Deaf" in order to distinguish between the physiological condition of not being able to hear (deaf) and a group of people who share a language and a culture (Deaf). Indeed, people who are unable to hear (or unable to hear well) but who communicate by speech, lip-reading or with the use of hearing aids generally refer to themselves not as deaf but as hearing impaired. Very often these are not people who were born without hearing or who lost it early in life, but people who have lost their hearing later in life or who have grown up without the knowledge and practices of Deaf culture.[32] Only those who are educated as Deaf children are true natives of the Deaf culture. Even I. King Jordan, a graduate of Gallaudet University who lost his hearing at the age of 21 and who later went on to become president of the university, has said, "I am not a real member of the Deaf community. I am a deafened hearing person."[33]

Carol Humphries and Tom Padden, Deaf people who have written about Deaf culture and identity, repeat the following story about the Abbé de l'Epee that was told to them during a visit to France. It was told to them many times in Deaf clubs throughout the country, but this version was told to them by one of the older members of a Deaf club in Marseilles.

> The Abbé de l'Epee had been walking a long time through a dark night. He wanted to stop and rest overnight, but he could not find a place to stay, until at a distance he saw a house with a light. He stopped at the house, knocked at the door, but no one answered. He saw that the door was open, so he entered the house and found two young women seated by the fire sewing. He spoke to them, but still they did not respond. He walked closer and spoke to them again, but they failed again

to respond. The Abbé was perplexed, but seated himself beside them. They looked up at him and did not speak. At that point their mother entered the room. Did the Abbé not know that her daughters were deaf? He did not, but now he understood why they had not responded. As he contemplated the young women, the Abbé realized his vocation.[34]

That vocation was to educate deaf children. The efforts of the Abbé de l'Epee led to the establishment of public schools for deaf children throughout France in the late eighteenth century. He also became well known for advocating the use of sign language to educate deaf children. For Padden and Humphries, however, what was most striking about the story was the reverence with which it was told. They suggest that it is not just a bit of history (in fact, the details are not entirely historically accurate) but rather a folktale, which in its telling and retelling over the years has come to symbolize the passage of deaf people from isolation to community, from a world where deaf people live alone or apart from one another to a world of solidarity where Deaf people have a language and culture of their own.

The Abbé's accomplishments, deaf residential schools and sign language, lie at the heart of Deaf culture. Because most deaf children are born to hearing parents, and because most deaf parents have hearing children, Deaf schools and universities are a crucial vehicle for the transmission of Deaf history and culture. They are also the places where the Deaf learn and teach signed languages. The ability to communicate in Sign, and the manner and fluency with which one does it, is perhaps the most crucial determinant of membership in the Deaf community. The languages of the Deaf community are signed languages, and as Harlan Lane writes, the Deaf community often does not look forgivingly on those who try to be "oral"—that is, who try to pass as hearing in the hearing world. Lane writes, "Deaf people who adopt hearing values and look down on deaf people are regarded as traitors."[35]

This helps explain the opposition of many Deaf people in recent years to the proposed treatment—or perhaps I should put "treatment" in scare quotes—of deafness with cochlear implants. A cochlear implant is an electronic device intended to simulate hearing for deaf patients. It consists of a speech processor, a headset trans-mitter, and a surgically implanted receiver-stimulator. Speech is processed and transmitted to the receiver-stimulator, which directly stimulates the auditory nerve, thus allowing the deaf person to "hear." Nonetheless, many members of the Deaf community have strongly opposed the use of cochlear implants, especially in prelingually deaf children, for whom the implants do not work as well as they do in postlingually deaf patients, and who are not themselves yet mentally competent to make medical decisions. Part of this opposition arises from the fact that while cochlear implants help patients hear, they do rather less well in helping them to recognize speech and learn to speak; part of it arises from the fact that learning how to "hear" with cochlear implants and speak orally requires years of training and habilitation, sometimes with less-than-impressive results. But part of the opposition from many members of the Deaf community comes from seeing deafness as part of their identities.[36]

The fact that Deaf people consider deafness a fundamental part of their identities changes the points of debate over cochlear implants. If you consider deafness a disability, as do many doctors, bioethicists and even patients who have lost their hearing later in life, then you will see the debate over cochlear implants as a matter of weighing the risks of the procedure versus the benefits of hearing. You will describe the issue with words like "restoration," "cure," "silence" and "loss." But if you see deafness as part of your cultural identity, then the issue will be far more personal. It will be about the loss or preservation of your people and your culture. If you conceptualize the debate in these terms you will use words like "sovereignty," "power," and "iden-tity." What is at stake will be like what is at stake in the debate over Quebec sovereignty or in the struggle to preserve Gaelic. To think about cochlear implants being made available to all prelingually deaf children means thinking about the slow disintegration of the lan-guage that gives expression to who you are, and to the habits of being that give your life its sense.

It is difficult for hearing people to imagine deafness as anything other than a handicap, because it is difficult to imagine it as anything other than a loss. The imagined world of deafness is an imagined world of silence. But the prelingually deaf will not experience deafness as a loss, of course, any more than those who were not born with absolute pitch experience that as a loss. Nor will they necessarily experience deafness as a deficit. What counts as a "deficit" is not absolute; it is only a deficit in relationship to some other real or imagined world. Deafness is a deficit only in the same sense in which we might say that not having the "sonar" that bats possess is a deficit. It is something we don't have, of course, but we don't really miss having it. We would think of its absence as a problem only if we had to negotiate our way through a world where most other people had it, and where they had built that world in such a way as to require it.

Which is, in some respects, much like what we have: a world constructed for the hearing. For some people the most persuasive argument for cochlear implants is that they would serve as a passport for deaf people into the hearing world. This is not to say that the world of the hearing is superior to that of the Deaf, any more than the world of the English is superior to that of the Scots, or that of the Walloons to that of the Flemish, or that of Anglophone Canadians to that of Francophone Canadians. It is only to say that the hearing world is that of the majority, to which the deaf, by virtue of their condition, are denied access.

Yet the reverse is also true. Deaf people have access to a rich and vibrant culture that is closed to anyone who does not use or understand a manual language. In fact, anyone who speaks only one language, like most Americans, will have only a limited ability to experience the world's cultural and linguistic diversity. Yet most Americans do not see this as regrettable enough to warrant learning a second language. I suspect that even if Americans understood that learning Sign as a first language would probably give their children superior visual and spatial skills, they would still not trouble to have them learn it.[37] If Deaf people do not regret living in the hearing world, this should be understandable to hearing people who do not regret living in a Deaf world.

What hearing people often fail to appreciate is the complexity and subtlety of signed languages. Sign is not simply a manual equivalent of English, nor is it a pantomine or gestural code. It is a manual language with its own syntax and lexicon. It is, moreover, a language that, unlike spoken languages, has evolved to suit the needs of its users. More than any other single feature, what distinguishes signed languages from spoken languages is their unique linguistic use of space. What takes place linearly and sequentially in a spoken language becomes, as Sacks puts it, "simultaneous, concurrent, multilevelled in Sign."[38] Signed languages may initially look to hearing people like pantomine, but in fact they involve an exceedingly complex range of spatial patterns connected to each other in three dimensions, signified (for example) by the directions and changes of direction of the hands, the wrists, the arms and the fingers, not to mention the nuanced movements of the head, the eyes and the face.[39] Even the mistakes and pathologies of spoken languages have signed equivalents. For example, users of signed languages experience "slips of the hand" in the same way that users of spoken languages experience "slips of the tongue." Deaf patients with schizophrenia exhibit "sign salad" similar to schizophrenic "word salad," the mixed-up grammatical formations and neologisms seen in patients with schizophrenia who use spoken languages.[40]

Users of signed languages have at their disposal a rich variety of spatial inflections to communicate nuances of meaning. To take only one example, Sacks points out that different movements of the hands can communicate the temporal variations on the American Sign Language (ASL) verb "look at," so that it signifies "stare," "gaze," "watch," "look at incessantly" or "look again and again." Still other spatial inflections are available for verbs like "reminisce," "prophesy," "predict," "look forward to," "anticipate," "sightsee," "browse," "look around aimlessly" and so on. The unique use of space in signed languages leads William Stokoe to believe that with Sign, language itself takes on a cinematic quality, which he compares to edited film. He suggests that the use of four dimensions in signed languages (three spatial dimensions plus time), as opposed to the single dimension of time in spoken languages, gives signed languages tools comparable to those of a film editor: flashbacks and flash-forward scenes, cuts from distant shots to close-up. Moreover, says Stokoe, each signer "is placed very much as a camera: the field of vision and quality of view are directed but variable. Not only the signer signing but also the signer watching is aware at all times of the signer's visual orientation to what is being signed about."[41]

The use of spatial, signed languages may contribute to the formation of a uniquely deaf way of experiencing the world through the inner world of meaning and thought that make up the mind. Oliver Sacks puts it this way: "It is through inner speech that the child develops his own concepts and meanings; it is through inner speech that he develops his own identity; it is through inner speech, finally, that he constructs his own world. And the inner speech (or inner Sign) of the deaf may be very distinctive."[42]

Yet deafness contributes to the formation of a child's sense of herself in another way: as an insider or an outsider, healthy or handicapped. In the Deaf community, Deaf children are not identified by their deafness. But living in the world of the hearing means being identified as disabled, not only by others but also by yourself. As Robert Crouch writes, "The child whose life is centered upon disability and the attempt to overcome it grows up in a context that continually reinforces this disability, despite his or her own best efforts to speak and despite the diligent work of the educators of the deaf and hearing-impaired. These children are always aware that they are outsiders, and not merely outsiders, but outsiders attempting to be on the inside."[43]

Must it be this way? Perhaps not. It was not this way on the island of Martha's Vineyard for over two centuries, as Nora Ellen Groce has documented in her remarkable 1985 book *Everyone Here Spoke Sign Language.* [44] As a result of isolation and a recessive gene for congenital deafness, for many years the population of Martha's Vineyard included a very high number of deaf people. In the nineteenth century, the incidence of congenital deafness was one in 5,728, but on Martha's Vineyard it was one in 155. In one small neighborhood of an isolated town, as many as one in four people were deaf. For this reason, nearly the entire population of the island used Sign. Hearing and deaf people were able to communicate freely with each other; in fact, hearing people were so fluent in Sign that they often shifted back and forth between English and Sign in midconversation.[45]

Islanders seem to have attached no stigma to deafness. At worst, deaf people regarded it as a nuisance. According to the older residents (the last deaf islander died in 1952) deaf islanders were in no way regarded as disabled or handicapped. One man told Groce, "I didn't think about the deaf any more than you'd think about anybody with a different voice." Another island woman in her eighties, responding to a remark about the handicap of deafness, said, "Oh, those people weren't handicapped. They were just deaf."[46] Many residents seemed surprised that outsiders seemed interested in the issue. Their memories of the way deaf people were treated do not appear to be the result of mere nostalgia for the past. A reporter for the *Boston Sunday Herald* wrote in 1895, "The kindly and well-informed people whom I saw, strange to say, seem to be proud of the affliction—to regard it as a plume in the hat of the stock."[47]

Illness and health, disability and difference, cure and enhancement: it is a mistake to think there can be rigid distinctions here. This is because illness, health, disability and difference all are connected to a person's identity, her sense of who she is. A person's identity is not formed in isolation. It is always formed against a certain background, a culture and a history, in dialogue with other human beings. My self-description is connected to your description of me, and our descriptions of one another are connected to the descriptions of others. Thus what counts as an illness or a disability—or on the other hand, as normal biological variation—will itself depend on its cultural and historical location.

But the reverse is also true. There may be no biology independent of culture, but neither is there culture independent of biology. How a given society conceives of its members, how they conceive of themselves, is connected to certain biological facts—like the incidence of congenital deafness, for example, or 5-alpha-reductase deficiency syndrome. To recognize this amounts to a twist on Clifford Geertz's contention that there is no such thing as human nature without culture: not the idea that one's identity is cultural rather than biological, but the extent to which the cultural is biological. It is to recognize, like Wittgenstein, that our concepts are tied to certain basic facts of nature.

Chapter 3

Lost at the Mall; or, The Use of Prozac in a Time of Normal Nihilism

And you may ask yourself/What is that beautiful house?
And you may ask yourself/Where does that highway go?
And you may ask yourself/Am I right?...Am I wrong?
And you may tell yourself/MY GOD!...WHAT HAVE I DONE?
——The Talking Heads

I

In his essay "Madness and Religion," the Irish psychiatrist M.O'C. Drury, a student and lifelong friend of Ludwig Wittgenstein, tells the story of a Catholic priest he once treated for depression.[1] The priest was widely considered a man with a gift for his work, but he had lost his faith. He had come to believe that his sermons were being delivered without true feeling, and that he was asking his parishioners to do and believe things in which he no longer had any faith. Saying Mass had become a great burden for him, and he felt that he should never have been ordained. He would awake each night at 3 A.M. and lie in his bed until sunrise worrying about the state of his soul. He lost his appetite and began to have stomach pains. He became convinced that he had cancer. In fact, he even began to hope he had cancer so that he would die. He consulted a physician, but a work-up showed no signs of organic disease, at which point he was referred to Drury.

The priest was showing the classical signs of depression: depressed mood, guilt, sleep loss, appetite loss, preoccupation with death. Yet he did not regard his condition as a medical problem. He thought of it as a spiritual problem and he resented Drury's presence. Drury concentrated on his somatic symptoms, the abdominal pain and the sleep loss, and eventually managed to get the priest to agree to a course of electroconvulsive therapy. After the first course of ECT the priest's abdominal pain had disappeared. Within a week he was saying Mass again. After seven courses of ECT he was sleeping well and had gained ten pounds. His spiritual problems disappeared.

Was this a therapeutic success? By the standards of psychiatry, yes. The symptoms of depression were gone. Yet Drury has worries about what he has done. He asks us to consider other men and women who had undergone spiritual crises, such as the author of these words:

> I felt that something had broken within me on which my life had always rested, that I had nothing left to hold on to, that morally my life had stopped. . . . An invincible force impelled me to get rid of my existence, in one way or another. . . .
>
> Behold me then a happy man in good health, hiding the rope in order not to hang myself to the rafters of the room where every night I went to sleep alone; behold me no longer going shooting, lest I yield to the too easy temptation to put an end to myself with my gun. . . .
>
> All this took place at a time when so far as all my outward circumstances went I ought to have been completely happy. I had a good wife who loved me, good children and a large property which was increasing with no pains taken on my part.[2]

The author of these words was Leo Tolstoy, and Drury has no doubt that, with the right treatment, Tolstoy's two years of suffering could have been terminated in two weeks. Yet he is not sure it would have been the right thing to do. The convictions that resulted from this episode determined the manner and spirit in which Tolstoy lived the rest of his life. Would Tolstoy have been an appropriate candidate for ECT? Would he have been an appropriate candidate for an anti-depressant? If he had been treated quickly and effectively, what would the rest of his life have been like? The question for a psychiatrist, says Drury, is when to say, "This man is mad and we must put a stop to his raving," and when to say, "Touch not mine anointed and do my prophet no harm."[3]

The moral problems presented by Drury's case may be particular to an older sensibility, even a nineteenth-century sensibility: Is a spiritual illness diminished by treating it as a psychiatric problem? If so, when can using the tools of psychiatry be morally justified? Certainly, most contemporary psychiatrists would not see treatment in this case as morally problematic. It is a straightforward case of major depression, successfully treated. Even Drury himself thinks that treatment was, in the end, morally justifiable, although it worries him. For most of us, I suspect, moral questions such as these do not arise because most of us do not feel the tremendous spiritual pull of religion in the same way that Drury and Tolstoy did. Whatever diminution a spiritual problem undergoes by being treated as a psychiatric problem is overshadowed by the physical and psychic relief that psychiatric treatment provides.

Yet we have not completely escaped the problem that Drury describes. The question of when to treat a problem as spiritual and when to treat it as psychiatric still arises, though it may not be as dramatic as the problem that Drury faced.

Suppose, for example, that you are a psychiatrist, and into your office comes a young Southerner who is now living in New York City. He is a healthy, amiable young man, slightly deaf in one ear, prone to long periods of vacancy and melancholy. He is handsome but rather shy and given to long silences, so that you don't quite know what to make of him. He doesn't strike you as remarkable. He says people often tell him the same joke two or three times. He did well in school and even now makes very high marks on psychological aptitude tests; his problem, he says, is that he doesn't know what to do between tests. You ask him what brings him to your office. He says he feels bad in good environments and good in bad environments. For example, when he is down in Alabama and looks around at his fellow Southerners, most of whom are happy and prosperous, his heart sinks. On the other hand, the happiest time he can remember was the previous summer when he was caught in a severe hurricane near Newport and was nearly killed. He feels fine in blizzards and blackouts and car accidents; what gives him problems are ordinary Wednesday afternoons.

He tells you he comes from an honorable and violent Southern family. His great-grandfather once met the Grand Wizard of the Ku Klux Klan in a barbershop and challenged him to a duel right there and then. Like all the other men in his family, this young man was sent up to Princeton for college. He did well in his studies, made the boxing team, joined a good eating club, but one afternoon during his third year while he was sitting in his dormitory room he was overtaken by a profound melancholy. This was supposed to be the best time of his life. He let out a groan, looked in the mirror, said this is no place to spend another half hour, much less another two years, and forty minutes later he was on a bus to New York City. For the past two years he has been living in the YMCA, working in Macy's as a "humidification engineer" and seeing an analyst five days a week.

Readers of Walker Percy's novels will recognize Will Barrett, the protagonist of *The Last Gentleman*.[4] Barrett's diagnosis, whatever it might be, is worth thinking carefully about, because it is representative of a condition common among Westerners in the latter half of the twentieth century. It appears in different guises in psychiatry, literature and philosophy: melancholia, ennui, *Alltäglichkeit*, Binx Bolling's malaise, James Edwards's normal nihilism. Those afflicted with such a condition tend to ask themselves questions like, "What is the purpose of it all?" or "Is this all there is?" or, as Will Barrett says to his analyst, "Look here now, this analysis is all very well but how about telling me the truth just between ourselves, off the record, that is, what am I really supposed to do?"[5]

Whatever name we give it, the condition has taken on more contemporary reverberations because at least some of those afflicted with some variation seem to respond to a new class of antidepressants, the selective serotonin re-uptake inhibitors (SSRIs), of which Prozac is the most famous representative. The SSRIs were developed to treat depression, of course, for which they work very well. But they have also become much more commonly prescribed for patients who are not clinically depressed, at least partly because the side effects of SSRIs are often not as burdensome as those of other classes of anti-depressants. Many of the patients who respond to the SSRIs do not have the profile of patients undergoing an episode of major depression. They are not tearful. They are not preoccupied with death. They do not feel excessively guilty or despairing. They aren't overly tired. They don't find it hard to concentrate. They are not losing sleep or losing weight. Rather, these are people who are compulsive, or anxious, or who have poor self-esteem, or who are simply rather sad. And some of them sound worryingly close to the alienated protagonists of Percy's novels, people who are empty and confused, whose lives don't seem to have any direction, who are searching for their place in the world. These are patients such as those in Peter Kramer's book, *Listening to Prozac*, who say things like "I don't know who I am," or "The whole world seems to be in on something that I just don't get."[6]

Unlike Drury or his priest-patient, Percy sees the condition that afflicts his characters as a clue to a broader cultural condition, a symptom not so much of the patient's illness but of the illness of the society in which he lives. In our society, spiritual matters no longer have the same resonance that they once did. (Percy would say this is true even for most ordinary Christians, although he was himself a Catholic.) And it is this very loss of spiritual resonance that produces the condition from which Percy's characters suffer: not so much depression as a peculiar sense of feeling lost in the world, the sense that all the old structures that once gave life sense have disappeared, that we have been abandoned and lost at sea, castaways on a lonely island. Thus for Percy, the question is whether this condition, whatever it is, belongs within the domain of psychiatry. Is there anything morally worrying about trying to change it with Prozac?

II

Subtitled "The Adventures of a Bad Catholic at a Time Near the End of the World," Percy's *Love in the Ruins* is narrated by Tom More, an alcoholic psychiatrist and self-described "lapsed Catholic" who writes from Feliciana Parish in the Louisiana bayous at a time when apocalypse seems imminent.[7] The reason for this imminent danger has to do with Tom More himself—or rather, with one of his inventions, which has fallen into the wrong hands. As More writes in his journal:

> For I have reason to believe that within the next two hours an unprecedented fallout of noxious particles will settle hereabouts and perhaps in other places as well. It is a catastrophe whose cause and effect—and prevention—are known only to me. The effects of the evil particles are psychic rather than physical. They do not burn the skin and rot the marrow; rather do they inflame and worsen the secret ill of the spirit and rive the very self from itself. If a man is already prone to anger, he'll go mad with rage. If he lives affrighted, he'll quake with terror. If he's already abstracted from himself, he'll be sundered from himself and roam the world like Ishmael.

The invention that More believes will cause this psychic fallout is the More qualitative-quantitative ontological lapsometer. The lapsometer is a diagnostic instrument developed by More, a "stethoscope of the human soul." Just as a stethoscope or an EEG diagnoses the infirmities of the body, More's ontological lapsometer can measure the ills of the spirit. Alienation, angst, terror, depression, rage—"In fact," says More, "with this device in hand any physician can make early diagnoses of potential suicides, paranoiacs, impotence, stroke, anxiety and angelism/bestialism. Think of the significance of it!"

More relates the case history of Ted Tennis, "a well-educated, somewhat abstracted graduate student who suffered from massive free-floating terror, identity crisis, and sexual impotence." "Every psychiatrist knows the type," says More, "the well-spoken slender young man who recites his symptoms with precision and objectivity—so objective that they seem to be somebody else's symptoms—and above all with that eagerness, don't you know, as if nothing would please him more than that his symptom, his dream, should turn out to be a text-book case. *Allow me to have a proper disease, Doctor*, he all but tells me."

Tennis suffers from "daytime terror and nighttime impotence." More passes the lapsometer over his head and takes a reading:

> He registered a dizzy 7.6 mmv over Brodmann 32, the area of abstractive activity. Since that time I have learned that a reading over 6 generally means that a person has so abstracted himself from himself and from the world around him, seeing things as theories and himself as a shadow, that he cannot, so to speak, reenter the lovely ordinary world. Instead he orbits the world and himself. Such a person, and there are millions, is destined to haunt the human condition like the Flying Dutchman.

Because he has not yet hit on a therapeutic breakthrough for "angelism"—"excessive abstraction of the self from itself"—More must rely on a rough-and-ready, short-term cure; he instructs Tennis to walk home six miles through the swamp. The only treatment for angelism is "recovery of the self through ordeal." And that evening, Tennis arrives home, "half-dead of fatigue, having been devoured by mosquitoes, leeches, vampire bats, tsetse flies, snapped at by alligators, moccasins, copperheads, chased by Bantu guerillas and once even cuffed about by a couple of Michigan State dropouts on a bummer who mistook him for a parent." The treatment was successful; "half-dead and stinking like a catfish, he fell into the arms of his good wife, Tanya, and made lusty love to her the rest of the night."

The source of More's worries about his lapsometer is a mysterious, Mephistophelian character called Art Immelman, who claims to be a government liaison interested in funding More's new instrument. After a bit of tinkering, Immelman converts the lapsometer into an instrument not only of diagnosis but also of treatment: a means of curing spiritual ills with ionizing radiation. Immelman approaches More in the hospital men's room and offers to demonstrate this new development. He aims the lapsometer at More's "red nucleus"; More's readings jump up a few notches on the anxiety scale. He reports: "My shoulders are rounded and I am gazing at my hands clenched in my lap. At last I raise my eyes. A horrid white light streams through the frosted window and falls into the glittering porcelain basins of the urinals. It is the Terror, but tolerable. The urinals, which are the wall variety, are shaped like skulls."

Immelman then reverses the lapsometer, beaming negative ions at More's skull. The lapsometer hums against his head. "When I open my eyes, I am conscious first of breathing. Something in my diaphragm lets go. I realize that I've been breathing at the top of my lungs for forty-five years. . . . Then I notice a hand clenched into a fist on my knee. I open it slowly, turning it this way and that, inspecting every pore and crease. What a beautiful strong hand! The tendons! The bones! But the hand of a stranger! I have never seen it before."

Like most of Percy's novels, *Love in the Ruins* is a book about people who feel ill at ease in the world, and, perhaps more importantly, about whether it might not be still worse not to feel ill at ease. (The epigraph for Percy's first book, *The Moviegoer*, was a remark by Kierkegaard: "The specific character of despair is precisely this: it is unaware of being despair.") In contrast to his other novels, however, *Love in the Ruins* is about the perils and absurdities of a certain way of looking at such problems, that of seeing spiritual ills as psychiatric disorders. For Percy, these spiritual ills are a consequence of the times and manner in which we late twentieth-century Westerners live. To see them as falling within the domain of psychiatry is not so much an error as a distortion, a narrowness of vision that reduces existential problems to configurations of brain chemistry. For Percy, one suspects, using Prozac to alleviate existential angst would be a mistake like the ontological lapsometer, a misguided effort to relieve the spiritual illnesses that our manner of living has produced.

III

In *The Gutenberg Elegies*, Sven Birkerts writes the following description of what he believes is a widely felt reaction to contemporary American culture, variably offered as an explanation for all manner of moral ills:

> We are living in a society and culture that is in dissolution. Pack this paragraph with your own headlines about eroded

> values, crime, educational decline, what have you. There are
> many causes, many explanations. But behind them all, vague
> and menacing, is this recognition: that the understandings and
> assumptions that were formerly operative in society no longer
> feel valid. Things have shifted; they keep shifting. We all feel
> a desire for connection, for meaning, but we don't seem to
> know what to connect with what, and we are utterly at sea
> about our place as individuals in the world at large. The maps
> no longer describe the territory we inhabit. There is no clear
> path to the future. We trust that the species will blunder on,
> but we don't know where *to*. We feel imprisoned in a momen-
> tum that is not of our own making.[8]

The condition may be widely felt, but the reasons behind the condition are hard to diagnose. For Birkerts, it is related to our sudden
movement over the past several decades from a culture of print to a
culture of electronic media. For Walker Percy, it is connected to the
gap between the concrete particularities of being in the world and the
abstract generalizations of science and systematic philosophy—a gap
filled for Percy by the word-become-flesh of Christianity. For others,
such as James Edwards, it is connected to the contingency of our own
structures of interpreting the world, and thus of our own selfhood.

In his extraordinary study *The Plain Sense of Things*, James Edwards
describes our contemporary predicament as one of "normal nihilism."[9]
According to Edwards (following Nietzsche), we all live by structures
of interpretation, which are necessary to make sense out of the chaos
of raw experience. These structures of interpretation are not merely
the filters through which we view the world, but also organizations of
action: the enduring practices and patterns of thought that underly
our form of life. These structures of interpretation, for Edwards, are
shot through with values. By values, Edwards means our most *fundamental* social practices, something close to what Richard Rorty calls a
"final vocabulary." Edwards says that "values are those ground-level
interpretations—patterns of comportment—upon which other interpretations are erected to form the edifice of a culture."[10]

By the term "normal nihilism," Edwards means neither doomed
pessimism nor the moral flatness of the sociopath, but simply the realization that our own values, these basic structures of interpretation on

which our lives are built, are themselves resting on nothing more than biology and history. They don't rest on the Christian's God or the philosopher's Truth, and so they are, says Edwards, "self-devaluating values." They are self-devaluating because of their contingency: they could well have been otherwise, and in fact, for other forms of life, they are. Edwards says,

> As normal nihilists we are aware of both the existence of radically alternative structures of interpretation and the fact that we ourselves lack any knockdown, non-circular way to demonstrate the self-sufficiency, solidity, or originality of our own. The only stories available to us to explain the values we hold (or better, that hold us) are causal stories; stories told by intellectual historians or by psychoanalysts, not by theologians or philosophers.[11]

This is not simply a matter of admitting that our own moral beliefs might have been different, or that they may be incorrect, or that other people in other places and times have had and will continue to have different moral beliefs. To think of values as *beliefs* is to make them too simple. Values (at least in Edwards's sense) are ways of interpreting the world. As such—and here is the most disturbing aspect of normal nihilism—they are the stuff out of which our very identities are made. We do not stand apart from our social and interpretive practices, coolly observing them from above. To say that my values are a matter of contingency is to say something not only about my beliefs but about the self who holds and acts on those beliefs. To acknowledge the contingency of my values is to acknowledge the contingency of who I am.

Does this mean that a normal nihilist is a moral relativist? Well, not exactly. Normal nihilism, for Edwards, is what happens to your *own* highest values, your most sacred sense of who you are and what you live for, on realizing that other values mean just the same to people whose forms of life are radically different from yours. It is the movement from Values in capital letters to values in the lowercase: the devaluation of values that happens on acknowledging that your own way of being in the world and seeing the world is not the only way, or the best way, or even the way that other people would choose if they were able. As Edwards says, "To be a normal nihilist is just to acknowledge that, however fervent and essential one's commitment to a particular set of values, that's all one ever has: a commitment to some particular set of values"[12]—not God, not Truth, not even a moral theory to which all rational human beings must necessarily agree.

This gap, this absence of any convincing story by philosophers or theologians as to how we got to where we are, can leave us staggered and a little punch-drunk, uncertain where to put our feet. The world loses whatever stability, whatever metaphysical completeness, it might once have had. Even this story that we tell ourselves, this story of "normal nihilism," is undercut. It may seem that to find ourselves normal nihilists is to have discovered our true selves, that normal nihilism is the inevitable result of realizing certain things about the world. But as Edwards points out, normal nihilism is not the True way of talking about ourselves. It is "just another way—our way—of cutting the cake."[13] What's worse, even these contingent values that we *do* have, our structures of interpretation, are *our* values only in the most trivial and superficial way. They are values that we have inherited from our families, our religion, our political system, our culture—all the forces that have created us. "Our" values are nothing more than clones of the behavioral and linguistic practices into which we were born. So we're tricked, says Edwards; we think we're living a life that is our own, when in fact we're acting out scripts written for us by somebody else. Thus, like Wittgenstein's ladder, this self-narrative dispenses with the very conditions which make it ring true for us; the values it embodies are themselves self-devalued. "Even our normal nihilism is just a banal contingency, not an uncanny insight into the Order of Things. There are no uncanny insights any more, not even this one. And so the Pathos of self-knowledge, even of our own self-knowledge as normal nihilists, seeps away. All that is left is the economic exchange, the making and buying and selling, of values."[14]

The symbol that Edwards uses for this condition, the contemporary alternative to Heidegger's *Schwarzwald* farmhouse, is the suburban shopping mall, where you see alternative values jostling right up against one another: a Christian bookstore next to a health club, a shop decorated to look like a tropical jungle side by side with one selling Colonial American knick-knacks, the Oxfam Third World Shop just across the corridor from the Disney store. For Edwards, this is not just the buying and selling of goods; it is the transformation of the clothing, the tools and the attitudes specific to particular times and places into commodities, which are sold to anonymous, rootless consumers. "Laid out before one are whole lives that one, if one has the necessary credit line, freely chose to inhabit: devout Christian; Williamsburg grandee; high-tech yuppie; Down East guide; great white hunter."[15] It is the transformation of forms of life into lifestyles to be bought and sold and eventually discarded or traded for another. What is being advertised and traded is not merely a commodity but an identity, a way of being.

The shopping mall is an auspicious metaphor for our spiritual condition. As Jackson Lears documents in his cultural history, *No Place of Grace*, twentieth-century Americans have seen generation after generation rebelling against what it sees as stifling mainstream values in an effort to establish more authentic and meaningful ways of living: the Arts and Crafts movement at the turn of the century, the Greenwich Village intellectuals of the pre-World War I era, the Beats, the counter-cultural movements of the '60s. But most of these movement have eventually failed, according to Lears, because they have had no anchor in structures of meaning outside the self. Where once these movements were motivated by religious or political goals, they have gradually come to be aimed instead at psychic harmony and personal fulfillment. And once these movements turned inward, they were easily subsumed into the broader consumer culture.[16] Thomas Frank puts it nicely in his critique of cultural dissent in the 1990s when he says that "existential rebellion has become a more or less official style of Information Age capitalism."[17]

What Frank realizes is how the market can gobble up and regurgitate any alternative or dissenting values, including the value of dissent itself. The story we contemporary Americans have been taught is that the enemy is conformity. According to this story the way to a more authentic existence is to break the rules, question authority, be yourself, subvert the established order. But business can exploit these values just as well as it can any other values. And so it does. Any value or idea can become part of the corporate world, including the countercultural ideals of rebellion and nonconformity. Business manuals exhort managers to challenge assumptions, to think outside the box. Television advertisements tell us that we assert our individuality through consumption. What we buy is who we are. "We consume not to fit in," Frank writes, "but to prove, on the surface at least, that we are rock 'n' roll rebels, each one of us as rule-breaking and hierarchy-defying as our heroes of the '60s, who now pitch cars, shoes, and beer. This imperative of endless difference is today the genius at the heart of American capitalism. . . ."[18]

Witness, for example, the late William S. Burroughs—Beat, homosexual drug addict, accidental killer and, most recently, spokesman for Nike. Frank writes that:

> as expertly as he once bayoneted American proprieties, as stridently as he once proclaimed himself beyond the laws of man and God, he is today a respected idealogue of the Information Age, occupying roughly the position in the pantheon of corporate-cultural thought once reserved strictly for Notre Dame football coaches and positive-thinking Methodist ministers. His inspirational writings are boardroom favorites, his dark nihilistic burpings the happy homilies of the new corporate faith.[19]

Did Burroughs sell out? Of course not. He could not have sold out, because his ideology is not appreciably different from that of American capitalism.

Frank thinks this story of rebellion and dissent is one that we were taught by the 1960s counterculture, but in fact it is a rather older story. Take, for instance, Malcolm Cowley's description of some of the values and ideas of Greenwich Village in the 1920s, which were themselves seen as a rebellion against the prevailing business-Christian ethic of the day: the idea of self-expression, or that our purpose in life is to realize our individuality through artistic creativity and living in beautiful surroundings; the idea of female equality; the idea of living for the moment; the idea of liberty, or that laws and conventions preventing self-expression should be abolished; the idea of psychological adjustment, that we are unhappy because we are psychologically repressed. Any one of these slogans of rebellion could

equally well have described the values of the countercultural movements of the 1960s and early '70s. And like those values, the values of
the Greenwich Village intellectuals were eventually appropriated by
the mainstream business establishment, which exploited them to
encourage people to consume just those goods that the Village had
made fashionable. Responding to the *Saturday Evening Post's* procla-
mation that Greenwich Village was dying, Cowley wrote: "It was dying
because women smoked cigarettes on the streets of the Bronx, drank
gin cocktails in Omaha, and had perfectly swell parties in Seattle and
Middletown—in other words, because American business and the
whole of middle-class America had gone Greenwich Village."[20]

The commodification of values can be seen as either cause or effect
of our normal nihilism: cause, in that reducing values to fungible
goods inevitably flattens them out and devalues them; or effect,
because only in a culture uprooted from its existential moorings
would the selling of identities and forms of life have the deep pull
that it has. Either way, for Edwards, it carries two dangers.

The first is related to the appeal of the market, the endless quest
for the new. The danger here is that of change for the sake of change.
We can become addicted to novelty, forever reinventing ourselves and
restructuring our way of seeing the world. The market is not a cause
of this restlessness so much as an efficient exploiter of it. And by so
doing, the market reinforces the contingency of our values, identities,
traditions, forms of life. The world loses its depth. As Edwards puts
it, "The Christian bookstore is for us just another shop in the mall."[21]

The second danger is the opposite of the first, that of sinking into
the everydayness of life. Rather than immersing ourselves in the variety and flux of life, we react against it by letting ourselves be defined
by ordinary social and cultural roles. Our responses to the world are
determined by what others think and say, our identities determined
by convention. This is the danger that Walker Percy's Binx Bolling
worries about, that of becoming Anyone Anywhere. Percy, echoing
Fromm, calls this a "pathology of normalcy," where a person may
meet every biological and cultural norm yet still feel alienated and
alone. [22]

IV

It is easy to misread the question of whether there is anything morally worrying about treating our normal nihilism with Prozac. The knee-jerk reaction is to dismiss Prozac as a kind of ennui-tranquilizer, a way of anesthetizing oneself against demands of living.[23] But Prozac is no anesthetic. If anything, people who use Prozac and the other SSRIs often say the opposite: that they feel energized, more alert, better able to cope with the world, better able to understand themselves and their problems. It is also too easy to insist that the SSRIs do not, in fact, rid people of their existential problems, because the issue is much more thoroughgoing than simply the SSRIs. That issue concerns the way that psychiatry looks at human beings and the way that view may be changing with the development of more effective chemical treatments.

It is a platitude that medicine is an art as well as a science, and the extraordinary growth of medical technology over the past half-century has prompted fear in many humanistically minded clinicians, including some psychiatrists, that medicine has swung much too far toward the scientific-technological. The cost of that swing has been a deteriorating relationship between physicians and patients, a shift that has left both parties uneasy about the state of present-day medical practice. As the surgeon and author Richard Selzer says: "You don't have to ask your patients anything. You order a hundred blood tests, get a hundred X-rays, hook them up to the machinery, and you don't have to look at them or ask them questions. . . . It's a different thing entirely. It's a mechanical, technical, more brilliant process, for which I am not at all suited."[24]

Nonetheless, despite the cost to the personal relationship between physicians and patients, technological medicine has had spectacular success in curing and controlling disease. And whatever the advantages of a closer understanding between doctors and patients, few of us, when faced with life-threatening or debilitating illness, would hesitate to trade that understanding for technical excellence. Its flaws notwithstanding, the biomedical approach to disease continues to achieve a sounder understanding of the ills and frailties of the human body.

Essential to this approach is a view of the human body as a mechanism. The task of biomedical science is to discover the pathophysiological mechanisms that underlie disease and dysfunction, and then to devise a remedy. The task of medical practitioners is to diagnose, by observing signs and symptoms, and to treat, using the appropriate technology, the diseases and dysfunctions that underlie the problems of a particular patient. The practitioner may have other tasks—comfort, friendship, emotional support—that may or may not influence this underlying pathophysiology. Some of these tasks may be morally obligatory, no matter what their influence. But regardless of these additional tasks, modern medicine has built whatever success it has achieved largely on mechanistic foundations—the human body as a vast, elaborate and sometimes mysterious machine.

This mechanistic approach to the human body underlies the peculiar status of psychiatry as a medical discipline. To see something mechanistically—be it a body, a brain or a blender—is to take up a certain attitude toward it, an attitude that entails certain beliefs, preconceptions and ways of behaving. This attitude is difficult to reconcile with much of the subject matter of psychiatry, which is concerned largely with human relationships and problems in living.

Some of these difficulties are simply the result of the assumptions that underlie science. To see something as an object of scientific inquiry is to see it as a product of causal forces, something to be tested, probed and experimented upon for the purposes of prediction and control. Most of us are able quite easily to picture the human body in this way, and even the human brain. This is not, of course, the way that we *ordinarily* see our bodies, and to see our bodies as objects of scientific inquiry may require that we suspend our ordinary attitudes. A clinician shifts from his ordinary attitude toward the body to a mechanistic one the moment he enters the examining room. But it is much more difficult to take up this scientific attitude (at least for very long) toward human behavior. No matter how hard we try to see behavior as the product of causal forces, governed by the laws of nature, and no matter how tempting such a view might be in clinically controlled, laboratory conditions, it is difficult to take the scientific attitude toward human behavior as it occurs, so to speak, in nature: people falling in love, telling stories, playing baseball, saying prayers.

A more important reason for the difficulties in reconciling psychiatry and mechanism relates to the contrast between what Peter Strawson has called reactive and objective attitudes.[25] Reactive attitudes are those attitudes that we take toward other human beings and that govern our relationships with them: "the non-detached attitudes and reactions of people directly involved with each other," such as "gratitude, resentment, forgiveness, love, and hurt feelings." Reactive attitudes are the currency of human life, and we attach great importance to them—both the attitudes that we take toward others, and the attitudes that they take toward us. As Strawson says:

> We should think of the many different kinds of relationships we can have with other people—as sharers of a common interest; as members of the same family; as colleagues; as friends; as lovers; as chance parties to an enormous range of transactions and encounters. And then we should think, in each of these transactions in turn, and in others, of the kind of importance we attach to the attitudes and intentions towards us on the part of those who stand in these relationships to us, and of the kinds of *reactive* attitudes and feelings to which we are prone.

Though much of ordinary life is characterized by these reactive attitudes, we are also able to take toward other human beings another sort of attitude, profoundly opposed to the first. To take an *objective* attitude toward another human being is to see him or her as an object—of social policy, of scientific inquiry, of medical treatment, or of many other things. The objective attitude may even be emotionally colored in some ways. According to Strawson, "(i)t may include repulsion or fear, it may include pity or even love, though not all kinds of love." However, to take up the objective attitude is to abandon the reactive attitudes that characterize our ordinary relationships with other human beings, such as forgiveness, resentment, gratitude, and a certain sort of love. As Strawson puts it: "If your attitude toward someone is wholly objective, then though you may fight him, you cannot quarrel with him, and though you may talk to him, you cannot reason with him. You can at most pretend to quarrel, or reason, with him."

To some extent we all take the objective attitude toward human beings who are immature or mentally disordered or handicapped beyond a certain degree. We suspend, for example, our ordinary judgments of responsibility, praise and blame. Less often, we take this attitude toward normal, mature individuals—perhaps as a way of studying them. But as Strawson notes, "what is above all interesting is the tension there is, in us, between the participant attitude and the objective attitude. One is tempted to say: between our humanity and our intelligence. But to say this would be to distort both notions."

Psychiatry straddles the border between objective and reactive attitudes, between our intelligence and our humanity. Like any other medical practitioner, the psychiatrist must look upon the patient as an object of inquiry and treatment; to do any less would be to do something other than psychiatry. But to an extent much greater than in the other medical specialties, the psychiatrist must also remain aware and take account of the reactive attitudes that characterize human life outside the therapeutic relationship. The encounter between a patient and her psychiatrist is a very different affair from that between, say, a patient and a surgeon. It bears a far greater resemblance, at least superficially, to those encounters that are familiar from ordinary human life. The balance between the reactive and the objective is a fragile one, and some psychiatrists are better at maintaining it than others. Many of us have had the slightly eerie experience of suspecting that we are being clinically examined during an ordinary conversation with a psychiatrist—the result of an inappropriate "I see," or, "tell me more about that," or, "and how did that make you feel?"

Percy's ontological lapsometer is comic precisely because it exploits the pretensions of the behavioral sciences toward objectivity; it objectifies those aspects of our experience that are most resistant to analysis in scientific terms. With the lapsometer in hand, any physican can "probe the very secrets of the soul, diagnose the maladies that poison the wellsprings of man's hope."[26] It is this same aspiration toward scientific objectivity that seems to underlie the jargon that behavioral scientists invent to describe the intercourse of ordinary life—jargon that, no matter how effective a means of communication between professionals, seems peculiarly inappropriate when we try to apply it to our own experience. As Percy says elsewhere, "Take these two sentences that I once read in a book on mental hygiene: 'The most profound of all human needs, the prime requisite for successful living, is to be emotionally inclusive. Socrates, Jesus, Buddha, St. Francis were emotionally inclusive.' These words tremble with anxiety and alienation, even though I would not deny that they are, in their own eerie way, true."[27]

The attitude of objectivity is one that all clinicians must, at certain points in the clinical encounter, take toward their patients, but for several reasons the objective attitude is a delicate one for psychiatrists. First, the means by which psychiatrists diagnose mental disorders is the same means by which they conduct the intercourse of ordinary life. Language is the psychiatrist's diagnostic instrument— the medium for objective attitudes as well as reactive. Laboratory medicine, radiology and physical diagnosis are largely (but not, of course, entirely) outside the psychiatrist's typical diagnostic armamentarium. Psychiatric diagnosis involves an intricate interplay of words, hints, cues, and gestures, similar to the language that we all use to conduct our lives but put to a different task. As Percy writes, "The psychiatrist not only enters into a conversation as other people do; he also preserves a posture of objectivity from which he takes note of the patient's behavior, and his own, according to the principles of his science."[28]

Second, the relationship between psychiatrist and patient is itself a focus of objective attitudes. The relationship of most clinicians to their patients is simply a *means* of getting at the patient's problems— a means by which to diagnose and treat. In contrast, the relationship of a psychiatrist to her patient is not only such a means, it is also a proper object of study. Percy himself wrote, "The social psychologist studies the interactions of person and groups. But the psychiatrist is largely concerned with the 'interaction' between the patient and himself. And so the psychiatrist has come to be called the 'participant observer.'"[29] Unlike many behavioral scientists, the psychiatrist studies not only the patient's life outside the clinic, but also the relationship that she and the patient share.

Third, insofar as a psychiatrist uses psychotherapy, he must maintain a balance between objective and reactive attitudes not only in diagnosis but also in treatment. For most nonpsychiatric practitioners, the border between objective and reactive attitudes in their treatment is clear. They treat illness or disability with drugs, surgery, radiotherapy or whatever, and they also provide encouragement, emotional support and guidance. Technological treatment requires an objective attitude; emotional support requires a reactive one. Both sorts of treatment and attitudes seem necessary for healing (although the reasons may sometimes be obscure). On the other hand, the psychiatrist, whose therapeutic tool may be largely or entirely psychotherapy, must treat the patient in a manner that combines both reactive and objective attitudes. The patient must be thought of as an object of treatment, but she cannot be thought of solely as an object; part of the reason that psychotherapy is effective is that the patient is treated as a person, a proper focus of reactive attitudes.

There is a tendency in medicine to devalue those aspects of practice that are not easily manipulated by technological means. Psychiatrists know all too well that within the typical US medical school hierarchy, psychiatry falls near the bottom. Even practitioners who are very sensitive to the emotional needs of their patients tend to see this aspect of medical practice as something intuitive and scientifically soft: the so-called "art of medicine." As a physician, Percy was very familiar with this prejudice. "Unfortunately, there still persists in the medical profession the quaint superstition that only the visible is real. Thus the soul is not real. Uncaused terror cannot exist. Then, friend, how come you are shaking?"[30]

In psychiatry itself there is much controversy over whether one should embrace a biological or a psychodynamic model of psychiatric practice. Implicit in a biological model is the assumption that most or many psychiatric disorders are the result of neurochemical abnormalities and that psychiatric research will eventually discover a way of rectifying these abnormalities, probably by chemical means. Percy's ontological lapsometer parodies the biological approach by taking it to its logical extension—electrochemically measuring the human soul, treating its ailments with ionized "heavy sodium." The irony, of course, is that what Percy intended as parody has, to some extent, been realized. Aspects of personality that once seemed fixed and part of a person's identity look much less fixed if they can be altered with medication.

Yet how far are we willing to take this logic? As prominent a psychiatrist as Samuel Guze has written that "there is no such thing as a psychiatry which is too biological."[31] By this, Guze meant to respond to the criticism that a biologically based psychiatry was in some way inadequate or incomplete, and he followed his assertion with a broad sketch of the way in which all of human life, culture and society can be thought of as the result of vast, complex permutations of human brain function. In one sense Guze is certainly right; if we view biology as the study of life, then the charge that psychiatry can be too biological would be an odd one. But surely to defend biological psychiatry on these grounds is to miss the point of the criticism.

Biological psychiatry has come into its own largely as a result of greater scientific knowledge about neurotransmitter function and the development of psychopharmacological agents: the phenothiazines, tricyclic antidepressants, lithium, the MAO inhibitors, the SSRIs. The impressive results of these investigations into brain function have meant that psychiatrically disordered patients now have a far greater chance of being successfully treated than they had in the past. But the aim of most critics of biological psychiatry, including Percy, is not to challenge the results of biological investigation, now or in the future, nor is it to question the therapeutic worth of psychopharmacological agents. Rather, the point of the criticism is to question whether the subject matter of psychiatry can be completely and fully explained in biological terms.

Psychiatry certainly has to do with things such as dopamine and serotonin—but it also has to do with things like worrying, teasing and grieving, with getting married, losing a job and joining the Marines. The problem for biological psychiatry is to explain things like the latter in terms of the former. Now, it is no doubt possible to devise an explanation of some sort—to account for the notion of "worry" in terms of brain function in the same way that it might be possible to account for my experience of listening to Tommy Dorsey's rendering of "I'm Getting Sentimental Over You" in terms of its effects on my ears, my acoustic nerves and brain. But the point is that an explanation of a biological sort, simply by virtue of its being biological, will not be able to account for *all* of the subject matter of psychiatry—at least not in the way that we wish to have it explained.

Much philosophical history has been built on the difficulties that emerge when we try to explain phenomena of one sort with the vocabulary of another. Percy was himself well aware of the troubled history of the philosophy of mind—of the difficulties of explaining the mind with the vocabulary of the brain, of explaining free will within the framework of causal laws. In *Love in the Ruins* More puts up his lapsometer as the culmination of this history: "the first hope of bridging the dread chasm that has rent the soul of Western man ever since the famous philosopher Descartes ripped body loose from mind and turned the very soul into a ghost that haunts its own house."

But it is not at all clear whether biological psychiatry can ever realize its implicit agenda—treating all psychiatric disorders by correcting neurochemical function. One reason is that even if we know all that there is to know about neurochemistry, we cannot explain everything about human behavior that is relevant to psychiatric disorders within the vocabulary of neurochemistry. Much of our interest in and knowledge of human behavior derives from a context much wider than neurochemistry: the context of human life and culture. Neurochemical and anatomical explanations are obviously related to psychological, anthropological and humanistic explanations, and they do seem, in some sense, more basic—but it would be naive to assume that all other descriptions of human life can ultimately be reduced to the vocabulary of brain function.[32]

For one thing, psychiatry is concerned with the human being not only as an object, but also as a subject of experience. Psychiatrists have the difficult task of reconciling what they know about human beings, so to speak, from "the outside"—their behavior, their neuroanatomy and neurophysiology, their language—with what it is like to be a human being "from the inside." It is debatable whether combining the subjective and the objective points of view is conceptually possible.[33] But it is clear that the subjective point of view cannot be discounted. Biological psychiatrists are in danger of forgetting that our interest in psychiatry arises largely from our interest in what it is like to be a human being.

A second problem for biological psychiatry is the fact that much of the vocabulary by which we describe and understand human mental life is logically interwoven into a much wider context than that of brain events.[34] It is impossible to understand beliefs, desires and intentions—not to mention fear, hope, love and anxiety—apart from the broader setting in which they occur. These are concepts that have evolved within a certain form of human life, and they make sense only against the backdrop of that life. Speaking of fear and remorse apart from the setting of human life is as unintelligible as speaking of bishops and checkmates apart from the game of chess. The concept "checkmate" is interwoven with a variety of other concepts such as "king," "chessboard," "game" and "rule," to the extent that some understanding of all of them is necessary for an understanding of any of them. In like fashion, the concept of "fear" or "remorse" or "love" will not be intelligible without some understanding of the setting in which people feel "fear" or "remorse" or "love," and the vast array of related concepts with which they are intertwined.

A third problem is simply that scientific explanations are often causal ones, and our interest in human behavior is not always an interest in causes. Suppose that I encounter, as I once did as a medical student, a patient whom I believe to be psychotic, and who has been brought to the hospital by the police for attending classical music concerts in his pajamas, without a ticket, drinking Johnny Walker Black Label scotch whiskey. When he is interviewed, I notice that he has a shirt pocket full of shaving cream, which he eats from time to time. I ask him about the reason he has been brought to the hospital; he walks over to the attending psychiatrist and begins to tug gently on this man's necktie. I probe further, and he says something to the effect: "Black is black? Reds are trump. I can't tell—yes or no?"

Now, this patient's behavior and his bizarre speech may or may not eventually be explainable causally—in terms of genetics, neurochemistry, environmental factors and so on. But even if this information allowed me to identify the causes of his actions and predict them infallibly, I will still not have understood his behavior or his speech; they will still not be intelligible to me. Understanding his behavior is more than understanding what caused it; it is placing his actions in some sort of wider context, establishing some sort of communicative link, seeing what it might be like to be in his situation, establishing some sort of kinship with him, understanding his reasons for acting and answering as he did (if he can be said to have reasons). This is why psychotic behavior seems so intriguing and mysterious: not because we do not understand its causes, but because it appears so disconcertingly alien.[35] We cannot understand the severely psychotic because we cannot take the same sort of attitude toward them as we do toward ordinary human beings.

In his *Philosophical Investigations*, Wittgenstein makes the remark: "My attitude towards him is an attitude towards a soul. I am not of the *opinion* that he has a soul."[36] At least part of what Wittgenstein is getting at with this comment is that our attitudes toward and relationships with other human beings are of a certain character, and that this character is different from that of our attitudes toward other things or beings. Our attitudes toward persons are attitudes toward souls. This does not mean that we have any beliefs about an immaterial substance that distinguishes humans from other beings—"I am not of the *opinion* that he has a soul"—but it does mean that we have certain ways of describing and understanding human behavior that are distinct from our ways of describing and understanding anything else.

To understand another "soul" is partly, of course, to understand the relationships that human beings enter into with each other—as friends, rivals, colleagues, confessors—and the sorts of activities that characterize those relationships—playing, celebrating, pretending, cheating. But it is also to understand those aspects of human life that we often call, for lack of a better word, "spiritual." To speak of the spiritual, of souls, is to speak not only of the religious but also of those things that surround a unique part of human life—that part of life where we speak of reverence and transcendence, and of alienation, meaninglessness and absurdity. A person's soul is not just his mind, or his brain, or even his psyche; it is his self. Soul implies—among other things—depth, moral constitution, one's true nature.

Thus when Percy speaks of treating the ailments of the soul, he is not simply speaking metaphorically; "spiritual illness" is the best description of an aspect of human life recognizable to all of us.

In the end, what may be most interesting about Prozac may not be what it tells us about depression but what it tells us about psychiatrists. Like those in most theoretical disciplines, psychiatrists are often tempted to consider their subject within the simplest possible conceptual framework. Thus some psychiatrists are inclined to think of psychiatric problems as a peculiar set of biological problems; others, like the so-called antipsychiatrists, argue that psychiatric problems are no more than the problems of life. Most psychiatrists realize that the truth falls somewhere in between these two extremes. Most psychiatric problems are not simply medical, or even social or psychological. In Harry Stack Sullivan's words, "psychiatry deals with living," and so psychiatric problems are also spiritual problems, ailments of the soul.[37] It may be that these problems are the inevitable consequence of human existence: of the sort of life in which one is able to step back and compare the way life is and the way one would like it to be. Perhaps psychiatrists are no better equipped to treat such problems than anyone else. But these ailments of the soul are so closely tied to the problems that psychiatrists encounter that they cannot be ignored. In Percy's words, these ailments are "the new plague, the modern Black Death, the current hermaphroditism of the spirit, namely: More's syndrome, or: chronic angelism-bestialism that rives soul from body and sets it orbiting the great world as the spirit of abstraction whence it takes the form of beasts, swans and bulls, werewolves, blood-suckers, Mr. Hydes, or just poor lonesome ghost locked in its own machinery."[38]

Chapter 4

Puppet-Masters and Personality Disorders: Psychopathology, Determinism and Responsibility

> *You sometimes see in a wind a piece of paper blowing about anyhow. Suppose the piece of paper could make the decision: "Now I want to go this way." I say, "Queer, this paper always decides where it is to go, and all the time it is the wind that blows it. I know it is the wind that blows it."*
>
> ——Ludwig Wittgenstein

I

Ask a group of psychiatrists what sorts of mental disorders excuse a criminal offender from responsibility, and the number of answers you get will usually equal or exceed the number of psychiatrists in the group. This is not surprising: mental disorders are varied, patients unique, and circumstances unpredictable. Even so, about two broad groups of mental disorders there is, if not unanimity, at least broad consensus. The first group are the psychotic disorders—schizophrenia, psychotic depression and the manic-depressive or bipolar disorder.

Given certain constraints, nearly everyone will agree upon these disorders as the paradigmatic excuse for criminal responsibility. The second group are the personality disorders, about which there will be consensus for just the opposite conclusion. Very few psychiatrists will count a personality disorder as an excuse from moral or criminal responsibility. This generally holds even for the psychopathic or antisocial personality disorder, which counts among its diagnostic markers deficiencies that clearly bear on moral concerns.

These two groups of disorders fall on opposite ends of a spectrum of psychiatric disorders, the tension between which sustains many controversies about how psychiatry should be done. At one end of the spectrum are those psychiatric disorders like schizophrenia and the manic-depressive disorder which many (perhaps most) mental health workers believe will eventually be shown to be brain diseases. At the other end are the personality disorders and others like them, which seem less like brain diseases and more like problems in living. The vocabulary with which the first sort of disorders are discussed often overlaps with those of biochemistry, neuroanatomy, neuroendocrinology, and pharmacology. The vocabulary with which the second sort are discussed borrows less from neuroscience than from abnormal psychology and psychoanalysis. It also bears a stronger resemblance to the vocabulary of ordinary life: less talk about pathophysiology, more about anxiety, guilt, social relationships and the like.

Personality disorders are deeply ingrained, long-standing patterns of behavior and thought that, at least as they are conventionally defined, lead either to distress or to impairment in the person's ability to function in social situations, at work, or in some other important area of life.[1] Thus the paranoid personality disorder is characterized by suspicion and distrust, the borderline personality disorder by impulsivity and instability in relationships and self-image, the antisocial personality disorder by disregard for the rights of others, the narcissistic personality disorder by grandiosity and a lack of empathy and so on. We all know people with personalities like these. In fact, a fair number of Hollywood villains would be diagnosable with personality disorders—say, Glenn Close's borderline personality in *Fatal Attraction*, or Dennis Hopper's paranoid personality in *Paris Trout*. Joe Pesci has made a career out of playing a particular sort of antisocial personality, most famously in Martin Scorcese's *Goodfellas*.

It should come as no great surprise that psychiatrists are more apt to regard psychotic illnesses as legitimate excuses from criminal responsibility than they are the personality disorders. Criminal responsibility hinges on the matter of intention, and the psychoses affect a person's intentions in a way that personality disorders do not. A person who suffers the psychotic delusion that his mother's body is inhabited by a malevolent alien from outer space might be excused from assaulting her, while a person with the borderline personality disorder would be held responsible. The difference is intention: the latter intended to cause his mother harm, while the former intended only to defend himself.

Yet this is not the whole story. There is more to the intuition that a certain sort of psychiatric disorder excuses a person from responsibility in ways that others fail to do. It is the notion that a disorder is medically legitimated by a biological explanation but not by a psychological one, and that only medical disorders can provide excuses from moral responsibility. This notion has fueled a generation of effort to gather a variety of conditions under the medical umbrella, from neurosis to alcoholism. These efforts have not generally been very successful; even if conditions like personality disorders are still *called* disorders, or illnesses, or diseases, they are still widely believed to be different.[2] But the reasoning behind the efforts is understandable. Biomedical descriptions engender different attitudes toward the responsibility of the agent for her illness and for her actions. Mention certain characteristic EEG patterns in persons with the antisocial personality disorder, for example, and attitudes instantly become much more forgiving. Similarly, as behavioral geneticists tell us that aspects of character such as shyness, sociability and novelty-seeking show some degree of genetic influence, our sense of a person's responsibility for his character starts to erode.[3] The same goes for any other associated objective, physical, "medical" characteristic of personality or character. As soon as medical concepts arrive at the front door, moral responsibility begins sneaking out the back.

II

There are two broad ways of speaking about the subject matter of psychiatry. The first is what might be called the language of mechanism. We speak this language when we talk about the pathophysiology of mental disorders, genetic inheritance patterns, and the effects on mental conditions of pharmacological treatment. Its central concepts are mechanism and causation: explaining how things work and why.

The second way of speaking is the language of persons. We speak this language when we talk about a person's reasons for acting, her motivation, her beliefs, intentions, desires and so on. A rich vocabulary has evolved in this language to describe psychopathology: delusions, hallucinations, phobias, obsessions, compulsions and so on. Like the language of mechanism, this language is often used for explanatory purposes, but its explanations differ in kind from mechanistic ones. Explaining a person's actions by referring to his voyeuristic desires or paranoid delusions gives one a type of understanding that differs from the understanding acquired by an explanation in terms of pathophysiology.

The problem for philosophers has traditionally been the relationship between these two sorts of languages: between talk about the brain, mechanisms, neurophysiology and the causes of a person's behavior; and talk about choice, experience, intentions and a person's reasons for acting. The debate over free will and determinism has been one of the most stubborn of these problems. To shift back and forth between the language of persons and the language of mechanism, as psychiatrists often do, is also to shift between the assumptions inherent in the two languages. The language of mechanism includes the tacit assumption that actions are caused, which implies that a person had no choice but to act, and hence no responsibility for acting. Contrast with this the language of persons, which gives a central place to concepts such as intending, willing and choosing—words that seem to embed just the opposite assumption: that persons are able to act freely and consequently should be held accountable for those actions which they have freely chosen.

Whether and how these two languages can be reconciled is, to put it mildly, debatable. A more subtle question is why they appear so irreconcilable. This is the question that Wittgenstein concerns himself with, rather obliquely, in his very sketchy and epigrammatic "Lecture on Freedom of the Will."[4]

Wittgenstein's later philosophy gives a central place to the notion of attitudes and especially to the subtle way that taking a certain attitude toward events, objects or beings can affect the way that we think about them. Consider, for example, a person whose picture of the world is colored by the notion of retribution. When he is ill, he thinks. "What have I done to deserve this?" When he is ashamed of himself he thinks, "This will be punished."[5] The notion of retribution casts a certain hue on the way he interprets events and deliberates about his actions.

Although attitudes are related to beliefs, taking an attitude toward something is not quite the same as holding beliefs about it. Wittgenstein makes this clear when he discusses religion, which he considers not a network of beliefs, acquired and held in the same way as beliefs about facts, but rather a certain way of looking at the world.[6] Miracles are a good example. Suppose two passenger planes collide in midair, explode and plunge into the ocean. Everyone is killed—except one child, who not only survives, but survives unhurt. Her father might well think that her survival is a miracle. An engineer might look at the same event and say that there must be a scientific explanation—something about the particular circumstances of the accident, where the child was seated, where the plane crashed and so on. In describing the differences between these two ways of looking at the child's survival, it would be misleading simply to say that the father and the engineer held different beliefs. Rather, they have different ways of interpreting the same events and the same evidence. No matter what scientific evidence was uncovered, the father might still insist that his child's survival was a miracle. And no matter how little explanation science could provide, the engineer might still insist that there must be *some* scientific explanation. It would be less misleading to say the father and the engineer have different attitudes toward the event. They perceive the event and think about it in different ways; they approach it with different sensibilities.[7]

In the "Lecture on Freedom of the Will," Wittgenstein suggests that we take up a certain attitude when we look at something mechanistically. This attitude is more a tacit assumption than a reasoned set of beliefs acquired under the weight of evidence. The attitude, suggests Wittgenstein, is one of "fatalism"—the notion that things could not have happened otherwise. To think of events as governed by natural laws suggests that they are inevitable, that "what will happen is laid down somewhere."[8] For instance, the use of the word "law," as in "the laws of nature," seems to contain within it the idea of compulsion, implying that things are forced to occur as they do. We tend to think of natural laws, says Wittgenstein, "as if they were rails, along which things had to move."[9]

These sorts of attitudes are noticeably absent from our dealings with persons. It would not occur to most of us, except in extraordinary circumstances, to think of a person's behavior as "on rails." To think of a person as a mechanism is to take a step back from the assumptions resident in our ordinary ways of associating with human beings. Again, these assumptions are not so much beliefs as attitudes. As Wittgenstein writes in the *Investigations*, "My attitude toward him is an attitude towards a soul. I am not of the *opinion* that he has a soul."[10] Within the framework of this attitude, an attitude towards a "soul," explaining a person's behavior is ordinarily not a matter of explaining its causes. We explain behavior, both our own and that of others, by talking about reasons for acting, beliefs, intentions, desires and so on.[11] This is true of pathological behavior as well. Making sense of behavior which appears unusual or bizarre is often a matter of understanding the agent's delusions, obsessions or phobias and trying to see how they affect the way a person sees the world.

Daniel Dennett suggests that we have a number of different ways of explaining the behavior of a system, any of which we can adopt when it is convenient, but none of which rules out other sorts of explanations.[12] For example, we can make predictions about physical systems from the "physical stance" based purely on our knowledge of the state of the system and the laws of nature. ("Sit on that chair and it will break.") With more complicated systems, we often take the "intentional stance," which presumes some degree of rationality in the system. We take this stance toward human beings, whose behavior would be impossible to predict with what little we know about the mechanism of the brain; but we can also take the intentional stance toward other complicated systems, such as computers. When we take the intentional stance toward a computer (as we might when we play chess against it, for example) we behave toward the computer as if it had beliefs, intentions, desires and so on—without asking whether or not it "really" has them. Explaining and predicting the computer's actions does not preclude a physical explanation; rather, in some situations the intentional stance is simply a convenient one to take.

The intentional stance seems to be a prerequisite for Peter Strawson's notion of reactive attitudes, as contrasted with the objective attitude (for example) of science.[13] Reactive attitudes are those which characterize the relationships that we share with other persons, as friends or enemies, colleagues or competitors. They are not detached; they may be morally or emotionally charged, and they are associated with engagement rather than observation: gratitude, resentment, forgiveness. Strawson's reactive attitudes go further and deeper than Dennett's intentional stance; they imply a *relationship* rather than an explanatory perspective. One would not take a reactive attitude toward a computer, for example. But the intentional stance is a necessary *prelude* to a reactive attitude. Before one can take a reactive attitude toward a person, one must presume that her behavior is, to some minimal degree, rationally explainable.

We often move from the intentional stance to the physical when something in the system goes wrong. When a computer does not behave as we expect, we look for a physical explanation ("it isn't plugged in" or "the hard drive has crashed"). The same applies to human beings, at least to some extent. It is only when a person's speech and behavior become sufficiently strange that we step back into the physical stance.

This physical stance is not the position that we ordinarily take toward other persons. Nor, for that matter, is the objective attitude. We do not ordinarily approach a person with the idea of explaining or interpreting his behavior. Ordinary associations between persons are, to a greater or lesser degree, *relationships*. One is aware of how the other speaks and behaves, but one is also slightly self-conscious, aware of how the other reacts to one's *own* words and behavior.

Embedded in this relationship are certain mutual assumptions about thought and behavior—for example, that they are rational and, if need be, explainable in terms of certain features of human life. But we do not ordinarily feel that the other's behavior *needs* to be explained; rather, these assumptions about thought and behavior are implicit in the relationship and in the reactive attitude that we take.

When a person's words and behavior stray outside certain bounds, however, this relationship is snapped. Our position shifts: where we once were on one end of a relationship, we now become observers of the other's behavior. Our tacit assumption that the other person's behavior is explainable becomes questionable. We feel the need to look for some sort of *explicit* explanation when a person begins to behave strangely; we cannot find our feet with a person without making sense of what he is saying, how he is acting.

We ordinarily search first for an explanation in the language of ordinary life. We look toward a person's beliefs, motivation, feelings, perceptions and such. ("Why does he keep looking at the door?" "Because he is worried that his wife will come in.") With the psychotic person, however, these sorts of explanations begin to falter. ("Why is he wearing earmuffs indoors?" "He thinks that the FBI is broadcasting signals to his brain through his ears." "But *why* does he think *that*?") And with the severely psychotic, these sorts of explanations often fail completely. When a person's thoughts and behavior are utterly incomprehensible to an outsider—when they do not fit together in the ways that one would ordinarily expect—an explanation in the language of ordinary life will be unsatisfactory, because the framework of beliefs, desires and motivations upon which that language is built can no longer be assumed. We cannot simply assume that a psychotic person's thoughts cohere in the same way as ours. It is at this point, when the language of ordinary life fails, that we are inclined to start asking questions about a person's brain function.

We rarely reach this point with personality disorders. Personality disorders are essentially problems of character: long-standing traits of personality that influence the way a person negotiates her way through the world. A tense, humorless, excessively defensive accountant who reads snubs or insults into every remark that her coworkers make; an envious, self-important departmental chairman who exploits others in order to rise in the university hierarchy; an overly sensitive, ingratiating, dependent housewife who is unable to make even trivial decisions about everyday matters without reassurance from other people—these are not the sorts of people toward whom we ordinarily take an objective attitude. Unlike many people who are psychotic, people with personality disorders do not typically behave in a way that prevents us from relating to them as one human being to another. They may be frustrating, or repellent, or even puzzling, but we quite naturally take a reactive attitude toward them. They are people with whom we can have some sort of relationship.

Psychoanalysis presumes a different type of attitude, one which is a curious hybrid between the attitudes one ordinarily takes toward persons (or "souls," to use Wittgenstein's term) and those one ordinarily takes toward mechanisms. On the one hand, psychoanalysis and other types of psychotherapy ordinarily use the language of persons, the vocabulary that we use to explain and describe human behavior in everyday life: a person's fears and desires, beliefs, anxieties and worries. It has a further specialized vocabulary to describe certain common types of behavior and psychological characteristics—projection, repression, transference and the like. However, these terms are typically shorthand for concepts that can be described in the vocabulary of ordinary life.

Psychoanalytic explanations may but do not necessarily compete with other explanations. A person's behavior might be explained, for example, both in terms of unconscious desires and in terms of neurophysiology. Psychoanalytic explanations notoriously lack the predictive power that we ordinarily expect of a causal explanation. However, it is also true that psychoanalytic explanation does not aim at prediction in the same way. It is interpretive, and its purpose is less prediction than therapy. If psychoanalysis helps a compulsive handwasher to explain his compulsion to himself psychoanalytically, and thereby rid himself of it, it is a valuable tool, even if it has no predictive power.

Yet on the other hand, the explanations provided by the concepts of psychoanalysis and, to a lesser extent, other sorts of psychotherapy often bear a striking resemblance to mechanistic explanations.

Psychoanalytic explanations use terms like fears and desires, but in a special sense: they are often unconscious fears and desires, hidden from the agent. Whereas in their ordinary use they give a person *reasons* for behaving in a certain way, in their psychoanalytic use they *move* the person to behave; they are like causes of behavior rather than reasons for it.

These are terms which, in contrast to those of neurophysiology, presume a subject: there must be *someone* who desires or fears. But the psychoanalytical subject lurks unseen by the conscious subject. It is an agent; it has the power of will and choice. But it wills and chooses unconsciously, moving the conscious agent in ways which, at least before psychotherapy, he does not suspect.

Thus the attitude of mechanism, the fatalism which Wittgenstein observed, is as present in the explanations of psychoanalysis as in those of biology. Psychoanalysis and, to a lesser degree, other sorts of psychotherapy assume that a person's conscious will is inclined one way or another by unconscious forces. This may help to explain why mechanistic assumptions—that events are guided as if they are "on rails"—often creep into discussions of character and personality. To say that a person's narcissistic behavior is an unconscious way of coping with feelings of inferiority may be a helpful way of understanding the behavior, but it also brings in the notion that a person is being caused to act, by suggesting that he is being moved by forces outside his conscious control.

It also helps to explain why the notions of intention and choice often get lost in discussions of the personality disorders. Neither a biological nor a psychodynamic view of the personality disorders has much room for the concept of agency. Both are attempts to understand human character and behavior causally, and the salient characteristics of agency—willing, choosing, intending—are difficult to describe in causal terms.

The very term "personality disorder" has mechanistic connotations which can be misleading for questions of responsibility. To say that a personality can be disordered is to imply that it can, at least in theory, be fixed. The model implicit in the term is that of a machine which, like the human body, can function well or poorly. If the machine breaks down through no fault of the operator, then she cannot be held responsible for what happens as a result. In the same way that a person with two broken legs would not be blamed if she failed to rescue a drowning child, a person whose mental functions are temporarily out of order would not be blamed if she behaves in ways which might otherwise be objectionable.

Some mental disorders fit into this model fairly well. A person with bipolar disorder, for example, might behave in unusual ways while he is in a manic phase of his disorder. This behavior may be completely out of character and controllable with lithium. In such a case, even though the behavior was intentional, we might be inclined to say that the person should not be held accountable, because the actions were not really his own. The behavior was the result of faulty machinery, not *mens rea*, and once the machinery of his mind is fixed and functioning normally, the behavior disappears.

But the notion of a disordered personality can confuse judgments of responsibility for two reasons. First, the personality disorders are problems of character, and despite the unarguable influence of inheritance and environment, any given individual exerts some control over the development of his character. With that control comes accountability. As Aristotle says of "careless men" in the *Nicomachean Ethics*: "Still they are themselves by their slack lives responsible for becoming men of that kind, and men are themselves responsible for being unjust or self-indulgent, in that they cheat or spend their time in drinking-bouts and the like. . . ." Indeed, Aristotle remarks (none too subtly) that to fail to realize that character is formed in this way "is the mark of a thoroughly senseless person."[14]

Second, if a personality can be compared to a machine, it is not a machine that is separate from and external to a person's identity. The function or failure of a kidney, for example, bears very little on the identity of the person herself; a person can lose a kidney, or have one replaced or repaired, and she is still the same person. But to repair a dysfunctional personality is another matter altogether. A person's identity *is* to a large degree her personality, and to change a personality is to change the person herself.

Some mental disorders can be thought of as largely separate from a person's core identity, especially disorders that are circumscribed in scope or short in duration. A phobia, for example, might influence a person's thoughts and behavior in certain focused aspects of his life. The manic phase of bipolar disorder might result in global changes in a person's character, but only for limited amounts of time. In both cases, it is convenient to conceptualize the person's underlying core identity as remaining intact. Curing the disorder is either a matter of restoring this underlying core identity, as in the manic-depressive disorder, or eliminating a flaw which is largely peripheral to the core identity, as in the phobia.

In cases like these, it is possible to characterize the mental disorder as an external influence on the person himself. It might be thought, for example, that a person would not have acted in a certain way but for the phobia, which placed constraints on what he would have otherwise preferred to do. Characterizing objectionable or self-defeating personality traits as "disorders" encourages this type of thinking: the personality is somehow separate from the person himself, an influence or a constraint upon his actions. But of course it would be a mistake to suppose that the personality is separate from the person. Indeed, most definitions of personality disorders focus on their long-standing nature, stressing that they usually begin in adolescence and persist throughout adult life. In fact, some sources (such as ICD-9) define personality disorders as maladaptive *behavior*, which would mean that personality disorders are not external constraints on behavior, but rather the behavior itself. And as Lady Wootton has famously pointed out, if personality disorders are simply long-standing maladaptive behavior, to say that a person should be excused from responsibility because of a personality disorder is to say no more than that he should be excused because he behaves very badly.[15]

III

Whether taking a mechanistic attitude toward natural events necessarily entails the "fatalism" that Wittgenstein described is a controversial question. Does the notion that events can be described by natural laws mean that they are compelled? Some writers believe that compulsion and freedom are concepts borrowed from the language of persons which make sense only against a background of concepts such as choice and the will. A remark from the "Lecture on Freedom of the Will" indicates that Wittgenstein believed something like this:

> But thinking this [that actions are predictable from natural laws] is no reason for saying that if the decisions follow nat-ural laws—that if we know the laws which they follow—they are in some way *compelled*. What on earth would it mean that the natural law compels a thing to go as it goes. The natural law is correct, and that's all. Why should people think of nat-ural laws as compelling events? If what I say is correct people would seem to have made a blunder.[16]

Much more important, however, is another point that Wittgenstein makes: even if human behavior were completely describable and predictable by natural laws, it would still make sense to ask questions about moral responsibility.[17] Even if we knew in advance how a person was going to act, it would still make sense to ask, "Did he intend to act?" The distinctions that we customarily make between doing something on purpose or doing it inadvertent-ly, between deliberating about it or doing it impulsively, between act-ing under duress or acting in order to avoid a worse alternative or being manipulated by another person: these would all be as valid if human behavior were predictable as they are when it is not.[18] If behavior were infallibly predictable, then it might be "inevitable" in some sense of the word, but that fact does not invalidate genuine dis-tinctions *within that framework*.

To see how this is so, consider a thought experiment that Wittgen-stein proposes. Wittgenstein says to imagine that he is in a room, moving about in the normal way. Below that room, however, you can see another man with some sort of mechanism, which he regulates with a crank. With this mechanism, says the man, he can make Wittgenstein do exactly as he pleases. Like a puppet-master with a puppet, he can make Wittgenstein walk this way and that, say one thing or another as he likes. With a mirror, you can see that what he says is true; the puppet-master turns the crank, and Wittgenstein moves just as he said he would. But of course, if you were to ask

Wittgenstein what had happened, whether he was dragged around or was free, he would say that he was free.

Now we would probably say that Wittgenstein merely thought he was free, but that actually he just did what the puppet-master wanted. Still, it would make sense for Wittgenstein to make distinctions between what he has done (or thinks he has done) and what has merely happened to him: there would still be a difference between accidentally dropping a kettle of boiling water on someone and doing it on purpose. Showing that *all* actions are compelled does not undermine the concepts of praise and blame. To do that you must undermine the *distinction* that we ordinarily make between action that is compelled and that which is not.

Of course, it is a distinction of just that sort which would probably incline us to say, in the puppet-master example, that Wittgenstein should *not* be held responsible for what he does. We compare the special case of a person being controlled by the puppet-master with the ordinary case where a person's will is his own. Against this background of ordinary cases, the person who is being controlled is distinctive; he is being controlled in a way that everyone else is not. But if *everyone* were controlled in the same way, there would be no such distinction to be made. Whether all people were responsible or nonresponsible, they would all be *equally* responsible or nonresponsible. Within this framework of equality, it would still make sense to make distinctions between intentional and unintentional actions, and between actions which deserve punishment and those which do not.

Wittgenstein's "Lecture on Freedom of the Will" is aphoristic and at times unclear. But it points toward two important ideas for psychiatry. First, undergirding any human practice are certain concepts and unspoken assumptions that may influence the attitudes that we take while engaging in that practice. When we look at something or someone mechanistically, as the practice of psychiatry often demands, we are apt to take up an attitude of "fatalism," the notion that events could only have happened as they did. Stepping back from a person and looking at her objectively with the aim of explaining or interpreting her behavior, we begin to speak in ways that encourage us to see her behavior as determined, as something beyond her control.

Whether a psychiatrist is sympathetic to a biological or to a psycho-dynamic model of psychiatry, the terms and concepts that she uses incline her toward a deterministic view of human behavior, which may in turn undermine the notion of moral responsibility.

Second, judgments about responsibility, excuses, praise and blame are made within a particular conceptual framework. Part of that framework is the assumption that there are distinctions to be made between actions that are intentional and those that are unintentional. It is for intentional actions that we hold people responsible. And when people with personality disorders behave badly or commit criminal offenses, it is ordinarily the case that they have intended to act as they did. Thus we normally hold them responsible.[19] Of course, we can still ask the question of why they intended to act as they did, and in trying to answer that question one might point to factors that contributed to their personality traits, such as their upbringing. But to ask this question is not to make a distinction within the framework; it is to ask a question that undermines the framework, by asking whether any of us can ultimately be held responsible for the characters that lead us to act, intentionally, in the ways that we act.

Yet another part of this framework underlying our notions of responsibility is the presumption that whether or not we can ulti-mately be held responsible for our characters, those characters are things for which we all bear the *same* degree of responsibility (or lack thereof). My genetic inheritance and the circumstances of my upbringing may be factors over which I exert little control, but I exert no less control than anyone else. So to show that a personality disor-der should excuse a person from responsibility for his actions, it is not enough simply to show that he bears no responsibility for his dis-ordered personality; it would be necessary to show that he bears less responsibility for developing a disordered personality than the rest of us bear for developing the personalities that we have. But as long as we are all equally capable or incapable (as the case may be) of influ-encing what sort of personalities we have, then there is no reason to excuse persons with personality disorders. They are no less responsi-ble for their characters, and their actions, than are the rest of us.

Our attitudes toward persons with personality disorders are ordinarily (to use Strawson's phrase) reactive. But there are a broad variety of reactive attitudes that we can take, depending on the person and the circumstances. We might forgive a person who has acted badly, even while judging him responsible for his actions, and we might think he deserves to be treated compassionately. On the other hand, we might simply resent him. These attitudes are richly complex and interconnected, and they will be linked to the person's own feelings about his actions—remorse, pride, shame, defiance. However, it is important to realize that taking these sorts of reactive attitudes— that of forgiveness, say—does not entail absolving the personality disordered from their actions. On the contrary, the presumption of responsibility for intentional actions is often a necessary part of taking a reactive attitude. Before we can forgive a person for his actions, we must admit that he is responsible for acting.

Chapter 5

Nothing Matters: Depression and Competence in Clinical Research

> *Madness need not be regarded as an illness. Why shouldn't it be seen as a sudden—more or* less *sudden—change of character?*
>   ——Ludwig Wittgenstein

> *I hope I am the one.*
>   ——Patient with major depression, on being told that ECT carries a one in 3000 chance of death.

I

People sometimes do inexplicable things when they are clinically depressed. They make self-destructive choices, alienate their friends, damage their marriages, lose their motivation and creativity at work. A recurring theme in memoirs of depression, typically written during periods of clarity, is the writer's sense of regret and often astonishment at the things she did and said when she was clinically depressed.[1] In *Darkness Visible*, William Styron remembers with some embarrassment his refusal to have dinner with the members of a French academy who had just presented him with a major literary prize.

Strangely enough, physicians, researchers and bioethicists have generally paid little attention to depression when it comes to evaluating competence. This is especially true for clinical research. Depressed patients are often asked to take part in research protocols, and sometimes this research carries risks. A depressed patient might be enrolled in a protocol to evaluate a new antidepressant, for example, or in a protocol that requires a washout period, in which their current medication will be discontinued. Many Institutional Review Boards enthusiastically approve protocols testing new antidepressants against placebo controls, in which a depressed patient may be taken off his medication for six to 12 weeks. I have seen at least one placebo-controlled antidepressant protocol that called for patients with major depression to be taken off their medication for a year. Any of these situations entail risks, primarily the risk that the depressed patient's condition will worsen. The potential harm can be considerable, and at the extreme end of the spectrum includes the risk of suicide.

Competence to consent to research is one of the most widely and thoroughly discussed issues in bioethics, of course.[2-6] But most clinical research protocols involving depressed patients do not even specify that the patients' competence needs to be evaluated before they are enrolled in the protocol. The reason depression is not considered a warning sign of incompetence, or so I suspect, is that depression is not ordinarily thought to be the type of disorder that would interfere with competence. It is only the rare depressed patient who is psychotic, and while depression may often interfere with a person's memory and concentration, very often this interference is not severe enough to raise any warning flags. Most accounts of competence focus on intellectual capacity and abilities to reason, and depression is primarily a disorder of mood. According to conventional thinking, depression is primarily about despair, guilt and a loss of motivation, while competence is about the ability to reason, to deliberate, to compare and to evaluate. These latter abilities are ones that depression is thought to leave intact.

I believe this view of competence is misguided. Depression may well impair a patient's competence to consent to research. Perhaps most crucially, it can impair a person's ability to evaluate risks and benefits. To put the matter simply, if a person is depressed, he may be *aware* that a protocol carries risks, but simply not *care* about those risks. This sort of intellectual impairment can be as important a part of competence as the more detached, intellectual understanding that most accounts of competence emphasize. If I am right, then clinical investigators need to take special precautions in allowing researchers to enroll depressed patients in research protocols.

II

Competence is conventionally defined as the ability to perform a task—in this case, to consent to enroll in a research protocol.[7,8]What counts as competence to consent, then, will then depend on what one counts as the abilities relevant to the task in question. According to a widely accepted account of competence, the 1983 U.S. *President's Commission Report*, the relevant abilities are (1) the ability to reason and deliberate, (2) the ability to understand and communicate information, and (3) the possession of values and goals.[9] As conceptualized within this framework, a potential research subject takes in the relevant information, weighs it according to his goals and values, and then reasons his way to an informed decision.

I believe that accounts of competence like these are incomplete. If competence to consent to research is defined simply as the ability to make a decision to enroll in a research protocol, we are still left with the problem of what *counts* as that ability—whether a person is incompetent by virtue of making a poor decision, or by virtue of making an irrational decision, or by virtue of coming to his decision in an unsystematic, illogical or erratic way. But since even competent people are sometimes stubborn, obtuse or unreasonable, we need an account of competence that explains why we sometimes feel that a person can both be competent and make bad, irrational or even unreasonable choices.

What we really want to know when we ask if a patient is competent is whether he is able to make a decision *for which he can be considered accountable*. What we want to know is whether the decisions that a person makes—whether they are good decisions or bad ones, rational or irrational—are decisions for which that person can legitimately be considered responsible. This is why we define certain mental abilities as relevant: we realize that certain conditions or disorders impair a person's mental abilities such that he is not a morally responsible agent. He can make decisions, but we would not feel comfortable calling him to account for that decision. If a person is making a decision that will affect his life in momentous ways, we will naturally be concerned that he makes a sound decision. But since we recognize that a person generally has the right to make even unsound decisions, a judgment about competence ensures that whatever decision a person makes, it is truly *his* decision: a decision for which he can finally be held accountable.

For example, a nine-year-old can tell us whether or not he wants to take part in a research protocol. In fact, it is probably a good idea to involve nine-year-olds in decisions like these. But we shouldn't consider a nine-year-old competent to consent. If he were harmed in the protocol, as a result of risks which he had been informed of in advance, we would not say (as we would with an adult) that he shares in the responsibility for those harms as a consequence of consenting to the protocol knowingly and freely. We do not ordinarily feel that a nine-year-old can be called to account for his choices in the way that an adult can.

Once we conceptualize competence in this way, it becomes clear that it is not just intellectual ability that is relevant to competence. A person's emotional state can also affect her decisions in ways that might lead us to say that she cannot be judged fully accountable for them. The criminal law recognizes this, for example, and often grants leniency when a person acts under severe emotional distress. We often make decisions in the heat of anger or under the cold weight of despair that are uncharacteristic, that we would not have made otherwise, that we later regret and for which we feel we should not be considered fully accountable. Likewise, we often recognize that it would be unfair to hold a person to a decision that he or she made in the face of overwhelming fear. In emotional extremes, we value, think and behave differently—sometimes so differently that we might later feel that the decisions we have made are not decisions for which we can be held completely and unproblematically responsible.

While bioethicists as a whole have not paid much attention to depression, the importance of emotion and mood for competence has not been lost on those who are trained in psychiatry.[10-14] For instance, some accounts of competence stipulate that a person must "appreciate" the consequences of her choice, rather than simply understand them factually, the term "appreciate" implying a fuller, deeper comprehension of how the decision will affect the patient's life.[15, 16] A patient who can flatly recite the effects of treatment may still seem to fail to appreciate fully just how the treatment is going to affect his or her health. Nor can affect be completely divorced conceptually from cognition. Bursztajn and his colleagues have pointed out how a patient's affect can influence competence by altering his or her beliefs.[17] For example, a depressed patient, convinced that his situation will never change, may refuse treatment based on the unrealistic belief that it will not help him.

However, while some patients may have affective disorders that disrupt their cognitive, rational, decision-making abilities, a slightly different sort of depressed patient presents other problems. This is the depressed patient who is capable of understanding all the facts about his illness and the research protocol in which he is enrolling, and who appreciates the risks and the broader implications of the protocol on his life, but who, as a result of his illness, is not *motivated* to take those risks into account in the same way as the rest of us. These patients, for example, might realize that a protocol involves risks, but simply not *care* about the risks. Some patients, as a result of their depression, may even *want* to take risks.[18]

Could depression lead some patients to overestimate the side effects of interventions and underestimate the likelihood of benefit?[17-20] While there are no good empirical studies examining the question of whether depressed patients are more likely than nondepressed patients to consent to risky or uncomfortable research,[21] Lee, Ganzini and their colleagues have studied the effects of depression and its treatment on the preferences of elderly patients for life-sustaining medical therapies.[22, 23] In one study of 43 depressed patients, a subgroup of 11 severely depressed patients were more likely to choose life-sustaining therapies after their depression had been treated than they were while depressed.[24] This suggests that severe depression might affect the way some patients evaluate risks and benefits, but it is not clear whether evaluation of life-sustaining therapy is similar enough to evaluation of research risks to bear much comparison.

Nonetheless, it seems unlikely that severely depressed patients are in the best position to make important decisions about their welfare. The Royal College of Psychiatrists in the United Kingdom is one of the few bodies to recognize this explicitly, offering the example of a patient with depressive delusions who consents to risky research because he thinks he is guilty and deserves to be punished.[25] Given the sense of hopelessness and worthlessness that characterizes some severely depressed patients, it doesn't seem unreasonable to be concerned about their decision-making. The novelist William Styron describes his own agonizing depressive episode as like "the diabolical discomfort of being imprisoned in a fiercely overheated room. And because no breeze stirs this cauldron, because there is no escape from this smothering confinement, it is entirely natural that the victim begins to think ceaselessly of oblivion."[26]

III

It might not seem controversial to say that mood and emotion affect a person's decision-making. For some people it seems clear that a person who is paralyzed by a fear she admits is unfounded, or who is soaring in a grandiose euphoria brought on by bipolar disorder, or who is gripped by depression-induced despair, is not exactly in the ideal position to make medical decisions. But not everyone agrees. On the orthodox view of competence defended by Hirschfeld and his colleagues, for example, overriding a severely depressed patient's choice to participate in a risky research protocol is a violation of his autonomy.[27] Moreover, even among writers who agree that emotion is an important part of decision-making, it is only the rare one who has tried to say *why* this is so.[28] It is not such an easy question to answer. Even if we concede that emotion and mood are part of ordinary decision-making, it is also normal for a person's mood to change from one time to another, and it is not immediately obvious why a depressed mood should invalidate a patient's competence. If mere sadness were considered a sign of incompetence, then some of us would scarcely have the authority to make any decisions at all.

Nonetheless, I believe there are at least two good arguments for the conclusion that some *severely* depressed patients are incompetent to consent to research, each of which is persuasive for a slightly different type of patient. The first might be called the argument from *identity*. When a person is caught in the grip of depression, his values, beliefs, desires and dispositions are dramatically different from when he is healthy.[29] In some cases, they are so different that we might ask whether his decisions are truly his. A decision may not be truly his in the sense that it reflects dispositions and values that are transient and inconsistent with much more deeply ingrained traits of his character. One might say, "I wasn't myself," when looking back on a time of despondency, and a caricature of the identity argument would hold that we should take this declaration literally: I was not myself, so that decision is not mine. Yet underneath that caricature is a grain of truth. If a person is so deeply depressed that his decisions are wildly inconsistent with his character, it seems problematic to abide by his decisions, particularly if the depression is dramatic and reversible.[30]

Here is where the notion of competence as accountability is helpful. If a person were to behave badly while mentally ill—say, in a full-blown manic episode—we would very likely feel it unfair to hold him fully responsible for what he has done.[31] His behavior was uncharacteristic; he would never have acted this way if he had not been manic; his mania was temporary and reversible with lithium. His actions in the manic state were not truly *his*. The same goes for the depressed patient who is asked to consent to research: his mental state is such that his behavior and choices do not seem to be truly his. If something untoward were to happen to him during the research, for instance, we could not in good conscience say that he bears the full responsibility for undergoing that risk.

Now, some philosophers might well dismiss the idea that we should see any mentally ill person, much less one who is merely depressed,

as a different person, even in a less-than-literal way. But we should not
reject the idea out of hand. If a person's personality changes dramatically as a result of trauma or illness, for example, his friends and relatives are often inclined to say that he has become a different person.
The classic case here is that of Phineas Gage, the nineteenth-century
railroad man whose name has become familiar to all psychiatrists and
neurologists. While Gage was blasting stone with dynamite, the charge
exploded in his face, driving a 16-foot rod upwards through his frontal
lobes and out of the top of his head. Gage survived; in fact, he was
talking rationally and coherently only minutes after the explosion. But
in time it became clear that his injury had left him with profound
problems. Where once he had been shrewd, energetic and persistent,
a solid worker and businessman, after his injury he was impulsive and
undisciplined. He became profane and often rude. His behavior was
sometimes obstinate, sometimes capricious. He spent the rest of his
life wandering from one job to the next, at one point even finding
employment as a circus attraction. Remarking on his plight, his friends
and acquaintances said "Gage was no longer Gage."[32]

Changes of personality as dramatic as this do not occur in depression the way they often do in frontal lobe injuries, of course. But even
in depression, particularly when it is severe, there comes a point where
a person's personality and thought processes become so different from
the way they ordinarily are that it seems reasonable to consider him,
at least from a standpoint of accountability, as a different person.
Especially since depression is reversible. Imagine, for instance, that a
person who has been successfully treated for a suicidal depression
were to say to a clinical investigator, "Why did you take my consent at
face value? You knew that I was not myself. I would never have con-
sented had I been thinking properly about my well-being." It would
be hard not to take his complaint seriously.

The identity argument presupposes a person with a stable character
and entrenched dispositions who, while depressed, makes decisions so
uncharacteristic that we feel bound to question whether those decisions
were truly hers. However, sometimes this break between the depressed
and predepression personality is not so dramatic. Some patients are
chronically depressed, and others are depressed periodically. It would

not be plausible to argue that the decisions of these depressed patients do not reflect their underlying characters—characters which are closely tied to their depression. Yet there comes a point where, if a person appears largely insensitive to her own welfare, we might feel that she is incompetent to consent to research. Why should this be so?

One answer lies in what might be called the argument from *self-interest*. Our ordinary relationships with other people are based on certain assumptions about their thoughts and behavior. One of these assumptions is that other persons have some minimal concern for their own welfare. For example, the assumption that other people ordinarily both have some minimal degree of self-interest and are best positioned to judge their own interests lies at the heart of the institution of informed consent.

However, if we have reason to believe that severely depressed patients do not have this minimal degree of concern, then a fundamental assumption underlying informed consent is undermined. We justify exposing patients to the risks of research by the assumption that the patient is evaluating that risk with some degree of concern for her welfare. A competent evaluation of risks involves taking into account one's own well-being—not necessarily taking it as an overriding or supremely important concern, but at least taking it into account. If a person is so depressed that she fails to take her interests into account in deciding whether to take a risk, then we can hardly feel comfortable saying that she is accountable for taking that risk.

These two arguments for taking depression seriously as a barrier to competence, the arguments from identity and self-interest, are based on what could be called the background assumptions about other minds. If severe depression calls those background assumptions into question, as I have suggested, then we have reason to consider severe depression a barrier to competence. But there is a far more radical (and ultimately more interesting) argument for taking depression seriously as barrier to competence, which calls into question the very idea that rational decision-making could exist in the absence of emotion.[33] We often think that clear and rational decisions are best made in a cool hour, without interference by the emotions. But Antonio Damasio argues that the *absence* of emotion can be just as damaging to decision-making. His arguments are based on clinical observation of patients with, for example, damage to the ventromedial region of the frontal lobes. He points out that patients (like Phineas Gage, for example) with neurological damage that has left them emotionally flat, far from being competent at making decisions about their personal lives, are often completely hopeless at it. One patient whom Damasio calls Elliot was referred to him for evaluation of a meningioma which was compressing his frontal lobes from below. When the tumor was surgically removed, along with a slight amount of healthy tissue that had been damaged by the tumor, Elliot's personality changed. He became emotionally detached. Damasio describes him as distant and calm, patient to a fault. He did not show any signs of sadness even when describing the most tragic events of his life. He made high scores on tests of intelligence and memory. He scored a good profile on the Minnesota Multiphasic Personality Inventory. He even made excellent scores on tests of moral development. Yet when it came to practical decisions about his life, his judgment was terrible. He needed prompting to get out of bed in the morning. Sometimes he would persist at trivial tasks at his workplace; other times he would be endlessly distracted from his main goal. When he was fired from his job, he took up with crooks. He started collecting junk. He divorced his wife, married another woman briefly, then divorced her too. Yet despite all this, he was able to perform very well on theoretical, pen-and-paper tests of decision-making. For Damasio, Elliot's defect, a deficiency in practical reason, suggests a flattened decision-making landscape where Elliot's very cold-bloodedness prevented him from being able to assign different values to different options.[34]

If writers like Damasio are correct, and emotional engagement is not merely a matter of motivation but is a necessary constituent of rational decision-making, we will need to think twice about the decisions of patients with major depression. William Styron, commenting on the trancelike stupor he experienced when he was clinically depressed, writes, "Rational thought was usually absent from my mind at such times, hence *trance*."[35]

What sort of practical conclusions should we draw from all these observations about depression? First, it seems clear that we need to see more empirical research on the ways in which severe depression might affect psychological factors relevant to competence. For example, it would be important to know the extent to which severe depression affects how much a person cares about his or her own well-being and how it might affect a person's willingness to expose himself or herself to potential harm. Moreover, if we take seriously Damasio's contention that emotions are especially bound up with practical rather than theoretical reason, then theoretical, pen-and-paper tests may give us misleading answers to these questions.

Secondly, these arguments suggest that we may need to alter our conventional ways of assessing competence. As I have argued, many conventional accounts of how competence should be assessed downplay the importance of emotional factors. However, if my arguments are convincing, it may not be enough for psychiatrists or researchers to evaluate competence simply by testing a person's memory and reasoning ability, such as with a Mini Mental Status Exam. Rather, it may be that evaluations should also be concerned with a person's affective and motivational state: whether a person's mood has dramatically changed recently, how concerned a patient appears to be about her own well-being, how carefully she looks at risks and benefits and so on. Of course, we will also need to find sound and uniform ways of assessing these affective and motivational factors.

Finally, on a more practical level, these arguments should lead us to rethink the conduct of clinical trials testing new treatments for major depression. For example, if it is concluded that severe depression does impair competence to consent, clinical research protocols involving subjects with depression will need to require explicitly that the competence of subjects be evaluated before entering the study. This would make studies of severe depression look more like studies testing new anti-psychotic drugs, which generally require that subjects either be competent to consent or that consent be obtained from an appropriate surrogate.

Also, this view of competence should make us rethink studies involving relatively poor risk-benefit ratios. If a severely depressed patient is incompetent to consent to research, riskier studies are much more difficult to justify. For example, sometimes severely depressed patients are enrolled in placebo-controlled studies in which their depression is likely to worsen as a result of receiving a placebo. Researchers argue that exposing competent adults to these sorts of risks is justified at least in part by the institution of informed consent, with the corresponding presumption that potential subjects understand the risks of the protocol, consent to them and can be judged accountable for undertaking them.[36] But if severely depressed patients are incompetent, exposing them to the risk of having their illness worsen is much more difficult to justify. Thus the view of competence I have argued for here would bolster the increasingly persuasive arguments that new therapies for severe depression should be tested against standard therapy, rather than placebo. [37, 38]

Chapter 6

What's Wrong with Living Heart Transplantation?

"I took an oath, dammit!"
——Television doctor

I

What would be wrong with transplantation from a living heart donor? Willing volunteers would certainly come forward. At a conference sponsored by the University of Utah after the total artificial heart implantation in 1982, the sociologist Renee Fox reported that the heart transplant team at Stanford University had been contacted by a number of healthy volunteers who wanted to become living heart donors, even though this would mean ending their lives. William De Vries, the surgeon who performed the first artificial heart implant at Utah, said that at the time of the heart implant surgery his team received a number of calls from healthy volunteers who wanted to volunteer for the procedure. These volunteers had no medical need for an artificial heart, but nevertheless wanted to volunteer to have one implanted, apparently solely to become test subjects for the sake of medical science. Some of these volunteers were death row inmates. Another was a 60-year-old woman who had raised her family, and evidently thought this would be a fitting way to end her life.[1]

No surgeon would do it, of course. But it is hard to level any moral criticism at the donors. If anything, offering to give up your life for the sake of another person seems morally admirable. In fact, it seems more than that—heroic perhaps, beyond the limits of duty. But if it is morally praiseworthy, even heroic, why do doctors have trouble with the idea? Why do *we* have trouble with the idea of doctors carrying out such a procedure? This wouldn't be puzzling if the refusal to carry out a living heart transplantation were simply a matter of custom, or avoidance of a malpractice suit, or just plain hardheadedness. But the reason doctors would not do such a procedure, I think, is based on moral grounds—that is, most physicians have the intuition that to participate in such a transplant would somehow be morally wrong. So the puzzle is why I, for instance, might have the dual intuitions that in this case it is morally praiseworthy for a person to offer to donate his heart, and that it would be morally wrong for me to help him do it.

Saying just what is wrong is not as easy as it might seem. In a moral framework whose dominant principle is respect for individual auton-omy, doubts about freely chosen but harmful procedures are difficult to defend. The volunteers are competent, and their sacrifices would clearly help people who otherwise would probably die. We also allow patients to *refuse* procedures, even when a refusal will be harmful. So when they *request* harmful procedures, why shouldn't we agree to perform them? John Harris, who professes to see no problem with such procedures, puts the case simply: "Should I be permitted vol-untarily to donate a vital organ like the heart? Again, if I know what I am doing then I do not see why I should not give my life to save that of another if that is what I want to do"[2]

II

Medical treatment is often painful, usually unpleasant and sometimes genuinely harmful. The administration of pain has become a routine part of diagnosis and treatment, from blood drawings, intravenous lines and lumbar punctures to chemotherapy, limb amputations and involuntary psychiatric confinement. Many doctors are understandably uncomfortable with this part of medicine, even when the patient agrees to it, especially when the harm is permanent or severe. Life may be short and the art long, but the art's most delicate aspect is not to shorten life further, and not to diminish it.

The bioethical literature of the past three decades has done a thorough job of exploring the rights of competent patients to refuse treatment, and it has struggled, not always successfully, with the question of when research or other risky procedures are justifiable on patients who are incompetent to consent. But it has tended to overlook a cluster of questions surrounding the opposite problem: competent people who consent to, or even request, procedures that are risky, painful or harmful. Part of the reason for this neglect may be the idiom in which bioethical questions are usually scripted and rehearsed, which is not well suited to the moral backdrop against which these issues are often played out. A vocabulary of rights and autonomy can be inadequate to represent the intimate bonds of family and friends, the delicate balance between sacrifice and self-interest and the complex, often awkward relationship between doctors and organ donors or research subjects. In a moral framework shaped by respect for patient autonomy, whether or not to undergo risk or harm can come to seem a matter solely for patients to decide. The worries that many doctors feel about exposing willing subjects to harm or great risk can be frustratingly difficult to express.

Although medical procedures that harm patients are ordinarily intended to serve the patient's welfare, there are two related exceptions. The first is nontherapeutic clinical research on human subjects, such as Phase 1 clinical trials for new medications. Phase 1 trials test a drug's safety, and many are done on healthy subjects. Others, such as Phase 1 trials for new chemotherapeutic drugs, are done on patients with incurable illnesses. Patients are at first given a small dose of the drug, which is increased until the patients begin to have toxic side effects. However, with the toxicity comes only an exceedingly small chance of therapeutic benefit; for example, one study put the rate of complete remission in Phase 1 cancer trials at 0.16%, and the likelihood of any objective response at all at less than 5%.[3]

The second type of medical procedure that does not serve a patient's welfare is organ transplantation from living donors. We don't need to go as far as living heart donors. Kidney transplantations from living donors have been performed since the 1950s, from children as well as adults, and liver lobe transplantations from living donors are becoming increasingly common. These procedures have had no shortage of critics, but the criticisms, oddly enough, have been couched in the language of autonomy. We ought to respect a person's autonomous choice to risk harm to herself, this argument goes, but are such choices truly autonomous? Such was the reasoning behind the chorus of wary voices at the early liver transplants from living donors at the University of Chicago. Many commentators expressed reservations about the Chicago transplant team's announced plan to transplant a hepatic lobe from a mother to her severely ill infant daughter. B.D. Colen told the *Los Angeles Times*, "Simply put, how can a parent be expected to make an informed, rational free choice when asked to consider donating an organ to his or her own dying child?" George Annas said, "The parents basically can't say no." "Does anyone really think parents can say no when the option is certain death for their own son or daughter?" asked Arthur Caplan.[4] The reasoning behind these reservations seems linked to the mother's emotional ties and moral commitment to her daughter. These ties prevented the mother's decision from being free, the argument goes, and thus from being truly autonomous.

To me, this sounds like a very strange way of framing the moral issue. It's an odd notion of autonomy which would count emotional ties and moral commitments as constraints on autonomy. That worries about self-chosen risks should emerge disguised as concerns about free choice—the idea that a parent is *coerced* by her love for and moral obligations toward her child—says something about the central place the ethic of autonomy holds in our culture. If you take a risk for someone you love, the reasoning goes, your love has "coerced" you. I suspect no one would have thought to call such a choice made out of love coercive if no risk of harm were involved.

The criticism also misses the point, of course. The question is not whether the donor (or subject) should have the right to expose himself to harm; this right is little disputed, at least in the libertarian United States. The point at issue is the physician's role in exposing that donor to harm.

In debates over euthanasia and abortion, many physicians defend their refusal to participate on grounds of conscience. A patient may have the right to be euthanized or to have an abortion, but this right has no claim on a physician, who may justifiably refuse to participate in a procedure which she conscientiously believes to be wrong. Some might say the same of living organ transplantation. But to cast the problem of dangerous organ transplantation in these terms merely sidesteps the real problem. The problem here is not whether a physician should have the right to obey her conscience; in the vast majority of cases she clearly will. The problem is how to justify one's conscientious choice—to say what accounts for the pervasive intuition that there is something wrong with a physician exposing a patient to such risk.

Doctors reflexively defend their refusal to participate in dangerous procedures on grounds of professional ethics. *Primum non nocere*, first do no harm. Sometimes dressed up as the "principle of nonmaleficence," this injunction appeals to the duties or obligations of physicians *qua* physicians, one of which has traditionally been the duty not to harm patients. But despite the frequency with which the *primum non nocere* argument appears in medical ethics, and the force that it often justifiably carries, it does not do much to *explain* the pervasive intuition that there is something wrong with a physician taking part in procedures like the one sketched out above. First, as a justification for refusing to participate in the transplant, it will not do merely to say that physicians ought not to do harm, for physicians justifiably do harm routinely, as a means to some greater good—say, a course of chemotherapy for cancer. Why shouldn't a physician simply view the willing death of a heart donor as a means to a greater good? Here, unlike situations where sacrificing one person for the sake of a greater good would violate widely shared values concerning personal autonomy, the patient actually wants to sacrifice his life, and maybe even for rational, altruistic reasons.

Besides, we do not have to imagine a case where the physician actually *does* any harm. It may be that the patient agrees to commit suicide on the condition that when he does, the physician will transplant his heart. But I doubt that this would do much to ease our discomfort with the physician's role. So the discomfort must be a result of something other than the harm that the physician actually *does*. The same goes for objections that a physician should not participate on the grounds that physicians must never kill. Our intuition that something is wrong with the physicians performing the transplant remains even if it is the case that the physician herself does not kill the patient.

In the end, any appeal to a professional code or oath in this case misses the crux of the problem. For our intuition here is not merely that it is wrong for a physician to help a person sacrifice himself for the sake of others, but that it would be wrong for *anyone* to help. This is not a puzzle only for medical ethics. We would have the same reservations about any person who helped another one sacrifice himself. We call a soldier a hero who throws himself on a grenade to save his battalion, but there is something ghoulish, for instance, about a man who throws a paralyzed colleague on a grenade, even if the colleague begs him to do it.

III

Graham Greene's novella, *The Tenth Man*, is a subtle reminder that self-sacrifice is often more morally complicated than it seems.[5] It tells the story of a French lawyer, Chavel, who is jailed by the Nazis during World War II. Chavel has been rounded up by the police for reasons unknown and imprisoned in a cell with 29 other men. Most of the men are poor, below Chavel's station in life, and this fact increases Chavel's agitation about his plight.

After a number of months, a guard enters the cell and tells the prisoners that there have been some murders in the town by the resistance movement. As a result, the commanders have ordered that one man out of every ten in the camp is to be shot. In a day's time, three of the 30 prisoners in Chavel's cell will be executed. The prisoners themselves must choose which three.

The prisoners decide to draw lots, and Chavel is among the three marked to die. Unlike the other condemned men, Chavel panics. He alone among the prisoners is a wealthy man and, fear-stricken, he begins to offer all his wealth and belongings to the other prisoners, if only one of them will change places with him. To the astonishment of all, one man accepts the offer. Michel Janvier says that if Chavel will sign over his house and all his wealth to him, so that he can in turn leave it to his impoverished mother and sister, he will take Chavel's place before the firing squad. He and Chavel draw up a will, and the next day, Janvier is shot.

This exchange takes place in the first chapter of the book, but it is the story's defining event. The exchange was freely agreed to by both men and witnessed by the other prisoners. Yet even though the deal was freely made, we know that Chavel was wrong to make it. Even though we might admire Janvier for sacrificing his life in order to provide for his mother and sister, we know that Chavel was wrong to take advantage of Janvier's selflessness.

Chavel knows this as well, and his actions torment him. *The Tenth Man* is a book about guilt and shame, and its plot turns on Chavel's efforts to purge himself of the guilt that he feels about bartering for his life. After the Nazis fall and Chavel is freed from prison, he is celebrating in a bar when he sees his face in a water decanter.

> It is the face of failure. It was odd, he thought, that one failure of nerve had ingrained the face as deeply as a tramp's, but, of course, he had the objectivity to tell himself, it wasn't one failure; it was a whole lifetime of preparation for the event. An artist paints his picture not in a few hours but in all the years of experience before he takes up the brush, and it is the same with failure.

Our ordinary moral and political vocabulary makes it natural to think of exchanges involving harm, such as the exchange made by Janvier and Chavel, as questions primarily of rights, freedom and fairness. Yet very often our private reservations about harmful practices bear only a tangential relationship to these questions. That this is so can be seen in the awkward terms in which contemporary debates about harmful practices are often played out: whether people have a "right" to act altruistically, or whether a research subject's "freedom" is compromised by payment. In *The Tenth Man*, a prisoner objects to the deal struck by Chavel and Janvier on the grounds that it is not fair. But argued in these terms, his legitimate moral concerns are bound to be frustrated. As Janvier angrily replies: "Why isn't it fair to let me do what I want? You'd all be rich men if you could, but you haven't the spunk. I see my chance and I take it. Fair, of course, it's fair. I'm going to die a rich man and anyone who thinks it isn't fair can rot."

While rights and freedom should not be ignored, they do not quite get at the real source of Chavel's shame nor at what is most troubling about subjects who volunteer for harmful procedures or research protocols. An exchange can be made fairly and freely yet still fail to be admirable or honorable. Certainly Chavel's actions were understandable; they were the actions of a desperate man, who grasped frantically at the only possible chance of surviving his imprisonment. But they were also the actions of a coward, a man who took advantage of his wealth and another man's selflessness in order to save his own skin. A person who attempted such an exchange might well be justified in demanding that no one prevent him from making it, but as Adam Smith remarks of this type of situation, "(N)o man, I imagine, who had gone through an adventure of this kind would be fond of telling the story."[6]

IV

In his essay, "Saints and Heroes," J.O. Urmson argued that traditional ways of evaluating moral worth classify actions into three sorts: first, actions that are duties, or that we ought to perform; second, actions that are not duties but are morally permissible; and third, actions that are morally wrong, that we ought not to do.[7] Urmson thought that this classification ignored another sort of morally important action, actions that he called saintly or heroic. We reserve high moral praise for saintly and heroic actions, so we could not say that they are merely morally permissible. But they are not duties either. Such actions are, if anything, beyond the call of duty.

Urmson claims that there are several sorts of actions which we generally call saintly or heroic, and some of these actions may well fall within the traditional classification. A person may be called a saint if he does his duty in a situation where considerations of self-interest or desire might cause most people not to do it. A person might be called a hero if he does his duty in cases where fear or the drive to self-preservation would cause most people not to do it. In these cases the common element is self-control. But Urmson would still be willing to call a saint or a hero the person who does his duty effortlessly in cases where most of us would fail. The person who is virtuous in this Aristotelian sense may also be a saint or a hero.

However, the person who is most obviously saintly or heroic, Urmson says, is not the one who does his duty in extreme circumstances. Rather, saints or heroes *par excellence* do morally praiseworthy actions which are plainly not duties. The soldier who throws himself on a grenade to save his battalion has clearly done something of moral worth, but we could not say that the action was his duty. If he had not done it, no one could say to him that he ought to have thrown himself on the grenade. So the person whose actions Urmson believes to be most plainly heroic or saintly is the one who goes "the second mile," whose actions "exceed the demands of duty."[8]

Whether or not you subscribe to Urmson's scheme, it should be uncontroversial that one reason that we consider saintly and heroic action morally admirable is the fact that the saints and heroes voluntarily sacrifice their own interests for the sake of something or someone else.[9] This is not to say that self-sacrifice itself confers moral worth on actions, for plainly a person might sacrifice himself for something morally bad, or even foolish. And the element of self-sacrifice will be missing from the actions of some persons whom Urmson is willing to call saints or heroes: namely, the person who does his duty effortlessly in situations that would be too much for most of us. Still, no one will dispute that self-sacrifice is one reason, among others, that we consider at least some actions heroic or saintly, and that this is especially true for those actions that Urmson calls saintly or heroic *par excellence*.

When for any reason we are inclined to say that an action is morally praiseworthy, it will usually be the case that we consider it more morally praiseworthy if the agent has sacrificed his own interests to accomplish it. This might be a sacrifice in fulfilling one's duty, as in the case of a military officer who refuses to reveal state secrets even when faced with torture. But self-sacrifice may also incline us to think more highly of an action which is clearly outside the bounds of duty. If a billionaire gives away ten thousand dollars to feed the hungry, he has clearly done a good deed and we might think highly of him. But we would probably think even more highly of the person who gave away his last ten thousand dollars.

Those actions for which we reserve our highest praise are those where the agent has sacrificed his own interests for another good. The sacrifice may not be the sole reason that we call the action morally good, but it is usually the reason that we call the action heroic or saintly. The soldier who sacrifices his life to save his battalion, the nurse who devotes her life to taking care of lepers, the civil disobedient who risks his life for the cause —these are the types of people whom we are most likely to call saints or heroes. Without self-sacrifice their actions might still be morally praiseworthy, but they will not be saintly or heroic.

The relationship of self-sacrifice to moral worth can help us to understand the intuition that there is something morally wrong with a physician exposing a willing patient to the risk of harm. We might well agree that a person who offers to donate his heart to another person—or for that matter, to donate his kidney, his bone marrow or part of his liver—is doing something which is morally praiseworthy. And it is not only praiseworthy because it helps another person; it is praiseworthy because in helping that person the donor is sacrificing his own interests. But this element of self-sacrifice, an element that is crucial to the moral worth of the donor's action, will be absent from the actions of the physician who performs the operation. The physician takes no risks.

The puzzle of the living heart transplant was a product of conflicting moral intuitions. On the one hand, it seemed that the person who wanted to donate his heart to another person was acting in a morally praiseworthy, even heroic, manner. On the other, it also seemed that perhaps it would be wrong for a physician to perform such an operation (or, at least, that a physician would be morally justified in refusing to participate). The element of self-sacrifice in the moral evaluation of actions helps us make sense of these conflicting intuitions. Self-sacrifice is precisely the element that inclines us to say that the donor's action is morally praiseworthy. And thus it is no wonder that we consider the physician's role less than praiseworthy since, in performing the operation, she makes no sacrifice.

We might think very badly of the soldier who threw a willing but paralyzed fellow soldier on a grenade to save the battalion. But what if to smother the grenade took two men, and the soldier threw himself on the grenade along with the willing colleague? I doubt we would criticize him for that action. In fact, we might well call both of the soldiers heroes. The fact that the soldier sacrificed himself seems to elevate him morally on our eyes. In a similar way, the way we morally evaluate the physician who performed a heart transplant would also change if the physician underwent a sacrifice—say, if she risked catching a fatal infectious disease by operating.

But this kind of reasoning will only get us so far. For example, mere self-sacrifice does not morally justify actions. Even if we think more highly of the physician who risks her own life, we might still object to her performing the operation. People can act nobly but wrongly. Some sacrifices are made in the service of an unjustified cause. More importantly, the fact that in assisting a saint or a hero, a physician has himself done nothing saintly or heroic does not mean that assistance is morally unjustifiable. It only means that the physician is not a saint or a hero. Thus to point out the absence of self-sacrifice in the physician's action only goes part of the way towards explaining the gut feeling that he ought not to take part in the transplantation. It helps explain how the physician's action differs from the patient's, and why this makes a difference in how we see each of their actions, but it does not shed any light on why we might feel that for the physician to take part would be positively wrong.

V

To get at what is troubling about a person who knowingly and willingly consents to a harmful medical procedure, it is necessary to look not simply at the person making the decision to participate, but beyond him to the other people involved in and affected by the exchange. In many ordinary, nonmedical cases, if a person chooses to risk his life or health, we feel that this is ultimately his decision to make. Miners, police officers and soldiers all take risks, often very dangerous ones. Our highest admiration, in fact, is reserved for those rare people who risk or even sacrifice themselves for the sake of others.

But while we honor self-sacrifice, we would rightly criticize a person, like Chavel, who willingly *took advantage* of another person's sacrifice. And this is what is hard to avoid in many harmful medical procedures: a person who stands to gain from a volunteer's selflessness. Altruistic acts benefit other people, both directly, as with an organ recipient, and indirectly, as with the clinical researcher whose reputation is made through the fruits of his research. And while it might be admirable to risk harm to oneself, it is not admirable to encourage another person to risk harm to himself for one's own benefit.[10]

Though the risks associated with organ donation from living donors vary from one procedure to the next, from very little to unknown, they are all undertaken for the good of a donor who, unless he or she is a child, has presumably agreed to be a recipient. Accepting a sacrifice of great magnitude is not mere passive acquiescence devoid of any moral import. If I allow someone else to risk his life or health for my sake, I am endorsing his self-sacrifice and agreeing to profit by it.[11] Now, of course, if the risk to the donor were very small, as in the case of bone marrow transplantation, and the alternative were death, an offer like this would be difficult to refuse, and accepting it would surely be justified. But what if the risk were very high? What would we think of a person who would take advantage of a donor's willingness to take life-threatening risks? What would we think of a person who would accept a heart from a living donor?

Unless the circumstances were extraordinary, most of us would think very badly indeed of a person who would agree to, and take advantage of, a sacrifice of this magnitude. Like Chavel's, his would be an act of failure: a failure of courage, a lapse of moral nerve. Chavel is ashamed because his hour came; he had the chance to behave honorably; and he betrayed himself. Like Conrad's Lord Jim, he was faced with a moral test and he floundered. If an ailing patient were to take advantage of a healthy donor's voluntary self-sacrifice, it might well be understandable but it would not be morally admirable. It would not be the sort of behavior that we would aspire to and want to encourage.

This point also helps to explain why we often feel very differently about a person who donates an organ to a family member. Chavel's life was saved through a bargain struck with a stranger, and we rightly feel that he was wrong to take advantage of Janvier's unusual wishes. But relationships between family members are colored by very different moral and emotional hues. Here talk of rights, obligations, respect and freedom gives way more naturally to talk of gratitude, grudges, devotion and kinship. If a father wishes to donate an organ to a child, or a sister to a brother, we can immediately understand the wish. It arises out of love. And accepting a gesture of love, even if it involves the risk of harm to the giver, is profoundly different from paying someone to harm himself or even from endorsing self-harm from a stranger. When a person is faced with serious illness, we *expect* her family to respond, and we can identify with the impulse to undergo whatever risks or harms are necessary to help the loved one. It is a legitimate question, of course, whether or not a person who truly loves another could in good conscience allow that person to take great risks for him. But we can understand and approve of the relationship out of which such an offer and acceptance might take place. If a person offers to risk his life for a stranger, even if we admire him we feel the need for him to explain why he is willing to take such grave risks. But if a sister offers to risk her life for her brother, the explanation "because he is my brother" will suffice.

For related reasons, it seems less problematic for a small child to be the recipient of an organ from a living donor than it is for an adult. Since a small child has no choice in the matter, unlike an adult, he cannot endorse or agree with a donor's decision to undergo risk or harm. Thus there is no worry that the recipient might be taking advantage of the donor.

It must be remembered that decisions about risking harmful procedures are always made within a web of social relationships: between family members, between strangers, between clinician and patient, researcher and subject. The nature of those relationships affects the moral standing of the decisions, as I have pointed out, but the reverse is also true: what sort of decisions we allow or encourage affects the nature of the social relationships. For example, it may be admirable for a person to place another person's interests above his own, but for doctors to encourage or endorse such decisions by their patients might undermine the already endangered assumption that doctors put the interests of their patients first. This might well change the relationship between doctors and their patients in general. Even those of us who resent being told by doctors how we should behave might be wary of doctors who had no qualms about doing significant harm to their patients for the benefit of someone else.

This points to another reason why we might worry about doctors taking part in risky living organ transplantations. A donor, we think, should be praised for valuing his own interests less than those of the transplant recipient. We give medals to heroes. But things are different for the doctor. A doctor is supposed to value the interests of his patients *equally*. Thus, while a doctor may think that the donor's offer to sacrifice his life for that of another is admirable, he may also believe that he would be violating his duty to value the interests of both the potential donor and the potential recipient equally if he performs the operation. By performing the transplant, he is endorsing the donor's sacrifice, and thereby valuing the interests of the recipient more than those of the donor.

This brings up a related question: What about the sale of organs, or paying people to take health risks? Would commercializing the transfer of human organs change the nature of the doctor-patient relationship? Perhaps, though just how it would change is not easy to predict. Organ transplantation is a practice in which a relatively small proportion of people ever take part, and it fits into our cultural landscape rather awkwardly. Both the language we use to describe the prelude to organ transplantation and our customary ways of proceeding suggest that we have begun thinking of the practice, however tentatively, as a variation on gift-giving.[12] We speak of "donating" organs; promotional campaigns encourage potential blood donors to "give the gift of life."

However, the anthropology of a practice is altered by the exchange of money for what would otherwise be undertaken for reasons of affection, charity or duty. We make important distinctions between favors and services, gifts and merchandise.[13] To put a price on organs and sell them alters, in a rather uncomfortable way, both the way we think of the organs themselves and the relationship between the organ donor and the recipient. The donor becomes a vendor, the recipient a customer, the organ a commodity, and the relationship a contract. Many doctors would be uncomfortable with this commercialized version of transplantation, even those who doubt that generosity can meet the demand for organs.

The Tenth Man also reminds us that few decisions affect only the person who makes them. Chavel eventually takes a job under an assumed name as a handyman at his old estate, which is now owned by Janvier's sister and mother. There he realizes how much his exchange has hurt Janvier's sister, who despises the unknown man whose bargaining led to her brother's death. She wonders how Janvier could have ever thought that she and her mother would have preferred the wealth they have inherited to his life.

That a person's decision to harm himself deeply affects a circle of people far beyond him seems so obvious a part of ordinary life that it seems almost trite to emphasize it here, but a recognition of this point is often strangely absent in philosophical writing. To emphasize the broader effects of a person's actions is not, of course, to deny that a person's liberty rights entitle him to harm himself if he wishes. It is rather to point out that these actions often extract a heavy toll on those who love and care about the agent, and that for this reason, they are not ethically uncomplicated. If I pay another person to harm himself for my sake, or if I agree to use him in a risky research protocol, I must recognize that my actions might very likely damage his family and friends very much. And even while I might defend that person's right to make the decision to harm himself, I would feel very awkward trying to defend myself against the criticism of his family and friends, whose resentment most of us could readily understand.

Finally, it is important to realize that the doctor is not a mere instrument of the patient's wishes. Analyses of living organ donation and risky clinical research are often simplified without much warrant by a failure to acknowledge outright that the doctor is also a moral agent who should be held accountable for his actions. If a patient undergoes a harmful procedure, the moral responsibility for that action does not belong to the patient alone; it is shared by the doctor who performs it. Thus a doctor is in the position of deciding not simply whether a subject's choice is reasonable or morally justifiable, but whether *he* is morally justified in helping the subject accomplish it.

This alters the doctor's perspective in at least two important ways. First, as a moral agent, the doctor must ask not simply whether a change in a given state of affairs would be morally better, as a detached observer might ask, but whether or not he should become the *agent* of that change. Answers to these two questions need not be the same. If I were faced with a dying person in intractable pain who wanted to be a heart donor, I might well judge that all things considered, it would be better if he were to die. But this does not mean that I would be willing to kill him, or that I believe that I (or anyone) would be morally justified in doing so. It is an essential part of our notion of agency that we distinguish between that which we do and that which merely *happens*. It is not at all unreasonable for a doctor to think that it would be good for an event to take place but bad for him to bring it about.

To take another, slightly different example: opponents of a market trade in human organs often argue that an organ market would exploit the poor, who would be tempted to alleviate their poverty at great risk to their health. Market defenders respond that the harms a poor person chooses to undergo should be a matter for that person himself to decide. A poor person might well think that it is better to be without a kidney than without money. But if I am the surgeon faced with doing the transplantation, this argument may still not win me over. Because even if I agree that the choice of harms should be up to the poor person himself, and that his choice to donate a kidney for money is reasonable, the fact is that I would not be responsible for his being poor, but I *would* be responsible for his being without a kidney. Greene makes this point in *The Tenth Man*. What torments Chavel is not a mere event, the death of Janvier, but the fact that he, Chavel, is at least partly morally responsible for bringing that death about.

The second important way in which the doctor's perspective differs from that of a patient or a detached observer is in the balance of harms and interests that he must weigh. A potential organ donor or research subject must decide whether to weigh the interests of other people over his own. To do so would be admirable, and not to do so would still be understandable. However, the doctor is looking at a different sort of balance. He must weigh not his own interests, but the interests of one person against another: in the case of organ transplantation, the interests of a potential donor against the interests of a recipient; or in the case of nontherapeutic clinical research, the interests of a potential research subject against the potential beneficiaries of the research. This shifts the moral balance of the problem in an important way, because while we admire the person who *undergoes* harm to himself for the sake of another, we do not necessarily admire the person who *inflicts* harm on one person for the sake of another. And the latter is what the doctor must do.

VI

Should these abstract points shape the way we approach policy decisions on procedures that involve the likelihood of significant harm to patients? Perhaps. For one thing, there is a legitimate distinction to be drawn between *allowing* a person to risk harm to himself and *encouraging* it. So, for example, even if we acknowledge the argument that a person has a right to risk harm to himself and that his action would benefit others, it does not follow that a system is justified which encourages people to harm themselves. Substantial payment to organ donors or volunteers for dangerous research arguably crosses the line between allowing and encouraging.

There is also an obvious difference between choosing to risk harm to oneself and choosing to aid another person in risking it. It is partly for this reason that we might admire a person who chose to risk his life or health for the sake of others, but at the same time criticize the doctor or researcher who exposed him to that risk. It is not unreasonable, then, for doctors to be reluctant to expose willing subjects to the risk of harm, even while acknowledging the legitimacy of a system which allows subjects to take great risks. In fact, we might be justifiably suspicious of the character of a doctor who had no such reservations.

At least part of the reason why we have reservations about patients who volunteer to be harmed is the possibility that other people might be taking advantage of the volunteer's selflessness—organ recipients taking advantage of donors, researchers taking advantage of volunteers, and so on. For this reason, any system of practices in which people are likely to be harmed should be set up in ways that minimize this possibility. Of course, there is a sense in which *any* person who benefits from such a system is taking advantage of those who contribute to it, but it is possible to draw some limits. For example, it would be better to have a system of living organ transplantation in which nobody is able to make a financial profit from the procedure, including transplant surgeons and organ procurement agencies. This would limit incentives for anyone to encourage potential donors to take risks.

So perhaps there is, after all, some substance to back the intuition that there is something wrong with helping or encouraging a person to do himself harm, no matter how heroic we think such an action might be. This is one reason for the resilience of medicine's injunction not to do harm, and despite the unthinking way in which it is often invoked, for its particular rhetorical force. It is doubtful that most of us want a society in which physicians are unreflectively willing to endorse their patients' suicides. Because physicians are in a special position, with the capacity to do great harm to patients both willing and unwilling, *primum non nocere* gives voice to the widely-shared belief that physicians must exercise special care in practicing their art, and abstain from practices which harm patients even if the patient, quite reasonably, wishes to be harmed.

Chapter 7

The Point of the Story: Narrative, Meaning and Final Justification

Just because you wander in the desert doesn't mean there is a promised land.

——Paul Auster

I

There is a sequence in Ross McElwee's documentary film, *Time Indefinite*, when Ross visits his brother Tom, a surgeon in Charlotte, North Carolina. His reason for visiting is to talk to Tom about their father, also a Charlotte surgeon, who had died suddenly of a heart attack only a few months previously. During the visit, Ross films Tom examining a patient with breast cancer. Her tumor is enormous, the size of an orange, and Tom asks her how long it has been there. She says she doesn't know, maybe a few months. Her tone is casual, matter of fact. Later, in his office, Tom tells Ross that a tumor that size must have been growing there for years.

Shortly after this conversation the camera turns to a cross section of the tumor, after it has been surgically resected from the patient's body. McElwee holds the shot for an uncomfortably long time. While you, the moviegoer, look at the cross section of this large, cancerous mass, you hear McElwee's voice asking himself how someone could possibly ignore a tumor this size for so long. The tumor had been growing larger and larger for years, invading her body, yet she had simply pretended that it wasn't there. This kind of self-deception seems hard to imagine, says McElwee; yet isn't it the same with death itself? All of us will die, yet we go about our day-to-day lives pretending we won't, ignoring the inevitable fact of our mortality.

It is a powerful moment in the film, both intimate and disturbing, the tumor suddenly transformed into a visual metaphor for your own inevitable death. I doubt it could have been as powerful with any medium other than film—an ugly tumor, a wry Southern voice addressing you in the dark and your own self-deception about death, all brought together in a single moment. Such moments are not uncommon in McElwee's films, which are often a strange hybrid of existential rumination and home movie. This particular moment is all the more moving in the context of the narrative in which it is set, one framed by the unexpected death of McElwee's father and the birth of his son. Thinking about McElwee's film started me thinking about the relationship between narrative and medium, particularly the way that moral communication is shaped by the way in which it is delivered. Does our understanding of life and death depend on the form and the medium in which we communicate about it? Does moral discourse delivered in an essay differ in any important way from that delivered in a novel, a film, the television news, an electronic discussion list?

In his early philosophical work Wittgenstein was captivated by the idea of language representing the world. His picture theory of language concerned the idea of representation: of language picturing the world, with the logical relationship between words mirroring the logical relationship between things in the world. Language pictured reality. But later in his life Wittgenstein came to reject this view of language. For the later Wittgenstein, language is an altogether messier and more complex affair, like the haphazard, mazelike streets of an old city. We are not picturing the world when we swear, or joke, or pray or do many of the quite ordinary things we do with words. For the later Wittgenstein, it is a mistake for philosophers to try to systematize language or to provide some kind of philosophical foundation upon which language can be constructed. Wittgenstein's own style of writing philosophy is radically unorthodox, an aphoristic array of dark warnings, abstract meditations and fanciful thought experiments.

Most bioethicists, or at least most philosophers and doctors, tend to use language in a more or less thoughtless way, assuming that the *way* that we describe the world is independent of the *content* of the description. We tend to assume that our task with language, and especially for ethics, is to represent the world in the best way that we can, and we make our ethical decisions accordingly. We may of course be faulted for what we include in our description and what we leave out, but the issue (we think) is about how closely our description matches the facts. It isn't how we say things; it is what we say. A growing minority of scholars in the medical humanities, on the other hand, want to make us self-conscious not just about what we say, but about how we say it.[1] Style is not innocent of theory, they suggest, and style cannot be fully separated from content. When we use language, we are not just representing the world; we are interpreting it, and in some ways, we are creating it.

II

Tod Chambers has been among the most innovative and original advocates of the idea that the style in which bioethicists write expresses their substantive philosophical views.[2] He points out that unlike most other philosophers, bioethicists often begin their articles with a case which is intended to present the reader with a moral problem. Often italicized or indented, the case is generally set off from the rest of the article, implying that the case and the philosophical analysis of the case are separate. But, as Chambers says, bioethicists write these cases themselves, adapting them from the literature or from their own experience. And just as, say, Albert Camus's "white" style mirrored his existentialist philosophy, the manner in which a bioethicist writes the case narrative—the setting, the narrator's voice, the use of irony and so on—will reflect his or her own philosophical arguments.

To demonstrate his point, Chambers examines a number of bioethics case studies, including the following case, titled "The Humane Murder of a Helpless Infant," from Robert Veatch's book *A Theory of Medical Ethics:*[3]

> Mrs. R arrived at the physician's office simultaneously depressed and agitated. She had been under Dr. T's care for a little over a year, but today was especially traumatic for her. Her breast cancer was developing rapidly. Since the birth of her daughter a few months ago, she had been rapidly losing strength. She feared that soon she would have to give up her baby in order that someone or some institution could care for her. She had no family, no husband, no one to turn to for help except Dr. T.
>
> In the privacy of his office, she reviewed her tragic story. None of the obvious options would work. Adoption would not meet the baby's needs adequately, and given the baby's problem with a malformed hip, probably no one would want to adopt her anyway. As for the institutions that care for the moneyless orphans of the street, Mrs. R said they could not possibly give the baby the care she needed. There were no friends or neighbors she could rely on. The city was large and anonymous.

Convinced that her child is doomed to a miserable life, Mrs. R. wants to kill her as humanely as possible. She asks Dr. T for help.

In setting out this case, says Chambers, Veatch doesn't simply give us a context for the moral problem; he creates a world. Veatch's world is that of the dangerous, uncaring city. Indeed, it is not Mrs. R's cancer or the baby's needs that lie at the heart of the moral problem but the perils of the city, which the omniscient narrator pronounces "large and anonymous." Chambers compares Veatch's hostile urban world to that of the hard-boiled detective novel, the literary landscape inhabited by Sam Spade and Philip Marlowe. The hard-boiled detective is an outsider in a corrupt urban domain, a man who lives by his own private moral code. He begins his adventures reluctantly. Like Dr. T, he is suddenly confronted with "a case," usually brought by a desperate client who stumbles into the detective's office because she has nowhere else to turn. Mrs. R comes to Dr. T because she has "no friends or neighbors" to rely on, and no faith in the "institutions that care for the moneyless orphans of the street." Veatch's characters don't trust the authorities; they must go outside the law for help. Like the characters in the hard-boiled detective novel, they cannot rely on conventional morality. They must make confidential arrangements with private individuals to ensure that justice is done.

As with Veatch's case narrative, says Chambers, so it is with his moral theory. Veatch's objective is to convince his readers to abandon ethics based on professional codes and opt instead for a contractarian approach, with individual doctors and patients coming to mutually agreed-upon understandings. The cold, cynical world Veatch constructs in his case narrative reinforces the need for such contracts. In such a world we should not assume that anyone can be trusted. We are alone in the naked city, and the streets are dark and menacing. Just as the client in the hard-boiled detective novel must establish a private contract with a stranger, so must a patient contract with her doctor, because she cannot simply assume that all physicians are morally trustworthy. The model of medical ethics Veatch advocates is one where doctor and patient contract together in fidelity and loyalty.

The point Chambers is driving at is not that bioethicists should try to present cases more "objectively." His point is that bioethicists should acknowledge (to themselves as well as to their readers) their authorship of the cases they present. Even seemingly "objective" case presentations will express a particular worldview. "Authors can never subtract how they tell the story from how they see the world," writes Chambers, "but they can destroy the illusion that an objective presentation of a case exists."[4]

What is problematic, then, is not that narrative style communicates a personal moral vision, but that it packages a personal moral vision in the surface wrapping of objectivity. Case studies can be especially deceptive in this regard because they appear to be laying out nothing but the facts. As Chambers says, "Narrative is a particularly seductive form of rhetoric, for it makes readers see another's way of seeing as natural and self-evident, as though there were no other way of seeing."[5]

Yet for this very reason narrative can be a more potent medium of moral communication than the philosophical essay. Martha Nussbaum has argued that there are certain aspects of morality which the essay simply cannot convey to us in the same way that narrative literature can. Thus to make a choice to write an essay rather than a narrative is to make a choice about the aspects of the moral life that you transmit.[6]

The moral life involves the unexpected, for example. It involves events that happen by surprise, which we can't predict or control: a dismissal letter from the Dean; a fishtailing car on the ice; an inheritance from a long-lost uncle; the birth of a child with cystic fibrosis. How would you convey these things, and the way they can turn your moral life upside down, in a philosophical essay? You can *write* in a sentence that surprise is part of the moral life, as I did earlier in this paragraph, but you can't actually express this sense of the unexpected or surprise in the absence of narrative. Surprise happens in stories. It is hard to surprise your reader in an essay without resorting to profanity.

Nussbaum relates this to the Aristotelian idea of learning by experience. We have to learn certain things by guidance, not by a formula; we have to experience them rather than simply having the concepts repeated to us. This is the difference between learning how to swim in a lake and learning how to swim by reading a manual. The novel can come much closer than an essay can to placing us in a situation and showing us what it is like. It can reproduce experience—including the experience of surprise, of the unexpected—in a way that the essay can't.

The novel can also better express the idea of the plurality of value. It can show us that values differ from each other in qualitative ways, and that the conflict between values may be a conflict between goods that cannot be directly compared with each other and weighed. Vronsky or Karenin? Family or revolution? Good health or good barbecue? Nussbaum suggests that a choice between two incommensurable goods is tragic in a way that a choice between different quantities of the same good is not.

Perhaps most crucial for Nussbaum is the way narrative can express the ethical value of the emotions. The novel, the story, the play, the film, all can engage the emotions in a way that is far more difficult for an essay. Reading Tolstoy puts into play a different set of mental faculties from reading Kant.

That a narrative can pull a reader emotionally into a particular situation in a way that an essay cannot is probably not controversial. What is more controversial is whether this emotional engagement is enlightening or whether it is dangerous. Those who worry about emotions clouding sound judgment will be suspicious of the narrative style; better to step back and view events in the cool, detached light of reason. But those who see morality as critically tied to sympathy and imagination will be equally suspicious of the emotional flatness of the philosophical essay. As Chesterton wrote, the danger with a reasonable man is that all he has left is reason.

Yet whatever your ideological take on this question, it should be clear which manner of writing is winning. Most Americans, I would venture to say, have never read a philosophical essay.

III

Not long ago I was approached by someone from Sony Pictures about the possibility of taking part in a Web discussion on genetic enhancement. Sony was releasing a new film called *Gattaca* with a roster of Hollywood stars, and it was set in a future state in which a child's genetic inheritance can be predicted and controlled through various medical technologies. The film raised moral questions about discrimination against individuals based on their genetic constitution, about parental control over the future of their children, about genetic determinism and individual responsibility. Portentous questions, these. I don't usually feel comfortable playing the role of bioethics pundit, but this project sounded different. It involved writing about ethics rather than speaking, and it would be interactive. Another academic and I would post comments on three ethical issues at the *Gattaca* Web site, which would be then be open for comments from other participants. We could reply to those comments in turn. The audience would be vast in comparison to, say, a graduate philosophy seminar.

It didn't exactly work out as I had anticipated. The film was no better than average, and the ethical questions we were given to answer had little to do with genetic enhancement. One was about cloning, another about abortion. What seemed as if it might be an electronic discussion turned out to be closer to an electronic bulletin board, with postings from people I was glad not to have met in person. One of the first postings I read said, "I am made of squirrel meat." Another one said, "Where are the pictures of naked women with animals?"

I have found myself agreeing more than I would like with Sven Birkerts, whose worries about electronic media were collected in his book *The Gutenberg Elegies*. Birkerts is concerned that the cost of our perpetually expanding world of electronic communications is a loss of inwardness and depth. In a relatively short time we have moved from a culture of print to one of electronic media, of television, radio, telephones, answering machines, video recorders, voice mail, fax machines, satellite dishes, portable computers, books on tape, e-mail, Web pages, virtual reality technologies and hypertext. "The ultimate point of the ever-expanding electronic web is to bridge once and for all the individual solitude that has heretofore set the terms of existence," writes Birkerts. Television, radio and the telephone compress space, bringing us voices and images from distant places; voice mail, video recorders and computer technologies compress time, bridging the gap between what is spoken or written and when it is heard or read. The absence of any physical substance or place leaves electronic words and images without the permanence of printed words and images. What does this do to our sense of time and place, our sense of history and culture? What does it do to our selves? Birkerts' worry is that electronic media are making us shallower, moving us farther away from the primary things that until now have given our lives meaning and, in the process, making us less capable of the depth and self-reflectiveness that seem essential to philosophical thinking. Of our dependence on electronic media Birkerts writes, "And in time—I don't know how long it will take—it will feel as strange (and exhilarating) for a person to stand momentarily free of it as it feels now for a city dweller to look up at night and see a sky full of stars."[7]

I wish Birkerts were wrong, partly because I am no less dependent on some of these technologies than other Americans, and partly because I like them. I am typing this essay on a laptop computer in my three-year-old son's bed, while he lies next to me listening to *Hansel und Gretel* in German on a cassette recorder. But I am afraid that Birkerts may be right. It is not simply that abstract philosophy doesn't play well on the Internet. Even concrete, practical ethical discussion takes on peculiar and unexpected forms on electronic media such as e-mail lists, Web sites and television.

At various times I have subscribed to electronic discussion lists for philosophical and ethical matters, the most active of which has been a moderated list for bioethical discussion open only to academics, professionals and students with demonstrable experience, background or knowledge in bioethics (thus avoiding the "I am made of squirrel meat" problem). The list generates dozens of messages daily on topics as abstract as the *telos* of medicine and as concrete as the withdrawal of ventilator support for dying children. Many of the regular contributors to the list have written books and articles that I admire. Yet the electronic discussion is frustrating to read, or perhaps I should say try to read, since any prolonged attention is difficult to sustain. There is none of the context and form that a book provides, for example. No chapters, no defined beginnings or endings, no physical pages or covers, often not even paragraphs. Just various threads of text, some a single line in length, others much longer, in disjointed and interrupted sequences, arriving at irregular intervals in my electronic mailbox, which is itself, of course, not even a real box, only a program on my computer. The messages are somehow ephemeral, disembodied, weightless. And endlessly repetitive. With an ever-changing body of contributors, and without the foundation of written texts with which everyone is familiar and to which everyone can refer, the messages turn to the same topics again and again, to which the same resolutions are offered, the same comments posted, the same questions raised. Far from the narrative forms that Nussbaum and others find crucial to moral discourse, this kind of electronic discussion resembles an antinarrative, in which time and linear sequence are undermined. I suspect Birkerts is onto something when he says the impermanence of electronic media alters our sense of time and history, fixing in the user a heightened awareness of the present moment but flattening out our historical perspective.[8] These days, most of the messages I delete without reading.

Like some computer communications technologies, television also fixes the viewer in the present, but unlike computer technologies, it relies heavily on the narrative form, not only for dramatic programming but for news broadcasts, which package current events into news "stories." On television, narrative is emphasized at the expense of explanation. Yet television narratives are generally short, self-contained and often unrelated to one another, whether they are the three-minute mini-narratives of the television news or the hour-long episodes of a dramatic series.

Bioethicists themselves are becoming fixtures on the television news, of course, providing commentary on morally controversial issues. Supposedly the purpose of these appearances is to educate the public. Whether they succeed is not obvious. Television is a visual medium. It trades in images rather than words, visual representations rather than linguistic ones. It creates moods, impressions, atmosphere, emotional responses. It is much less effective at communicating arguments and propositions, the tools of the philosopher's trade. Bioethicists deceive (and flatter) themselves when they say that their television appearances educate the public. Arguments cannot compete with images on television, and still less can an eight-second sound bite; whatever is spoken on television has far less an impact than the images that accompany it. The only effective response to an image is another image, and if an idea cannot be communicated effectively with images it will generally lose the game.

Bioethical problems on the television news come without history or context. Because the news is organized into brief stories announced by punchy headlines, moral issues often appear devoid of past and future. Absent is any sense of place and personality, much less the institutional and cultural subtleties that give a moral problem its shape. The immediate predominates over the long-term, the simple over the complicated. A moral position that can be justified in a few sentences or images wins out over those that are more subtle, complex or less easily illustrated.

Television is very good at generating a visceral moral response to a concrete, particular state of affairs: the brutality of war, the plight of a woman in need of a heart transplantation, the child trapped in a collapsed building. But it is much less suited for communicating abstract and impersonal moral claims. The categorical imperative would never have made the evening news. Fine, one might say; when you choose your method you must think about the medium. Philosophy should be reserved for the classroom, not the television studio. Sometimes, however, the essential *point* of a moral problem involves abstract, impersonal, moral claims: duties toward strangers, the impact of present actions on future generations, the injustice embedded in institutions or systems. And these aspects of moral problems are absent on television, or might as well be, simply because of the nature of the medium. Stalin said that one death is a tragedy, a million deaths a statistic. But on television any number of deaths are tragedies as long as they are seen and not merely said. Those that are merely spoken about might as well have been passed over in silence.

IV

It is often said that contemporary Western life is fragmented and confusing, that we have somehow lost our cultural moorings. One reason for this, argues Alasdair MacIntyre, is that we have lost a sense of the narrative character of human life and human traditions. Human actions are embedded within the narrative of a human life, and human lives are in turn embedded in larger social narratives. Our sense of fragmentation and confusion is at least partly the result of our failure to take proper notice of the narrative structures that give life its unity.[9]

We tend to think of human action atomistically, as discrete, brute events. But as MacIntyre points out, actions are always actions under a description. If I were asked what I was doing yesterday at 10 A.M., I might reply accurately in a number of ways: "speaking," "lecturing," "emitting noises from my mouth," "explaining Wittgenstein's private language argument," "boring my students," "carrying out my duties as a professor" and so on. Each of these descriptions may be true; the accuracy of one doesn't rule out the accuracy of others. However, the accuracy of a description does depend on my intentions. It wouldn't be accurate to say that what I was doing would count as "trying to get tenure" unless that is what I am in fact trying to do, and it would not be accurate to say that I was "carrying out my duties as a professor" unless that is what I intending to do.

It is with the notion of intention that MacIntyre makes the link to narrative. He says it is natural for us to describe actions in relation to certain contexts: the narrative history of the self and the narrative history of the setting. The description "trying to get tenure," for example, has to be set in relation to my own future plans, which presupposes the narrative of my self; and it also has to be set in relation to the setting of the university and its narrative history.[10] Some actions are intelligible to us only within the context of some kind of narrative. To take MacIntyre's own example: a man at a bus stop turns and says, "The name of the common wild duck is histrionicus histrionicus histrionicus." This is going to be unintelligible to us unless we are told something like, "He is a Russian spy waiting for a rendezvous who is speaking in code to the wrong person," or "His psychiatrist told him to break down his shyness by saying something (anything) to a complete stranger," or "He has mistaken you for the person who asked him yesterday what the name of the common wild duck was." When we place the action within such a narrative, what was previously baffling becomes intelligible.

For MacIntyre, the narrative of a life is placed within a social narrative. "I am born with a past," MacIntyre says; my story is always embedded within the story of those communities from which I derive my identity.[11] For this reason, I, as a white Southerner, would be wrong in claiming no responsibility whatsoever for wrongs that my fellow Southerners have done, such as owning slaves, even if these actions were undertaken before I was born. Slavery and racism are things of which I should be ashamed, because they are part of my identity and the social role that I have inherited. We learn how to (and how not to) live our lives from these larger social narratives, the stories and histories that we are told and which we tell others. Stories, says MacIntyre, are our shared mythology.

Narratives have both an unpredictable and a teleological character. We don't always know how a narrative will turn out, but a narrative moves towards an end. As MacIntyre writes, we live our lives, by ourselves and with others, in light of some shared future, towards which we are moving or failing to move. There are constraints on how the story can continue, but within those constraints there are infinitely many ways it can go. We cannot understand a life, and what it might mean, without referring to the individual's narrative and also to the social and cultural context in which it is lived.

James Lindemann Nelson has described a dramatic example of a way in which a narrative understanding of human life is essential to an understanding of a person's good or well-being.[12] Nelson asks us to consider a case, first introduced by Andrew Firlik, of a woman named Margo, who is suffering from Alzheimer's disease.[13] By all accounts Margo is demented but happy, able to have conversations with other people but often forgetting who they are, reading mystery novels but skipping from place to place in the book, painting pictures but often painting the same simple picture every day. Nelson asks us to imagine further that this kind of life, when Margo's mental functions were intact and she was able to reflect critically about it, would have been deeply repugnant to her. Nelson puts it this way: "Dementia, let us say, was always her personal version of Dante's Ninth Circle; and at the exact center of her fear was the thought that *she might lose that very repugnance* and end her life in a state where she was not merely demented, but also content to be so."[14]

Suppose Margo develops a treatable pneumonia. The pneumonia can be life-threatening if it is not treated, but it will clear right up with an easily tolerated course of intravenous antibiotics. In the absence of an advance directive telling doctors and family members how to proceed, should the pneumonia be treated? Or should Margo be allowed to die? If we abide by her current interests, we would seem to be obliged to keep her alive. But if we abide by her past opinions about the kind of life she is now living, it seems we are obligated to allow her to die.

Cases like that of Margo have generated a lively and often puzzling debate. Ronald Dworkin argues that people have both "experiential interests" and "critical interests," and these interests may conflict.[15] Experiential interests are not much more than preferences, and might include things like playing baseball and watching *Casablanca*. But critical interests are much more important, and serve things that we think are good in themselves. As Dworkin says, these are interests the satisfaction of which would make a person's life genuinely better, and that a person would be genuinely mistaken about if they did not recognize. As Nelson says, critical interests outline the very structure of our selves; they go into the narrative construction of our identities. A proxy decision maker should thus try to identify a person's critical interests and make a treatment decision accordingly. Given Margo's history, it would seem, this would mean not treating her pneumonia.

Rebecca Dresser takes a very different stance.[16] For her, a person like Margo may have critical interests but those interests are in the past, and so they are less important now than her present experiential interests. We need to focus on the person she is now, try to construct what the world of that person is like; and the interests of that current person should take priority. Dresser bolsters her argument by suggesting that there may be so little psychological continuity between a demented person's former self and her current one that we have reason to question whether or not she is the same person. And if Margo isn't the same person now as she was when her mental faculties were fully intact, then we have less reason to think that the wishes of the former person should take priority.

But Dresser's account of personal identity fails to take account of (for instance) MacIntyre's narrative understanding of a person's life. Am I the same person I was when I was 10? The question arises because of a lack of the proper background. That background to the problem of personal identity, says MacIntyre, is the "notion of a story, and kind of unity of character that a story requires."[17] MacIntyre says that in the same way that we can't understand an action without referring to narrative context—my intentions, my story, my social and cultural narrative—we can't understand the concept of a "person" without referring to narrative context. The reason we can't is the concept of accountability, or moral responsibility. The fact that I am responsible for my past actions—the very idea that I can be called to account for them, and that we take this for granted—assumes the unity of selfhood over time. If there were no unity of selfhood, no narrative of which I am the subject, there could be no such calling to account. The notion of saying that I am responsible for my past actions, especially actions in the distant past, would make no sense.

I am not sure what MacIntyre would say about a case like Margo's, where (to use language he might object to) there seems to be a dramatic break between former and present selves. One may well say that Margo, given her condition, could *not* be called to account for her past actions. She has changed irreversibly; she may well not remember many of her actions; and when she carried them out, her personality and mental functions were radically different from her present ones. But MacIntyre's point is a valuable one nonetheless, because it highlights two very different views of the self. As Nelson points out, Dresser implicitly endorses a view of the self as existing in a discrete moment in time, a view that Nelson, after Charles Taylor, calls the "punctual self."[18] But Dworkin's view of selfhood is very different. It extends over time; for him, the character of the self is caught up with things that have happened in the past. One could call this a "narrative self." The problem for Dworkin, thinks Nelson, arises when he is confronted with a radical psychological break such as the one Margo has had. Dworkin's account suggests that when this happens her critical interests stay as they were before the break. A demented patient has no sense of a whole life connected by time. Former critical interests may have final authority, but they don't change once certain mental capacities are lost.

Here is where Nelson's account is most persuasive. Unlike Dworkin, Nelson thinks that critical interests can change. He thinks that they can change because the self is not self-contained but instead intimately bound up with other selves. A person's critical interests can change even after she has become demented and no longer self-consciously aware of those critical interests, because situations and social contexts change.

Nelson says: suppose Margo were a devout Jehovah's Witness, and believed that to accept a blood transfusion would be morally wrong. According to conventional thinking we might then say that even after she had become demented, she ought not to be given any blood transfusions, even if she cannot remember her former beliefs. But what if the Jehovah's Witness community itself, as a formal body, changed its position on blood transfusions—say, because of a new scriptural interpretation? Wouldn't this mean that Margo's critical interests here would change as well? Or suppose that there were a split in the church, with some members coming out against blood products and others in favor of them. How would we decide what Margo's critical interests were then? According to Nelson, we need to look at Margo's relationships, the community with whom she worshipped, and who guided her worship. If that community has changed its position, it seems reasonable to think that her critical interests here might change as well.

The same might be said of her intimate relationships. Say, for example, that her daughter has changed her own mind about the dignity of living with dementia. Wouldn't it be reasonable to think that if Margo thought of herself as a good mother and valued her daughter's judgment very highly, her interests here might change? Interests do not necessarily remain static. If one's interest is in something that changes, writes Nelson, then one's interests should track that change. As MacIntyre puts it, we are never more than coauthors of our life narratives. "We enter upon a stage which we did not design and we find ourselves part of an action that was not of our making."[19] We are actors in other people's narratives, and they are actors in ours.

V

All human lives are played out against a particular cultural and historical background. This background is what gives meaning to the philosophical question "How should I live?" and in particular, to a subset of that philosophical question. This subset consists of questions like "What gives my life meaning?" or "What is the purpose of life?" or "How does it all fit together?" The answers to these questions, such as they are, I will call "final justifications." I don't want to suggest that such final justifications will be the same for all people at all times in history, or even that they are always well articulated. Often they aren't. Some people never even ask such questions. But many do, and I simply have in mind the answers one might give in trying to understand the shape and sense of one's life as a whole.

A narrative understanding of human life is one way to make sense of these kinds of questions and of the final justifications that one might give. It is only by thinking of a life and a self as extending through time that questions about the purpose, sense, or meaning of life are intelligible. To say that God has a plan for my life, or that my purpose in life is the liberation struggle, or that my reason for living is to raise my children and take care of my family, or even that I can see no meaning in life whatsoever, requires that I think of my life not as a series of discrete actions and events but as a unified whole. Alasdair MacIntyre suggests that one thing people are getting at when they complain that their lives are pointless is that they have lost their way in the narrative, that there no longer seems to be any reason to do one thing rather than another.[20]

To say that I must think of my life as a unified whole to make sense of final justifications is not, though, to say that I must think of my life as a narrative—that is, as having a structural unity with a beginning, a middle and an end.[21] Nor is it to say that most people (or even very many of them) plan out their lives in advance, that they live out their lives in pursuit of an unchanging vision of the good, or that they devote their lives to the realization of a meaningful personal project. (In fact, to plan out my life in advance and live it according to plan sounds suspiciously close to my own personal version of Dante's Ninth Circle.) All the notion of final justifications requires is that we think of a life in its entirety, with its parts connected in some sort of unity. Just as a thread may not be held together by any single fiber, a life might not be held together by any single narrative. As Wittgenstein puts it in another context, "the strength of the thread does not reside in the fact that some one fibre runs through its whole length, but in the overlapping of many fibres."[22]

Yet it is the absence of a coherent narrative that often makes a life seem meaningless, at least to those of us in the West. That dementia might destroy our memory of the past and our ability to anticipate the future is part of what makes dementia so terrifying. We fear becoming endlessly fixed in the present, with no memory of the past and little ability to anticipate the future. Oliver Sacks writes of a patient with Korsakov's syndrome whose short-term memory is damaged and who cannot remember any events taking place after 1945.[23] He cannot even remember events from 15 minutes previously, and so is permanently stuck in 1945, shocked each time he looks in the mirror and sees his own aging face. His life seems dreadful because he is endlessly stuck at one point in the narrative with no possibility of ever moving forward.

But if a life whose narrative is stuck in the present can be terrifying, so might a life whose narrative winds endlessly and pointlessly into the future. The image of Sisyphus pushing the stone up the mountain again and again, only to have it roll down again, is such a powerful symbol of meaninglessness precisely because the narrative has no end. Sisyphus pushes for eternity.

Conceptualizing a life as a whole also allows us to articulate a kind of moral description that lies somewhere between the domains of moral philosophy and psychology. I have in mind the kinds of descriptions which might once have been called virtues or vices, but are now more often called (rather weakly) "differences in values." For example, some of us might criticize or look disapprovingly at a person who devotes his life to the accumulation of material things, or who is single-mindedly focused on advancement in the company at the expense of his family. Others might look with sadness or even pity at someone immersed in a life of quiet suburban desperation, a soul-deadening sequence of watching television, shopping at the mall and obsessively tending the lawn. If we are critical of such people (and I realize not everyone will be) we are not criticizing any particular action. (Some philosophers would say we are not even levelling *moral* criticism, properly speaking.) We are making a judgment about the shape of their lives as a whole. We are saying that their lives are steered by the wrong stars.

MacIntyre thinks that in order to decide (or discover) what the good life is, I have to have some idea of the unity of my life. The good life is not going to be the same for everyone. As MacIntyre says, it will differ for a fifth-century Athenian general, or a medieval nun or a seventeenth-century farmer. This is not only because their circumstances differ, but because everyone inhabits a partly inherited social identity. I belong to a certain family, a certain profession, a certain nation, which means that I inherit a variety of debts, obligations and expectations. To ask how I should live, says MacIntyre, is to ask how I can live out the unity of my life and bring it to completion. I can answer the question "What is the good for me?" only if I can answer the question "In what does the narrative unity of my life consist?" MacIntyre compares human lives to medieval quests. A quest is not merely a search, like a miner searching for gold. It is also an education, both in self-knowledge and in the character of that which is sought. Quests can fail, or be thwarted or abandoned. But the "only criteria for success or failure in human life as a whole are the criteria of success or failure in a narrated or to-be-narrated quest."[24]

I am not so sure. It is one thing to say that a human life is usefully described as a narrative. It is another to say that we *must* describe our lives as narratives in order to decide how to live them. As Tom Tomlinson points out, any choice that a person makes, no matter how good or bad, foolish or wise, will become an intelligible part of her narrative.[25] Any action, in retrospect, will make narrative sense, even if that action is unpredictable or inconsistent with a person's values and dispositions. When I finished medical school in South Carolina, it might have seemed strange or inconsistent with my own history as the medically trained son of a doctor and a descendant of generations of South Carolinians to quit medicine, move to Scotland, study philosophy and marry a German. But in retrospect it makes perfect narrative sense. Perhaps even more than that, in fact; it makes for a more interesting narrative than if I had stayed in South Carolina to practice medicine. Some people don't plan their lives. Some people don't script out a narrative in advance. Others do, but deviate from the script. Or improvise on it, or rewrite it or simply throw it away. Yet however the narrative unfolds, it will still be a unified narrative as we look back on it and describe it. What seemed at one point in my life to be an action in one story may later look like an action in a very different story; a person who seemed to be a central character may later look like a bit player. Unpredictable events with no rhyme or reason to them may come to look unified and coherent.

Perhaps most people ask themselves questions about the sense and shape of their lives. Perhaps many of them, if pressed, would even be able to give some kind of final justification for the kind of life they have chosen to live. But I doubt that it is necessary for all people in all times and places to have conceptualized their lives as a narrative quest for the good before they can ask such questions or give such justifications. And I doubt that describing life as a narrative unity can tell us how to live it. The real question, the most important question, is how to say which narratives, which lives, are better or worse than others. This cannot be done except by appealing to some standards external to a life's narrative unity.[26] If we want to criticize a life of inherited wealth spent on lavish toys, or a life whose promise is compromised by moral weakness or the life of a person whose single-minded dedication to career advancement has involved the instrumental use of her juniors, we will have to appeal to some kind of standards or ideals apart from the unity of the life. It is only against some such background understanding that we can say that lives are tragic, or wasted, or heroic or even meaningless. Which is to say: my life can have narrative unity but still not be worth living.

Chapter 8

A General Antitheory of Bioethics

> *In spite of many attempts, no satisfactory definition of garden and of gardening has been found; all existing definitions leave a large area of uncertainty about what belongs where. We simply do not know what exactly a garden and gardening are. To use these concepts is therefore intellectually irresponsible, and actually to garden even more so. Thou shalt not garden. Q.E.D.*
> ——Leszek Kolakowski, "The General Theory of Not-Gardening"

I

The mystery at the center of Paul Auster's detective novella *City of Glass* surrounds an ex-professor of religion from Columbia University called Peter Stillman.[1] Stillman was involuntarily hospitalized in a psychiatric institution after it was discovered that he had locked his son in a darkened apartment for nine years, isolating him, like Kaspar Hauser or the wild boy of Aveyron, from any contact with human language. Many years later, Stillman has been released from the hospital, and his son, now an adult, has hired a private detective to protect himself from his father, who he fears will try to harm him.

Stillman is a man preoccupied with language. He has written a book titled *The Garden and the Tower: Early Visions of the New World*, which argues that the first explorers to visit America believed they had found a second Garden of Eden. Part of Stillman's book is devoted to a new examination of the Fall, which, for Stillman, is the story not just of the fall of man but of the fall of language. Adam's task in the garden had been to invent language, to name all the things and creatures of the earth. But Adam's words were not mere representations of the things he named. They somehow penetrated to the very essence of things, bringing them to life. After the Fall, however, names became detached from things. Words became mere collections of arbitrary signs. Whereas words once carried no moral significance, once Eve had tasted the forbidden fruit those words became ambiguous and shaded with the knowledge of evil.

Stillman's mission is to restore language to its state before the fall. The world is in fragments, he says. "Not only have we lost our sense of purpose, we have lost the language whereby we can speak of it." When the world was whole, our words could express what we needed to say. But little by little the world has broken apart, and our words have not adjusted themselves. "What happens when a thing no longer performs its function?" asks Stillman. "Is it still the thing, or has it become something else? When you rip the cloth off the umbrella, is it still the umbrella?" No, he says, it isn't. So when we speak of such things our words are false, hiding the very things they are supposed to reveal. New York is the ideal place for Stillman's mission because it is the most abject and forlorn of places. "The broken people, the broken things, the broken thoughts."

Stillman's utopian quest is to devise a new language, to invent new words that will correspond to this broken and fragmented world. The prophet of Stillman's vision is Humpty Dumpty, anti-Wittgensteinian philosopher and the purest embodiment of the human condition. For Humpty Dumpty, the speaker of a language is sovereign, the master of his words and what they mean. He is bound by nothing other than his own judgment.

> "There's glory for you!"
> "I don't know what you mean by 'glory,'" Alice said.
> Humpty Dumpty smiled contemptuously. "Of course you

don't—till I tell you. I meant, 'there's a nice knock-down argument for you!'"
"But 'glory' doesn't mean 'a nice knock-down argument,'"
Alice objected.
"When I use a word," Humpty Dumpty said in rather a scorn-
ful tone, it means just what I want it to mean—neither more
nor less."
"The question is," said Alice, "whether you *can* make words
mean so many different things."
"The question is," said Humpty Dumpty, "which is to be master—that's all."[2]

Humpty Dumpty is a philosopher of language, a private language
theorist who constructs his own personal vocabulary. He is a prophet
to a man like Stillman, whose mission is to invent words that will correspond to a changing, decaying world. In his speech to Alice, says
Stillman, Humpty Dumpty "sketches the future of human hopes and
gives the clue to our salvation: to become masters of the words we
speak, to make language answer our needs." He is a theoretician who
"spoke truths the world was not ready for."

II

One of the most alarming aspects of describing an ethical problem
and of hearing it described by others is discovering just how many
ways it can be done. How a moral problem is described will turn on
an array of variables: the role and involvement in the case of the person who is describing it, with her particular profession or discipline,
with her religious and cultural inheritance—indeed, with all of the
intangibles which have contributed to her character. What is more,
the description any person offers will also vary—notoriously—
according to whether an ethical decision has been made, or whether
it is still to come, with whether that decision is now judged to be a
sound one or a poor one, with whether the consequences which have
resulted were intended or unforeseen.

Consider a case of a sort relatively common in the United States: a
middle-aged man with multisystem organ failure, poor but not hope-

less prognosis, now incompetent, experiencing what seems to be considerable pain, who has no health insurance, and whose family is faced with the decision about whether to continue his medical treatment. Think of the possible alternatives to the brief and inadequate description I have offered here. A clinician will describe the patient's medical problems, his hospital course, his treatment, his laboratory work and so on. A moral philosopher will be less interested in the medical details of the case than in the moral ones, and his description will be constructed from a vocabulary of terms such as autonomy, justice and beneficence, and the patient's goals, values and wishes. The patient's wife will describe not a "case" but a continuing chapter in her life. A chaplain, social worker, nurse or hospital administrator will offer still different descriptions, as will the patient's daughter, his minister, his friends, his colleagues and his enemies. The perceptions of each of these will change as the patient's story unfolds: what seemed to be minor decisions at one time now appear disastrous; incidents which might have been overlooked now seem to be portents. And any description which is offered will reflect whether the patient is in a Tel Aviv teaching hospital, a Heidelberg *Krankenhaus* or a Chicago V.A.

Perhaps the most frustrating problem in describing a moral problem is the gulf between moral description and moral experience. No description, it seems, can do justice to the realities of our moral problems. It is extraordinarily difficult, if not impossible, to capture the countless subtleties which go into the perceptions and judgments of each person involved: the hopes, fears, prayers, guilt, pride and remorse, the conflicting emotions which accompany irrevocable decisions, the self-imposed pressure to carry through with an action once a decision has been made. Much of what goes into actual moral choices remains unarticulated. To express these things, even to perceive them consciously, requires a talent possessed by few of us other than novelists and poets.

A second problem comes from the realization that, in describing a given case, one has done much of the ethical work already. A person's moral judgment is reflected in what he chooses to include in a description—whether he mentions that the patient's wife has visited her critically ill husband only twice over the past three weeks, whether he reports a bed shortage in the ICU, if he notes that the patient's children stand to inherit the dying man's estate, how he describes the patient's prognosis, whether he brings up the option of palliative care, if he notes that the nursing staff feels strongly that treatment should be stopped, whether he mentions that the patient was an IV drug abuser. One of the most interesting and disturbing discoveries to be made in a medical ethics case conference is how one's moral intuitions change as each player in the drama says his piece, as another perspective is added to one's own. One begins to suspect that it is self-deception to think any description free of ideology, to believe that any viewpoint can approximate that of an impartial spectator.

A third problem is that in order to make sense of a particular case, one must have some sort of conceptual framework in which to place it. This conceptual framework structures one's perception of the case. Medical students know this as well as ethicists; it is only with time, as more patients are encountered and filed within certain conceptual categories, that one begins to understand how to think about particular cases—what to ask, what to examine, what is relevant and what is not. But concepts, of necessity, involve generalities, not particulars, types of cases, not individual ones. We swap precision for simplicity; as Nigel Barley says, "Generalizations always tell a little lie in the service of a greater truth."[3] But in ethics, while general, conceptual frameworks may be psychologically useful, they also make it easy to overlook those aspects of our moral experience which are not easily generalized. Let me mention only a few examples. In theory, it is often said that moral concerns override other concerns, but in practice, one can often readily understand them being overridden by other (perhaps practical) considerations. In theory, it seems that moral dilemmas can, at least in principle, be solved, but in practice they often cannot. In theory, we speak of beings who rationally choose what they believe to be the best action, but in practice, we find ourselves making irrational decisions, under the sway of seemingly inscrutable desires. In theory, guilt is an emotion that we feel (or rationally should feel) when we have acted wrongly, but in practice, we sometimes feel guilty when we have done nothing at all. Indeed, a caricature history of ethics could be written

merely by cataloguing various attempts to describe our moral experience, for the sake of making it more intelligible, in terms of something
else: moral goodness can be defined in terms of happiness; our moral
sense is like our physical senses; moral judgments are like expressions
of approval or disapproval. All this is not to imply, I hasten to say, that
all theories are caricatures. To do that would itself be a caricature. It is
only to point out that moral theories trade in generalities and simplifications, which make it easy to forget that our moral experience is
particular and complicated.

Implicit in these problems is a tension between, on the one hand,
the ethics of description and, consequently, of theory, and on the
other, the experience of making ethical judgments in concrete cases.
The ethics of description and theory seems necessary to make sense
of such a wide range of cases, but as with narrative fiction and reality, moral description differs from our actual moral experience. When
we describe ethical problems, in order to make sense of them we
must impose some sort of artificial order on the story we tell, whether
we do it in terms of a narrative, or ethical principles or a medical case
history. The order imposed on it affects how we respond to it; thus
we treat differently those cases which we have heard described and
those cases which we have actually experienced. In fact, not even
those cases which we experience firsthand are innocent of theory; our
moral judgments change with how we describe the case to ourselves.
Joan Didion puts this well:

> We look for the sermon in the suicide, for the social or moral
> lesson in the murder of five. We interpret what we see, select
> the most workable of the multiple choices. We live entirely,
> especially if we are writers, by the imposition of a narrative
> line upon disparate images, by the "ideas" with which we have
> learned to freeze the shifting phantasmagoria which is our
> actual experience.[4]

For those who make a living by talking and writing about ethics,
it is often easy to forget that ethics never came in flavors of deontol-
ogy and consequentialism; the principles of justice and autonomy
and utility are not intrinsic properties of ethical problems. When we
speak of ethical principles—or more fashionably, of a communitarian

or a narrative ethic—we do so because we find these useful ways of thinking about ethics: as a self-standing conceptual system by which we can impose some sort of order upon ethical problems. But in reality, ethics does not stand apart. It is one thread in the fabric of a society, and it is intertwined with others. Ethical concepts are tied to a society's customs, manners, traditions, institutions—all of the concepts that structure and inform the ways that a member of that society deals with the world. When we forget this, we are in danger of leaving the world of genuine moral experience for the world of moral fiction, a simplified, hypothetical creation suited less for practical difficulties than for intellectual convenience.

III

It is sometimes thought that the job of applied ethics is to apply normative ethical theories to particular practical problems. Recent years have seen growing dissatisfaction with such an approach, and the reason is simple: it does not work. The problems are becoming increasingly well rehearsed.[5] One familiar problem is that there is no shortage of ethical theories, and for a given ethical problem one must be able to adjudicate between rival theories in order to decide which to apply. This can be difficult, especially when intuition does not incline us in a particular direction. When we do have strong moral intuitions, they are usually concerned with a particular case and not with a theory.

Moreover, theories are not tested only against moral intuitions; they are also tested against other theories. Because within moral theories there are the problems of adjudicating between conflicting moral principles and of accounting for exceptions to principles; adjudicating between rival theories is usually done by appeal to tests such as clarity, economy, comprehensiveness and coherence. But while it is obviously easier to understand and apply theories that are clear, economical, comprehensive and coherent, it is not at all plain why we should expect a moral theory to measure up to such tests when our own moral beliefs are often genuinely unclear, uneconomical, incomprehensive and incoherent. To put it rather bluntly, the conflict here is one between tidiness and truth; we want our theories to be simple and elegant but also true, and the only measure of the "moral truth" of a theory seems to be our own inconsistent, untidy moral intuitions.

But the most trying problem for ethical theorists is how we should understand the equilibrium in a particular case between our moral intuitions and the mandate of an ethical system. On the one hand, ethical theories are supposed to corroborate and justify our moral judgments, but on the other, particular judgments are also supposed to count against theories. That is, theorists expect particular moral judgments to be backed up by principles and theories, but it may also be considered a failing for a theory if that theory yields an especially counterintuitive judgment. Most of us would consider it sufficient to dismiss a given ethical theory, for example, if it told us that betraying one's friends and torturing the innocent were morally obligatory. Yet why do ethical theories justify some moral judgments and not others? How are we to decide if the theory counts against the judgment, or if the judgment counts against the theory? Our problem is understanding this practical check on ethical theory. For clearly, if we do in fact have moral disagreement on a given problem, then any theory that does its job will be counterintuitive for someone by yielding a judgment that runs squarely against that person's sincerely held moral beliefs.

The practical difficulty with applying ethical theories is that ordinary people pay little attention to theories when they make their moral decisions. Moral decisions are, of course, influenced often by theories of one sort or another, but this influence is usually indirect rather than explicit. (I refer to no systematic moral theories or doctrines in making moral judgments, but I have no illusions that these judgments are independent of the fact that I grew up as a Presbyterian in South Carolina.) What is more, different rules for moral argument seem to carry more weight in the ethics of theory than in the ethics of ordinary life. In theory, one is likely to be criticized for making illogical jumps and deriving illegitimate conclusions. In ordinary life one persuades, cajoles, jokes, threatens, coerces, reminds, harasses, begs and forgives. One tells stories, makes analogies, sermonizes, moralizes, holds grudges and gets righteously indignant. This is not to say that these distinctions are exclusive, of course—or that all forms of moral argument are equally valid. But one need only compare the discussion of an ethical issue in a medical journal, a theology journal and a philosophy journal to see that even in the circumscribed world of the American academy and even in the subculture thereof that has devoted itself to discussing ethics, there are strikingly different methods of ethical argument. And the differences between the customary ways of proceeding with a moral argument, especially the difference between that of ordinary experience and that of academic ethics, present certain barriers to the academic who is concerned with influencing practical decisions. It is difficult to say how a theory can be applied, or even whether it should be applied, if it is alien not only in content but in structure to the way that people are accustomed to making their moral choices.

What, then, accounts for the attractiveness of moral theories? For clearly, a notion which has entrenched itself so deeply into moral philosophy cannot be entirely useless. One obvious answer is their psychological appeal. This is not just to say that most of us seem to have some sort of ground-level preference for simple explanations, though there is probably some truth to that. It is also that we need some degree of order to our moral judgments, and theory gives us that order. We do not need order to the degree conventionally required of a moral theory, but it would be psychologically impossible to have a completely random, unrelated, orderless set of moral judgments. We speak and think in terms of concepts, and concepts impose at least a minimal degree of order onto our moral experience.[6]

But another reason for the appeal of moral theories, one which moral antifoundationalists tend to overlook, is the extent to which moral theories are genuinely helpful. Simplifying a complicated case to "autonomy versus beneficence" does tell a little lie (many little lies, in fact), but we should not ignore the truth in that simplification—or its usefulness. I can remember the clarity which emerged out of the seeming chaos of endless cases when, as a student, I learned to classify them in certain ways: autonomy and beneficence, beneficence and truth-telling, acting and refraining. The simplifications eventually crumble, but it is only because the cases have first been simplified that a critique of simplification is possible. What is more, the truths carried by these simplified ways of seeing cases often help to sort their problems out; they capture and summarize the sort of intuitions that we (at least we in the West) often come to when we think about such problems. It may not help a doctor "solve" an ethical problem to know that it exemplifies a conflict between beneficence and autonomy, but it does often help her to clarify her own thoughts about the matter—not least because it orders and focuses a wide range of disparate intuitions.

And finally, we should not forget theory's rhetorical power. Even if a moral theory is not the sort of thing which can be rigidly "applied," it is one of the tools of rational persuasion, and thus powerful fuel for moral argument. The consistency of a moral theory may point out inconsistencies in conventional moral thinking, which may then in turn result in real changes in moral values. (Think of natural rights theory and the French and American revolutions—or, to take a more recent example, Peter Singer's utilitarianism and the animal rights movement.) Where we go wrong, on the other hand, is when we begin to expect more from a moral theory than it can provide.

IV

When we analyze ethical problems, we are able to choose the ethical principles, values and beliefs that we think should apply to that problem and govern its resolution. Thus we sometimes tend to see ethics not as an intrinsic part of a society, but as some sort of abstract system to be chosen by, rejected or even imposed upon a society. This temptation can be especially strong in the United States, where one is likely to encounter individuals with moral beliefs varying over a wide range. Ethics becomes a microcosm of politics, and the question "What shall I do?" becomes instead "What is the best moral system for us to have?"

In some cases this approach is fine—if, for instance, the question to be addressed is what sort of policy we want in general for our society, and if this a question about which we are genuinely undecided. And it would be foolish to think that the ethical decisions of individuals in particular cases do not influence the moral values of other individuals and thus of society in general. The question of how a particular moral judgment will affect the course of moral thinking in a society is always a legitimate one to consider. This is why, in the previously mentioned case, it is appropriate not only to consider what would be the morally best course of action, but also whether that course of action reflects the sort of policy one would like to see influencing similar decisions elsewhere. The objections of some writers to active euthanasia reflect these sorts of concerns: the recognition that euthanasia may well be the best course of action in some few, individual cases, but the fear that disastrous consequences would result if active euthanasia were a widely endorsed policy.

But in other situations the notion that ethics can be chosen might be quite misleading. We do not—we cannot—choose our moral values at will, and consequently a society has only limited and indirect control over the moral values it embraces. Here the contrast between morality and politics is helpful, because political structures, when they are not tyrannical, are to some extent the product of willful control. In a democratic society we can change our laws, policies and less easily, our political institutions. Our moral values, on the other hand, are at least partly the result of cultural factors beyond our reach— subject to rational scrutiny, to be sure, and also subject to change, but, like the broader aspects of character of which moral values are a part, largely out of our voluntary control.[7]

The point here is that, although they are often concerned with the same problems, questions about personal moral values differ fundamentally from questions about political and institutional policy. And while ethical theories are often genuinely helpful in political and institutional questions, they are much less helpful in particular cases. The reason, of course, is that while we make policy, we do not make our values. We can quite easily choose the sort of principles that we think should guide general policy about, say, the allocation of resources, or about abortion, but we cannot choose, at least in the same way, to change people's values, and we cannot simply choose the values upon which our own decisions about policy are made. Values are rooted much deeper than that.

Thus it is, at least in some sense, misguided, even futile, to call for a new "ethic," as seems to be increasingly common nowadays—be it a communitarian ethic, a return to premodern virtue, a narrative ethic, a family or a citizen ethic—if what is intended by such call is an actual change in our society's moral values.[8] To be sure, sometimes this is not what is intended; what is meant by a new ethic is sometimes a new ethical *theory*, a call for writers and consultants in ethics to pay attention to forgotten or overlooked values. But often, it seems, the point of a call for a new ethic is to promote some new value, or way of thinking about values, in moral agents—to effect real change in the values of a society. And while one small step toward changing moral values is to criticize them and call attention to new ones, we cannot simply return to an Aristotelian worldview or adopt a communitarian ethic. Such sweeping changes in a society's moral values come about only with broader changes in a society's way of life, its traditions, political institutions, family structures and so on—changes that occur, to a disturbing degree, as a consequence of events that are rarely planned and often undesired.

Calling for society to adopt new moral values is one way of responding to moral pluralism, where a diversity of values seems to be the barrier to agreement. A similar and more common way of responding is to construct moral theories which reduce individuals to their lowest common denominator, to the broadest and most general values that they share, and then to construct a theory on the foundations of these shared values. People are replaced by rational deliberators, bundles of pure will. The solution to moral disagreement is to construct a theory based on principles with which all rational persons can agree, and which will in turn yield conclusions with which they must also agree, if they are rational and consistent.

However, while this may well be an adequate approach to political (policy, institutional, legal) differences, where the aim is a minimal degree of cooperation necessary for peaceful coexistence, moral agreement requires more than a theory, and it requires more than peaceful coexistence. Contemporary moral debate often seems to overlook the fact that ethics is often a very intimate affair; it involves not only respecting rights, but also things such as gratitude, hurt feelings, embarrassment and love. These things are deeply intertwined with culture and individual character. Policy and law set boundaries for human behavior, but because morality is bound up so tightly with family ties and cultural inheritance, with character, communication and self-perception, moral agreement requires shared values above a basic minimum. It also requires shared institutions, cultures and traditions. Moral differences are usually settled not by simply blunting individual differences, but by becoming individuals more like each other. (For all of the hostility that United States patriotism—or nationalism—understandably arouses abroad, it at least serves this effect: providing shared ideals that individuals of wildly divergent cultural backgrounds can embrace.)

V

It is often taken for granted that the moral concepts of a society should reflect some underlying standards of order. If they do not, it is up to those who work in ethics to point out the disorder (incoherence, inconsistency) and perhaps to work at correcting it, for this lack of order is at the root of moral disagreement. For instance, when, in *After Virtue,* Alasdair MacIntyre argues that moral language is in a "state of grave disorder," he cites the existence of widespread, apparently irresolvable, moral disagreement as evidence.[9] "The most striking feature of contemporary moral utterance is that so much of it is used to express disagreements; and the most striking feature of debates in which these disagreements are expressed is their interminable character."[10]

MacIntyre goes on to suggest that the reason for the disordered state of moral discourse is that we have inherited the conceptual fragments of a multitude of moral traditions, concepts which have been severed from those traditions which grounded them.[11]

Part of the appeal of MacIntyre's account of moral language stems from the extent to which it is obviously true: moral disagreement grows as traditions change, and when individuals of divergent cultural traditions live together. But part of its appeal also comes from the way that it plays upon the tacit assumption, widely shared among writers in ethics, that moral beliefs and values in a society should reflect standards of order of the sort which we expect in a moral theory—consistency, coherence, simplicity and so on—with the result being that disorder becomes a phenomenon which needs explanation. Thus some philosophers, like Auster's Professor Stillman, see their task as one of fixing the disorder and disarray of our language, polishing and refining our words until they are restored to a state of crystalline purity.

But what sort of order should we expect in our moral language? Or perhaps even more importantly—what is it for a moral language to be in a state of disorder? Surely it does not mean that individuals in a society have moral beliefs which are inconsistent with each other, or which conflict with the moral beliefs of others; in the West, anyway, this seems historically to have been a fairly constant feature of moral discourse. MacIntyre compares the state of contemporary moral discourse to that of a society which, through some catastrophe, has lost all knowledge of the content and methods of science and whose scientific discourse must therefore struggle along with the remnants of scientific knowledge and methods left from the old society.[12] The image of a disordered language of morality called up by MacIntyre's scenario resembles that described by Stillman in *City of Glass*, where the world has collapsed from the order of Eden into confusion, leaving in disarray the language which describes it: "Nature became detached from things; words devolved into a collection of arbitrary signs; language became severed from God."

> For our words no longer correspond to the world. When things were whole, we felt confident that our words could express them. But little by little things have broken apart, shattered, collapsed into chaos. And yet our words have remained the same. They have not adapted themselves to the new reality. Hence, every time we try to speak of what we see, we speak falsely, distorting the very thing we are trying to represent.

But surely this is not the sort of state in which we see contemporary moral language: a language which has somehow remained static while the world has changed, and by which human beings can barely understand each other. Whatever moral disagreement we find in society, contemporary moral discourse allows for communication between individuals with minimal confusion as to what is *meant* when a moral judgment is expressed.[13] When I say that active euthanasia is wrong, you may disagree, but you understand what I mean. In fact, disagreement of this sort, far from being evidence of a disordered language of morality, *presupposes* understanding between speaker and hearer about what is meant when a moral judgment is expressed. Before I can disagree with your judgment that active euthanasia is wrong, I must know what you mean when you say it. Unlike Humpty Dumpty, who needs to explain to Alice what his words mean, we Westerners use our moral languages with a fair degree of mutual understanding.

Yet the point at which MacIntyre's account goes awry contains an important clue to the extent to which we should expect order in a moral language. We should not expect our moral language to reflect the underlying standards of order that we might expect of a moral theory—for all of our moral beliefs to be consistent with each other and with those of others, formulable in principles for behavior upon which all rational persons would agree. Rather, we should expect our language to meet the minimal standards of order which would allow communication and understanding between those who use it.

How much order will this be? Quite a lot, as it turns out—and this order will place limits on the extent of our moral disagreement. In order for a moral term such as "humane," "cruel," "wrong" or "perverse" to gain currency in our language, speakers must understand what the term means. That is, they must understand that using the word to describe actions or persons reflects a certain *attitude* on the part of the speaker. Not merely an attitude, of course, but an attitude of a certain sort, the sort which carries all of the baggage that we normally attach to moral terms—extreme importance, certain characteristics related to universalizability and objectivity and so on. Even if we sometimes disagree as to the sorts of things to which the word "kind" should be properly attached, we still agree as to what "kind" means; it reflects the same attitude for each of us.

And agreement as to what moral words *mean* places some constraints on the things to which they can be *applied*. My understanding of what is meant by "kind" or "cruel" is determined by the sorts of things to which these words are applied by the broader community of speakers. If there were not at least some minimal overlap as to the sorts of things to which this community of speakers applies the words "cruel" and "kind," I would be unable to learn what these words meant. Mutual understanding of the word "cruel" would be impossible if one person applied it to the practice of causing needless pain, another used it to designate the practice of punishing and rewarding only people who deserve it, and a third used it to describe self-sacrifice in the service of one's fellows. Of course, because moral words do reflect attitudes which differ from one person to the next, we will not always have *complete* agreement about what actions of persons the words should be applied to. But we must have some minimal amount of agreement about certain, paradigm examples of cruelty or kindness or perversity, or else moral words would cease to be tools of communication.[14]

It is not always easy, however, to see just how moral concepts are tied to a way of life—especially when that way of life is one's own. Clifford Geertz offers an instructive example from Balinese life with the concept of *lek*, which is occasionally translated into "shame," but which Geertz says is probably closer to "stage fright." However, to understand what the Balinese mean by *lek*, one must also have some understanding of the Balinese concept of the self. The Western notion of the self (or at least what is sometimes called, somewhat disparagingly these days, the Enlightenment concept of the self) is roughly something along these lines: circumscribed, independent, free, self-governing and (more or less) rational. The Balinese notion of the self, says Geertz, is quite different; in contrast to the independent individualism of the Western self, in Bali "anything idiosyncratic, anything characteristic of the individual merely because he is who he is physically, psychologically or biographically, is muted in favor of his assigned place in the continuing, and, so it is thought, never-changing pattern that is Balinese life".[15] A person is identified by various labels: birth order, caste titles, kinship markers, sex indicators. These identify him as "a determinate point in a fixed pattern, as the temporary occupant of a particular, untempory, cultural locus."[16] In Bali, says Geertz, life is theatre. As such, "It is dramatis personae, not actors, that endure; indeed it is *dramatis personae*, not actors, that in the proper sense, really exist."[17]

Lek, then, is not just shame; it is the fear of exposure, that fear that "the public performance to which one's cultural location commits one will be botched and that the personality—as we would call it but the Balinese, of course, not believing in such a thing, would not—of the individual will break through to dissolve his standardized public identity."[18] Geertz says: "When this occurs, as it sometimes does, the immediacy of the moment is felt with excruciating intensity and men become suddenly and unwillingly creatural, locked in mutual embarrassment, as though they had happened upon each other's nakedness."[19]

The point here, of course, is that a moral concept such as *lek* cannot be understood apart from the Balinese concept of selfhood, which cannot be understood apart from Balinese ritual life, which cannot be understood apart from the Hindu, Buddhist and Polynesian religions of Bali, and so on. Moral concepts are interwoven into the tapestry of a life. Oddly enough, this is easier to see by looking at another culture than by looking at one's own. We look at Bali through American eyes, with American values; but to look at American life requires that we do it with equipment made from the very stuff which we are trying to judge.

Jacques Barzun once remarked that if you want to understand America, you must first understand baseball. There is some truth to that remark—some truth about baseball, to be sure, but also some truth about how American concepts, and American problems, are inseparable from their broader cultural context. For instance, non-Americans occasionally find it difficult to understand all the furor over the "right to die" debate in America, and the vehemence with which it is sometimes argued. Why would anyone want to continue treating a patient in a persistent vegetative state with virtually no chance for recovery? Ah well, I usually explain, you must also understand how the right to die is related to the right to life, and to the debate over abortion, and to American churches and to the role of the church in small-town life; you must also understand something about American hospitals and feminism and libertarianism and fundamentalism and natural rights and John Locke and Thomas Jefferson, and so on and so on, *ad infinitum*. To understand America, I explain, you must first understand baseball.

VI

It would be a mistake to caricature the primary use of theory in bioethics as a sort of top-down, deductivist application of abstract theory to particular cases. The theoretical sensibility runs much deeper in bioethics, and it surfaces in more subtle ways. It surfaces, for example, in abstract questions such as "What is a person?" or less commonly but in the same spirit, "What is a human being?" Usually the reason for asking such questions is connected to an ethical issue at the end or the beginning of life, such as when it is ethically acceptable to remove vital organs from a patient who is irreversibly unconscious. In the earlier days of transplant surgery, it was a matter of controversy whether vital organs could be removed from a patient who was brain-dead (by whole-brain criteria); in recent years the controversy has surrounded irreversibly unconscious patients whose lower brain functions may have been preserved, such as anencephalic children. In such cases bioethicists have asked whether some patients are "persons," the implication being that if they are not, our ethical duties towards them should be different.[20]

Arguments for stopping aggressive, life-sustaining treatment for such patients commonly run along the same lines. If an anencephalic child, or a permanently vegetative adult, is not a person, then it is felt that the grounds are stronger for stopping treatment over the objections of the family. And conversely, bioethicists who write about abortion or new reproductive technologies ask the same questions about the beginning of life. Questions such as "Is the fetus a person?" or (more commonly) "When does human life begin?" are thought to be ethically important, the reason being that if the fetus or conceptus is a person, or has begun its human life, then our moral duties toward it will be different from what they would otherwise be.

These kinds of discussions take a fairly predictable form. Like Humpty Dumpty and Professor Stillman, bioethicists conventionally take concepts like "person" and define (or redefine) them so that they can be strictly and consistently applied. Once language is thus refined, we will know how words should be used and thus how we should act. Once we get straight about the meaning of the words, their correct use will follow.

In the abortion debate, for example, it is often argued that "persons" have certain necessary characteristics (the ability to use rational thought is a favorite), and that fetuses, who do not have these characteristics, are thus not persons. Having failed the personhood test, fetuses do not have the full complement of rights and interests that persons have. This is the approach that Mary Anne Warren uses in arguing against prohibitions on abortion. She argues that fetuses do not meet any of what she regards as obvious criteria for personhood: consciousness, reasoning ability, self-motivated activity, the capacity to communicate, and the presence of self-concepts. Since the fetus is not a person, we would be mistaken in ascribing it with the rights of a person. Most importantly, we would be mistaken to ascribe to it a right to life that would trump a woman's right to choose what to do with her body.[21]

Now, I don't want to question what the criteria for personhood might be, or whether Warren has gotten them right. In fact, I suspect the most interesting thing about these tests of personhood might not be what they tell us about persons in general but what they tell us about the person who made up the test. (Joseph Fletcher, one of the earlier writers in bioethics to propose the personhood test, included among his fifteen rather eccentric criteria for personhood "curiosity" and a "sense of time.") Nor is my point necessarily to question the conclusions that these list-makers have reached. Far be it from me to suggest that we ought to treat fetuses, anencephalics or vegetative patients the same way we treat competent adults.

My point is rather to question the theoretical sensibility behind this way of reasoning. This way of reasoning says: we can figure out what to do in this case if we can just get straight about what a person is. That is, we know how to treat a person, so if we decide that this marginal being is a person—a fetus, an anencephalic or a neurologically damaged adult—then a conclusion about how we should morally treat that marginal being will logically follow. But what is wrong here is the notion that we can somehow define what a person is apart from our *moral attitudes* towards persons, and that once we get the definition right, this will tell us what our moral attitudes should be. According to this picture of moral thinking, we can reason in this way: killing people is wrong; X is a person; therefore killing X is wrong. Or: only human beings have a right to life; X is not a human being; therefore, X does not have a right to life. The structure of the argument is such that our task is to lay out the conditions for personhood, then look at the particular cases about which we were previously uncertain in order to see if they fall into the class of persons.

But this is not the way our moral grammar works. In fact, just the opposite. Our moral attitudes are not *grounded* by a theory of persons; they are *built into our language.*[22] Part of what we mean by the word "person" entails a certain moral attitude. A "person" is a type of being about whom we have certain moral attitudes and towards whom we ought to behave in certain ways. When we use the word person, we use it to refer to beings whom we must generally treat in certain ways. Persons are beings whom we generally cannot justifiably kill, lie to, steal from and so on. This is not to say, of course, that persons are not also generally beings whom can reason, form self-concepts and do all the other things whom Warren and the other list-makers suggest. My point is simply that our moral attitudes are no less a part of the meaning of the word "person" than these other criteria. Trying to define what a person is in order to get moral guidance about the acceptability of ending a being's life is like a man trying to define what "sister" is in order to get moral guidance about whether it would be morally acceptable to have sexual relations with her.

Another example may help make the point clearer. We typically use the word "friend" to describe a person toward whom we have a certain kind of relationship and toward whom we behave and think about in certain ways. Among these ways of thinking and behaving are certain moral attitudes that we might not have toward, say, strangers or mere acquaintances. Attitudes of loyalty, for example: I might not apply for a job if I believed that a friend who needed it more might lose out as a result. Or I might feel obliged to defend a friend's reputation to others in a way that I would not feel obliged to do for a casual acquaintance. Similarly for attitudes involving honesty: I might feel obliged to tell a close friend that his marriage plans are a terrible mistake, while I would not presume the same for a mere acquaintance. And so on.

Suppose, though, that I am unsure how I should behave towards a person who is not quite a friend and not quite a mere acquaintance—a person I know very well from work, for example, but with whom I have had little social contact. Taking a cue from the kind of reasoning the theoreticians of personhood use, my ethical task should be to set out a list of criteria for friendship and see whether this person counts as a friend. The results of this list, and how this person matches up to it, will then tell me how to behave. One has only to outline such an activity to realize how peculiar it would be. Not simply the fact of setting out criteria for friendship—an activity peculiar enough in itself—but the image of how such a list might look. To avoid circularity, it would have to give a description of friendship without saying anything about our moral attitudes towards friends, and would thus exclude the very things at the heart of friendship.

It is important to realize the power of this picture of moral thinking. The underlying mistake here is the implicit idea that our language is built around facts, and that values have nothing to do with the matter. This picture tells us: if we can just get straight on the definitions of the words we use based on facts, we will then be logically compelled to change the moral attitudes that go along with using the words. Put this way, the picture looks faintly absurd, but it has been a powerful idea in philosophy. The idea that language is fundamentally about facts, or states of affairs, was the guiding idea behind Wittgenstein's *Tractatus Logico Philosophicus*. According to the Tractarian picture theory, language represents the world, or states of affairs. Ethics, however, is not about states of affairs. Ethics is not about facts, and thus, for the early Wittgenstein, ethical discourse was one of the things about which we cannot meaningfully speak. "That which we cannot speak about we must pass over in silence."

Few philosophers (including the later Wittgenstein) would agree that we should consign talk of ethics to the realm of silence, but the picture of language as the means through which the mind represents the world is one that continues to exert a curious hold. Grant Gillett compares this view with the picture of the mind as a camera, which mechanically detects and records information.[23] This picture is very misleading, of course, as Gillett points out. Concepts are not simply factual categorizations. The mind doesn't just record information and peg it into various conceptual slots. Rather, concepts are also about *significance*.

To say that concepts are also about significance means two things. First, it means that understanding a concept involves not just rationally understanding it, but directing your attention in certain ways. To understand a concept—say, the concept of a bourbon whisky's "mouth"—involves not just passive perception, but also selectively focusing your attention on certain things when you drink the bourbon. Second, it means that the meaning of concepts is bound up with significance for those who are using the concepts. Gillett writes that "the things a culture values are built into and structure the thinking and action of a human being."[24] We learn to attend to certain things around us, and ignore others. Our mind does not simply record everything. And what we attend to, what we find significant, is reflected in the language we use. (This might help explain, for example, John Shelton Reed's observation that linguists have recorded over 100 different words for "cornbread" in South Carolina.)

VII

The difficulty with moral concepts, of course, is that when we look at them in this way, as part of a society's form of life, then they start to seem "merely" one sort of concept among many, as "only" relative to the way in which a people live—hence relativism, hence the subjectivity of morals, and hence all of the myriad debates in which moral philosophy has mired itself over the years. I believe that the constraints placed on morality by language and concepts prevent such a slide into relativism, but this is debatable, and a debate stale enough to keep me from rehearsing it here. Suffice it to say that in the United States at any rate, provincialism is at least as much a danger as relativism. More important for our purposes is the relationship of moral pluralism to practical action. It is all very well to say that morality is embedded in a form of life, but how should we respond?

For one thing, it is important to realize that the bare fact of moral pluralism does not minimize the importance of moral conviction.

Whatever else a moral judgment is, it is something that we take seriously; it is no accident that we speak of moral *values*, with all of the weight which that word carries. And moral conviction need not be diminished by the recognition that others have moral convictions which they take equally seriously. My recognition that others have differing moral beliefs about a given problem does not require me to sit back in respectful silence. One important mechanism for dealing with moral pluralism in the West is argument and rational persuasion. After all, communal living does require a certain amount of moral agreement.

Another more obvious but less often discussed consequence of recognizing pluralism is a redirection of our intellectual energy. If moral concepts, and thus moral problems, are dependent on a culture's institutions, then clearly one important way to deal with those problems is to deal with the institutions. Of course, cultural institutions are highly resistant to change, as I have stressed, and it is not always clear what changes will solve problems and what changes will create them. But can anyone doubt that a great number of the problems in medical ethics are the result, for instance, of the way that American doctors and medical students are trained? Or that many of these problems are fuelled by the threat of malpractice lawsuits? Or that the abortion debate will ever be resolved without some broader changes in the circumstances which make abortion seem a necessary choice to so many women?

Yet if moral concepts are bound up with a society's way of life, then unless we expect all of the institutions, customs and traditions of that society to be ordered and systematic, we should not expect moral concepts to meet the standards that we would require of a systematic theory. Like other institutions, morality evolves in haphazard fashion, and moral disagreement inevitably emerges in response to broader societal changes. In fact, disagreement is so much a part of our notion of morality that we should reflect for a moment on what else we would lose if moral disagreement were to disappear. The result would bear little resemblance to what, at least in the West, we call morality. The concept of conscientious objection would vanish; we would have no moral reformers and no civil disobedience. We would lose the notion of one's moral ideals being self-chosen, of making up one's own mind about a matter of moral discretion. Also gone would be the idea of moral maturity, which would instead become a matter of conforming to the moral consensus. Moral reasoning would become like mathematical reasoning; all competent adults would agree which actions were right and wrong, and moral maturity would simply be a matter of acquiring the mental skills to reason correctly.

Moral disagreement will be with us as long as there is disagreement about what way of life is best for human beings. It is not at all obvious that this is a question which is answerable, even in principle.[25] There may be no best life, only better and worse lives. And if morality is tied to a form of life, then it is a mistake to think that we can eliminate moral differences without eliminating the differences in cultures, and in individuals, to which morality is tied. Though the biological characteristics which humans share will mean that some lives, and some features of lives, are necessarily good or bad for human beings, there is no compelling reason, universally applicable, for adopting any one particular form of life over all others—even if we had the choice, and we do not. For this reason, we should expect diversity in the sort of lives that people live, as well as the moral differences which inevitably follow.

Notes

Introduction

1. Richard Rorty, *Contingency, Irony and Solidarity* (New York: Cambridge University Press, 1989), p. 73.
2. Ludwig Wittgenstein, *Philosophical Investigations* (New York: Macmillan, 1953), §217.
3. Tom Beauchamp and James Childress, *The Principles of Biomedical Ethics* (New York: Oxford University Press, 1979), p. 5.
4. Wittgenstein, *Philosophical Investigations*, §255.
5. Wittgenstein, *Philosophical Investigations*, §119.
6. Ludwig Wittgenstein, *Remarks on the Foundations of Mathematics*, trans. G.E.M. Anscombe (Oxford: Basil Blackwell, 1956), p. 57.
7. James Edwards, *Ethics Without Philosophy: Wittgenstein and the Moral Life* (Tampa: University Presses of Florida, 1985). See esp. pp. 112–114 and 153–154.
8. Wilfrid Sellars, *Science, Perception and Reality* (London: Routledge and Kegan Paul, 1963), p. 1. I owe the reference to Jim Edwards, who discusses this conception of philosophy and cites Sellars in *Ethics Without Philosophy*.
9. Wittgenstein, *Philosophical Investigations*, §109.
10. See Friedrich Waismann, *Wittgenstein und der Wiener Kreis*, ed. B.F. McGuiness (Oxford: Basil Blackwell, 1967), pp. 116–117. See also

James C. Edwards's extraordinary *Ethics Without Philosophy: Wittgenstein and the Moral Life* (Tampa: University Presses of Florida, 1985).

11. Wittgenstein, *Philosophical Investigations*, §124.

12. See especially Edwards, *Ethics Without Philosophy*, p. 113.

13. Ludwig Wittgenstein, *The Blue and Brown Books* (Oxford: Basil Blackwell, 1958), p. 18.

14. Ludwig Wittgenstein, *Culture and Value*, eds. G.H. Von Wright and Heikki Nyman, trans. Peter Winch (Chicago: University of Chicago Press, 1980), p. 7.

15. Wittgenstein, *Philosophical Investigations*, §133.

16. Wittgenstein, *Philosophical Investigations*, §106.

17. Wittgenstein, *Philosophical Investigations*, p. vi.

18. For example, the editors of *After Philosophy: End or Transformation* include essays by Rorty, MacIntyre and Derrida, among others, but they make no mention of practical philosophy. See K. Baynes, L. Bohman, and T. McCarthy, eds. *After Philosophy: End or Transformation* (Cambridge, MA: MIT Press, 1991).

19. Bernard Williams, "On Hating and Despising Philosophy," *London Review of Books*, April 18, 1996, p. 17.

20. Clifford Geertz, "Common Sense as a Cultural System," in *Local Knowledge: Further Essays in Interpretive Anthropology* (New York: Basic Books, 1983), p. 167.

21. For an influential account of this, see Stephen Toulmin, "How Medicine Saved the Life of Ethics," *Perspectives in Biology and Medicine* 25:4 (Summer 1982):736–750.

22. Judith Jarvis Thomson, "A Defense of Abortion," *Philosophy and Public Affairs* 1:1 (Fall 1971).

23. See Clifford Geertz, "Thick Description: Toward an Interpretive Theory of Culture," in *The Interpretation of Cultures* (New York: Basic Books, 1973); and Gilbert Ryle, "Thinking and Reflecting" and "The Thinking of Thoughts," in *Collected Papers* (New York: Barnes and Noble, 1971.)

24. Tod Chambers has written extensively on this and related issues involving the style in which bioethicists write. See especially his comparison of Howard Brody's style to that of Beachamp and

Childress in "The Bioethicist as Author: The Medical Ethics Case as Rhetorical Device," *Literature and Medicine* 13:1(1994):60–78.

25. Hilde Lindemann Nelson and James Lindemann Nelson, *The Patient in the Family* (New York: Routledge, 1995).

26. Stephen Toulmin, "The Tyranny of Principles," *The Hastings Center Report* (December 1981):31–39.

27. Ludwig Wittgenstein, "Lecture on Ethics," *The Philosophical Review* 74 (January 1965), reprinted in Anthony Kenny, ed., *A Wittgenstein Reader* (Oxford: Blackwell, 1994), pp. 290–296.

28. Wittgenstein, in Kenny, ed., *A Wittgenstein Reader*, p. 291.

29. Charles Taylor, "A Most Peculiar Institution," in J.E. Altham and R. Harrison, eds., *World, Mind and Ethics: Essays on the Ethical Philosophy of Bernard Williams*. (Cambridge: Cambridge University Press, 1995), p. 134.

30. Stanley Hauerwas, *God, Medicine and Suffering*. (Grand Rapids, MI: William B. Eerdmans Publishing, 1990) p. 99.

31. Richard Rorty, "Solidarity or Objectivity?" in Michael Krausz, ed., *Relativism: Interpretation and Confrontation* (Notre Dame, IN: University of Notre Dame Press, 1989), pp. 35–50.

32. Rorty, *Contingency, Irony and Solidarity*, p. 74.

33. Raanan Gillon, ed., and Ann Lloyd, asst. ed., *Principles of Health Care Ethics* (Chichester: John Wiley and Sons, 1994), p. xxii.

34. In Gillon, *Principles of Health Care Ethics*, p. 251.

35. Rorty, *Contingency, Irony and Solidarity*, p. 77.

36. Charles Taylor, *Sources of the Self* (Cambridge, MA: Harvard University Press, 1989), p. 4.

CHAPTER 1

1. John Lantos, *Do We Still Need Doctors?* (New York: Routledge, 1997).

2. Lantos, *Do We Still Need Doctors?* p. 7.

3. Lantos, *Do We Still Need Doctors?* p. 183.

4. Lantos, *Do We Still Need Doctors?* p. 167.

5. See Stanley Hauerwas, "Communitarians and Medical Ethicists, Or

'Why I Am None of the Above,'" in Stanley Hauerwas, *Dispatches from the Front: Theological Engagements with the Secular* (Durham, NC: Duke University Press, 1994), pp. 156–164; Alasdair MacIntyre, "Patients as Agents," in *Philosophical Medical Ethics: Its Nature and Significance*, eds. Stuart Spicker and H. Tristram Englehardt (Dordrecht: D. Reidel, 1977), pp. 197–212; and Alasdair MacIntyre, "Medicine Aimed at the Care of Persons Rather than What . . .?" in *Changing Values in Medicine*, eds. Eric Cassell and Mark Siegler (New York: University Publications of America, 1979), pp. 83–96.

6. MacIntyre, "Medicine Aimed at the Care of Persons Rather than What...?", pp. 83–96.
7. Lantos, *Do We Still Need Doctors?* p. 167.
8. Hauerwas, "Communitarians and Medical Ethicists," p. 162.
9. Benjamin Freedman, "Where Are the Heroes of Bioethics?" *Journal of Clinical Ethics* 7:4(Winter 1996): 297–299.
10. Bruce Charlton, "Medicine and Post-Modernity," *Journal of the Royal Society of Medicine* 86(September 1993):497-499.
11. Charlton, "Medicine and Post-Modernity," p. 497.
12. Charlton, "Medicine and Post-Modernity," p. 498.
13. Charlton, "Medicine and Post-Modernity," p. 498.
14. Charlton, "Medicine and Post-Modernity," p. 499.
15. Charlton, "Medicine and Post-Modernity," p. 499.
16. Alasdair MacIntyre, "Relativism, Power and Philosophy," in Michael Krausz, ed., *Relativism: Interpretation and Confrontation* (Notre Dame, IN: University of Notre Dame Press, 1989), pp. 182–204.
17. See, for example, Paul Starr, *The Social Transformation of American Medicine* (New York: Basic Books, 1982).

CHAPTER 2

1. Anthony Appiah, "The Multiculturalist Misunderstanding," *New York Review of Books* XLIV, No. 14, October 9, 1997, p. 30.
2. Willard Gaylin, "Faulty Diagnosis," *Harper's*, October 1993, pp. 57–64.

3. Gaylin, "Faulty Diagnosis."

4. Erik Parens has edited an excellent collection of essays provisionally titled *Enhancing Human Capacities*, forthcoming from Georgetown University Press.

5. See Little's essay in the forthcoming *Enhancing Human Capacities*, ed. Erik Parens (Washington, DC: Georgetown University Press, in press.)

6. Peter Kramer, *Listening to Prozac* (London: Fourth Estate Limited, 1994).

7. Kramer, *Listening to Prozac*, pp. 1–21.

8. Kramer, *Listening to Prozac*, p. 291.

9. Arthur Frank, *The Wounded Storyteller: Body, Illness and Ethics* (Chicago: University of Chicago Press, 1995).

10. See, for example, Bernard Williams's essay "Moral Luck" in *Moral Luck: Philosophical Papers 1973–1980* (Cambridge: Cambridge University Press, 1981).

11. Ludwig Wittgenstein, *Remarks on the Philosophy of Psychology, Volume I*, eds. G.E.M. Anscombe and G.H. Von Wright (Oxford: Blackwell, 1980), §48.

12. Julliane Imperato-McGinley et al., "Steroid 5-alpha Reductase Deficiency in Man: An Inherited Form of Male Pseudohermaphroditism," *Science* 186 (1974); Julliane Imperato-McGinley et al., "Androgens and the Evolution of Male-Gender Identity among Male Pseudohermaphrodites with 5-alpha Reductase Deficiency," *New England Journal of Medicine* 300(1979):1235–1236.

13. Gilbert Herdt, "Mistaken Sex: Culture, Biology and the Third Sex in New Guinea," in *Third Sex, Third Gender: Beyond Sexual Dimorphism in Culture and History*, ed. Gilbert Herdt (New York: Zone Books, 1996), pp. 419–445.

14. Herdt, "Mistaken Sex," p. 428.

15. See, for example, Walter Williams, *The Spirit and the Flesh: Sexual Diversity in American Indian Culture* (Boston: Beacon Press, 1986), and Will Roscoe, *The Zuni Man-Woman* (Alberquerque: University of New Mexico Press, 1991).

16. W.W. Hill, "The Status of The Hermaphrodite and Transvestite in Navaho Culture," *American Anthropologist* 37(1935):273–279.

17. Clifford Geertz, "Common Sense as a Cultural System," in *Local Knowledge: Further Essays in Interpretive Anthropology* (New York: Basic Books, 1983), pp. 73–93.

18. Clifford Geertz, "Common Sense as a Cultural System," p. 85.

19. See Anne Fausto-Sterling, "The Five Sexes," *The Sciences* 33 (March/April 1993), and *Building Bodies: Biology and the Social Construction of Sexuality*, forthcoming, cited in Dreger, "Ethical Issues in the Medical Treatment of Intersexuality and 'Ambiguous Sex,'" *The Hastings Center Report* 28(May-June 1998), pp. 14–24.

20. Melvin Grumbach and Felix Conte, "Disorders of Sex Differentiation," in ed. Jean D. Wilson and Daniel W. Foster, *Williams Textbook of Endocrinology*, 8th edition (Philadelphia: W.B. Saunders Company, 1992), p. 937,

21. Grumbach and Conte, "Disorders of Sex Differentiation," p. 937.

22. Dreger, "Ethical Issues in the Medical Treatment of Intersexuality and 'Ambiguous Sex.'"

23. The Intersex Society of North America can be reached at the Web address http://www.isna.org or at ISNA, P.O. Box 31791, San Francisco, CA 94131.

24. One of the earliest and most important articles was Suzanne Kessler, "The Medical Construction of Gender: Case Management of Intersexed Infants," *Signs* 16(1990):3–26. See also Anne Fausto-Sterling, "How to Build a Man," in Vernon Rosario, ed., *Science and Homosexualities* (New York: Routledge, 1997), pp. 219–225; Julia Epstein, *Altered Conditions: Disease, Medicine and Storytelling* (New York:Routledge, 1995), pp. 79–122.

25. Dreger, "Ethical Issues in the Medical Treatment of Intersexuality and 'Ambiguous Sex,'" p. 18.

26. Maria I. New, "Congenital Adrenal Hyperplasia," in *Endocrinology*, ed. Leslie J. De Groot et al. (Philadelphia: W.B. Saunders, 1995), p. 1829.

27. Epstein, *Altered Conditions*, p. 81.

28. Ludwig Wittgenstein, *Zettel*, ed. G.E.M. Anscombe and G.H. Von Wright, trans. G.E.M. Anscombe (Berkeley, CA: University of California Press, 1967), §371.

29. An alternative interpretation would be that Wittgenstein is speculating about societies with limited or no means of communication.

30. Harlan Lane, *The Mask of Benevolence: Disabling the Deaf Community* (New York: Alfred A. Knopf, 1992), p. 82.

31. Robert Crouch, "Letting the Deaf Be Deaf: Reconsidering the Use of Cochlear Implants in Prelingually Deaf Children," *Hastings Center Report* 27:4(1997): 14–21.

32. Carol Padden and Tom Humphries, *Deaf in America: Voices from a Culture* (Cambridge, MA: Harvard University Press, 1988), p. 2.

33. Quoted in Beryl Lieff Benderly, *Dancing without Music: Deafness in America* (Washington, DC: Gallaudet University Press, 1990), p. 13.

34. Padden and Humphries, *Deaf in America*, p. 27.

35. Lane, *The Mask of Benevolence*, p. 17.

36. I am grateful to Robert Crouch for making these issues clear to me. See his discussion in Crouch, "Letting the Deaf Be Deaf."

37. Oliver Sacks, *Seeing Voices: A Journey into the World of the Deaf*, (New York: HarperCollins, 1990), pp. 98–104.

38. Sacks, *Seeing Voices*, p. 88.

39. Sacks, *Seeing Voices*, pp. 88, 90.

40. Sacks, *Seeing Voices*, pp. 78, 85.

41. Sacks, *Seeing Voices*, p. 90.

42. Sacks, *Seeing Voices*, p. 74.

43. Crouch, "Letting the Deaf Be Deaf," p. 18.

44. Nora Ellen Groce, *Everyone Here Spoke Sign Language: Hereditary Deafness on Martha's Vineyard* (Cambridge, MA: Harvard University Press, 1985).

45. Groce, *Everyone Here Spoke Sign Language*, pp. 3, 43.

46. Groce, *Everyone Here Spoke Sign Language*, p. 5.

47. Quoted in Groce, *Everyone Here Spoke Sign Language*, p. 52.

CHAPTER 3

1. M.O'C. Drury, *The Danger of Words and Writings on Wittgenstein*, ed. David Berman, Michael Fitzgerald and John Hayes (Bristol: Thoemmes Press, 1996). I owe the title of this essay to Jim Edwards, who speaks of being "lost at the mall" in his book *The Plain Sense of Things: The Fate of Religion in an Age of Normal Nihilism* (University

Park: Pennsylvania State University Press, 1997).
2. Drury, *The Danger of Words and Writings on Wittgenstein*, p. 119.
3. Drury, *The Danger of Words and Writings on Wittgenstein*, p. 129.
4. Walker Percy, *The Last Gentleman* (London: Panther Books, 1966). I have taken this description of Barrett mainly from the first chapter of the book. For the most part, the words are Percy's, not mine.
5. Walker Percy, *The Last Gentleman*, p. 36.
6. Peter Kramer, *Listening to Prozac* (London: Fourth Estate Limited, 1994), p. 224.
7. Walker Percy, *Love in the Ruins* (New York: Farrar, Straus and Giroux, 1971).
8. Sven Birkerts, *The Gutenberg Elegies: The Fate of Reading in an Electronic Age* (New York: Fawcett Columbine, 1994), p. 20.
9. James C. Edwards, *The Plain Sense of Things: The Fate of Religion in an Age of Normal Nihilism* (University Park: Pennsylvania State University Press, 1997).
10. Edwards, *The Plain Sense of Things*, p. 37.
11. Edwards, *The Plain Sense of Things*, p. 46.
12. Edwards, *The Plain Sense of Things*, p. 47.
13. Edwards, *The Plain Sense of Things*, p. 47.
14. Edwards, *The Plain Sense of Things*, p. 49.
15. Edwards, *The Plain Sense of Things*, p. 50.
16. T.J. Jackson Lears, *No Place of Grace: Antimodernism and the Transformation of American Culture, 1880–1920* (Chicago: University of Chicago Press, 1981).
17. Thomas Frank, ed. *Commodify Your Dissent: Salvos from the Baffler* (New York: HarperCollins, 1997), p. 20.
18. Frank, *Commodify Your Dissent*, p. 34.
19. Frank, *Commodify Your Dissent*, p. 37.
20. Malcolm Cowley, *Exile's Return* (New York: Viking, 1934). The part of the book from which I quote is excerpted in the *Utne Reader*, December 1997, pp. 48–49.
21. Edwards, *The Plain Sense of Things*, p. 51.
22. Walker Percy, *Signposts in a Strange Land*, ed. Patrick Samway (New York: Farrar, Straus and Giroux, 1991), p. 252.
23. For a good example of what I mean by this, see David Rothman,

"Shiny Happy People," *New Republic*, 210:7(Feb. 14, 1994):34–35.

24. Peter Joseph, "An Interview with Richard Selzer," *Medical Humanities Review* 5:1(1991):24–40.

25. Peter Strawson, "Freedom and Resentment," in *Freedom and Resentment and Other Essays*. (London: Methuen, 1974), pp. 1–25. All quotations are from this essay.

26. Percy, *Love in the Ruins*.

27. Walker Percy, "The Man on the Train," in *The Message in the Bottle*. (New York: Farrar, Straus and Giroux, 1975), pp. 83–100.

28. Walker Percy, "The Symbolic Structure of Interpersonal Process," in *The Message in the Bottle* (New York: Farrar, Straus and Giroux, 1975), pp. 189–214.

29. Walker Percy, "The Symbolic Structure of Interpersonal Process."

30. Percy, *Love in the Ruins*.

31. Samuel Guze, "Biological Psychiatry: Is There Any Other Kind?" *Psychological Medicine* 19(1989):315–323.

32. Bruce Charlton, "A Critique of Biological Psychiatry," *Psychological Medicine* 20(1990): 3–6.

33. Thomas Nagel, "What Is It Like to Be a Bat?" in *Mortal Questions* (Cambridge: Cambridge University Press, 1979), pp. 165–180.

34. For a Wittgensteinian exploration of this and related ideas see Ihlam Dilman, "Wittgenstein on the Soul," in *Understanding Wittgenstein* (London: Macmillan, 1974), pp. 162–192.

35. Paul Johnston, *Wittgenstein and Moral Philosophy* (London: Routledge, 1989).

36. Ludwig Wittgenstein, *Philosophical Investigations*, trans. G.E.M. Anscombe (New York: Macmillan, 1958), p. 178.

37. Harry Stack Sullivan, *The Interpersonal Theory of Psychiatry* (London: Tavistock Publications Limited, 1956).

38. Percy, *Love in the Ruins*.

Chapter 4

1. American Psychiatric Association, *Diagnostic and Statistical Manual of Mental Disorders*, 4th edition (Washington, DC: American

Psychiatric Association, 1994), pp. 629–630.

2. J.L.T. Birley, "Psychiatrists and Citizens," *British Journal of Psychiatry* 159(1992):1–6; P. Tyrer, P. Casey and B. Ferguson, "Personality Disorder in Perspective,'" *British Journal of Psychiatry* 159(1991):463–471.

3. Stephanie Sherman, John DeFries et al. "Behavioral Genetics '97: ASHG Statement. Recent Developments in Human Behavioral Genetics: Past Accomplishments and Future Directions," *American Journal of Human Genetics* 60(1997):1265–1275.

4. Ludwig Wittgenstein, "Lecture on Freedom of the Will," *Philosophical Investigations* 12:2(1989):85–100. The lecture is in fact just a short collection of notes made by Yorick Smythies on a lecture that Wittgenstein delivered in Cambridge, probably in 1945–1946 or 1946–1947. These notes record a series of very loosely connected remarks that are even more epigrammatic than Wittgenstein's other published writings. For this reason, they are particularly difficult to interpret and probably represent only very tentative thoughts on the problem of freedom of the will.

5. Ludwig Wittgenstein, *Lectures and Conversations on Aesthetics, Psychology and Religious Belief*, ed. Cyril Barrett (Berkeley: University of California Press, 1966), pp. 54–55.

6. See Ludwig Wittgenstein, "A Lecture on Ethics," *Philosophical Review* 74(1965):3–12; and Wittgenstein's *Lectures and Conversations on Aesthetics, Psychology and Religious Belief*, pp. 54, 60–61.

7. Wittgenstein, "A Lecture on Ethics," p. 11.

8. Wittgenstein, "Lecture on Freedom of the Will," p. 86.

9. Wittgenstein, "Lecture on Freedom of the Will," p. 85.

10. Ludwig Wittgenstein, *Philosophical Investigations*, trans. G.E.M. Anscombe (New York: Macmillan, 1958), p. 178.

11. Many philosophers, of course, believe that reasons *are* causes. See, for instance, Donald Davidson, "Actions, Reasons and Causes," *Journal of Philosophy* 60(1963):685–700.

12. Daniel Dennett, *Brainstorms* (Sussex: Harvester Press, 1979.

13. Peter Strawson, "Freedom and Resentment," in *Freedom and Resentment and Other Essays* (London: Methuen, 1974), pp. 1–25.

14. Aristotle, *Nicomachean Ethics*, trans. D. Ross (Oxford: Oxford University Press, 1987), iii.5.1114a3–11.

15. Barbara Wootton, *Social Science and Social Pathology* (London: Allen and Unwin, 1959).

16. Wittgenstein, "Lecture on Freedom of the Will," p. 86.

17. Wittgenstein, "Lecture on Freedom of the Will," pp. 90, 92, 93.

18. Logical problems arise when knowledge of such predictions is made known to the agent. See, for example, Dennett, *Brainstorms*; and D.M. Mackay, "Determinism and Free Will," in *The Oxford Companion to the Mind*, ed. R. Gregory (Oxford: Oxford University Press, 1987), pp. 190–192.

19. One notable problem for accounts of moral responsibility is the psychopath or sociopath (or to use a related concept, the antisocial personality disorder). Some writers have argued that psychopaths are unable to understand morality, which casts doubt on whether they "intend" to act wrongly. The classic text here is Hervey Cleckley, *The Mask of Sanity* (St. Louis, MO: C.V. Mosby, 1976). I have written about the moral understanding of psychopaths in Carl Elliott, *The Rules of Insanity: Moral Responsibility and the Mentally Ill Offender* (Albany, NY: State University of New York Press, 1996); and in Carl Elliott and Grant Gillett, "Moral Insanity and Practical Reason," *Philosophical Psychology* 5:1(1992):53–67.

CHAPTER 5

1. See, for instance, Elizabeth Wurtzl, *Prozac Nation: Young and Depressed in America* (New York: Houghton Mifflin, 1994); John Bentley Mays, *In the Jaws of the Black Dogs: A Memoir of Depression* (New York: Viking, 1995); William Styron, *Darkness Visible: A Memoir of Madness* (New York: Random House, 1990).

2. Paul Appelbaum, Charles Lidz and Alan Meisel, *Informed Consent: Legal Theory and Clinical Practice* (New York: Oxford University Press, 1986).

3. James Drane, "The Many Faces of Competency," *Hastings Center Report* 15:2(1985):17–21.

4. Willard Gaylin, "The Competence of Children: No Longer All or None," *Hastings Center Report* 12:2(1982):33–38.

5. C. Lidz, A. Meisel, E. Zerubavel, M. Carter, R. Sestak and L. Roth, *Informed Consent: A Study of Decisionmaking in Psychiatry* (New York: The Guilford Press, 1984).

6. Albert Jonsen, Mark Siegler and William Winslade, *Clinical Ethics,* 3rd edition (New York: Macmillan, 1992).

7. Ruth Faden and Tom Beauchamp, *A History and Theory of Informed Consent* (New York: Oxford University Press, 1986).

8. Allan Buchanan and Dan Brock, *Deciding for Others: The Ethics of Surrogate Decision Making* (Cambridge: Cambridge University Press, 1989).

9. US President's Commission for the Study of Ethical Problems in Medicine and Biomedical and Behavioral Research, *Making Health Care Decisions: The Ethical and Legal Implications of Informed Consent in the Patient-Practitioner Relationship* (Washington: US Government Printing Office, 1983).

10. C.M. Culver, R.B. Ferrell and R.M. Green, "ECT and the Special Problems of Informed Consent," *American Journal of Psychiatry* 137:5(1980):586–591.

11. T.H. Gutheil and H. Bursztajn, "Clinician's Guidelines for Assessing and Presenting Subtle Forms of Patient Incompetence in Legal Settings," *American Journal of Psychiatry* 143:8 (1986):1020–1023.

12. K.W.M. Fulford and K. Howse, "Ethics of Research with Psychiatric Patients: Principles, Problems and the Primary Responsibility of Researchers," *Journal of Medical Ethics* 19(1993):85–91.

13. L. Ganzini, M.A. Lee , R.T Heintz and J.D. Bloom, "Is the Patient Self-Determination Act Appropriate for Elderly Persons Hospitalized for Depression?" *Journal of Clinical Ethics* 4 (1993):46–50.

14. Jan Marta, "The PSDA and Geriatric Psychiatry: a Cautionary Tale," *Journal of Clinical Ethics* 4 (1993): 80–81.

15. Thomas G. Gutheil and Paul Appelbaum, *Clinical Handbook of Psychiatry and the Law* (New York: McGraw-Hill, 1982).

16. Paul Appelbaum and Loren Roth, "Competency to Consent to Research: A Psychiatric Overview," *Archives of General Psychiatry* 39(1982):951–958.

17. H. Bursztajn, H.P. Harding, T.G. Gutheil and A. Brodsky, "Beyond Cognition: The Role of Disordered Affective States in Impairing Competence to Consent to Treatment." *Bulletin of the American Academy of Psychiatry and the Law* 19:4 (1991):383–388.

18. The epigraph at the beginning of this chapter is one example. It is taken from Culver et al., "ECT and the Special Problems of Informed Consent," pp. 586–591.

19. L. Ganzini, M.A. Lee, R.T. Heintz and J.D. Bloom, "Do-Not-Resuscitate Orders for Depressed Psychiatric Inpatients," *Hospital and Community Psychiatry* 43:9(1992):915–919.

20. M.D. Sullivan and S.J. Youngner, "Depression, Competence and the Right to Refuse Lifesaving Medical Treatment," *American Journal of Psychiatry* 151:7(1994):971–978.

21. Hirschfeld, Winslade and Kraus believe there are such studies, but they fail to mention that the study they cite included only three patients with depression. See R. Hirschfeld, W. Winslade and T. Krause, "Protecting Subjects and Fostering Research: Striking the Proper Balance," *Archives of General Psychiatry* 54:2(1997):121–123. The study they cite (among others) which they apparently believe supports the claim that to consider severely depressed patients incompetent is to violate their autonomy is B. Stanley, M. Stanley, A. Lautin, J. Laine and N. Schwartz, "Preliminary Findings in Psychiatric Patients as Research Participants: A Population at Risk?" *American Journal of Psychiatry* 138(1981): 669–671.

22. M.A. Lee and L. Ganzini, "Depression in the Elderly: Effect on Patient Attitudes toward Life-Sustaining Therapy," *Journal of the American Geriatric Society* 40:10(1992):983–988.

23. M.A. Lee and L. Ganzini, "The Effect of Recovery from Depression on Preferences for Life-Sustaining Therapy in Older Patients," *Journal of Gerontology* 49:1(1994):15–21.

24. Ganzini et al., "The Effect of Depression Treatment on Elderly Patients' Preferences for Life-Sustaining Medical Therapy," *American Journal of Psychiatry* 151: pp. 1631–1636.

25. Royal College of Psychiatrists, *Guidelines for Ethics of Research Committees on Psychiatric Research Involving Human Subjects* (London: Royal College of Psychiatrists, 1989.)

26. Styron, *Darkness Visible: A Memoir of Madness.*
27. Hirschfeld et al., "Protecting Subjects and Fostering Research," pp. 121–123.
28. One notable exception is Louis Charland in his innovative paper, "Is Mr. Spock Mentally Competent?: Competence to Consent and Emotion," *Philosophy, Psychiatry and Psychology* 5(March 1998), pp. 68–81.
29. A.E. Buchanan and D.W. Brock, *Deciding for Others.*
30. A. Shamoo and D. Irving, "The PSDA and the Depressed Elderly: 'Intermittent Competency' Revisited," *Journal of Clinical Ethics* 4 (1993):74–79.
31. For a fuller discussion of this sort of case, see my own book: Carl Elliott, *The Rules of Insanity: Moral Responsibility and the Mentally Disordered Offender* (Albany, NY: State University of New York Press, 1996).
32. Antonio Damasio, *Descartes' Error: Emotion, Reason and the Human Brain* (New York: Avon Books, 1994), p. 8. This narrative is based on Damasio's account.
33. Louis Charland takes the work of emotion theorists and neurologists such as Antonio Damasio in fascinating directions in the paper cited above, "Is Mr. Spock Mentally Competent?"
34. Damasio, *Descartes' Error*, pp. 34–51.
35. Quoted in Damasio, *Descartes' Error,* p. 37.
36. Loren Roth and Paul Appelbaum. "Obtaining Informed Consent for Research with Psychiatric Patients," *Psychiatric Clinics of North America* 6:4(1983):551–565.
37. Benjamin Freedman, "Placebo-Controlled Trials and the Logic of Clinical Purpose," *IRB: A Review of Human Subjects Research* 12:6(1990):1–6.
38. K.J. Rothman and K.B. Michels, "The Continuing Unethical Use of Placebo Controls," *New England Journal of Medicine* 331(1994): 394–398.

CHAPTER 6

1. M. Shaw, ed., *After Barney Clark: Reflections on the Utah Artificial Heart Program* (Austin: University of Texas Press, 1984).

2. John Harris, *Wonderwoman and Superman: The Ethics of Human Biotechnology* (New York: Oxford University Press, 1992) p. 113.

3. M. Markham. "The Ethical Dilemma of Phase 1 Clinical Trials," *CA—A Journal for Clinicians* 36:6(1986):367–369.

4. For Colen, see the *Los Angeles Times*, December 11, 1989; for Annas, *The New York Times*, November 27, 1989; and for Caplan, see Knight-Ridder Newspapers, December 14, 1989.

5. Graham Greene, *The Tenth Man* (New York: Simon and Schuster, 1985).

6. Adam Smith, *The Theory of Moral Sentiments*, (Indianapolis: Liberty Classics, 1982 [originally 1759]), p. 333.

7. J.O. Urmson, "Saints and Heroes," reprinted in *Moral Concepts*, ed. Joel Feinberg (Oxford: Oxford University Press, 1969), 60–73.

8. Urmson, "Saints and Heroes," p. 65.

9. For a sampling of objections to Urmson's scheme, see Elizabeth Pybus, "'Saints and Heroes,'" *Philosophy* 57(1982):193–199; Yogendra Chopra, "Professor Urmson on Saints and Heroes," *Philosophy* 38(1963):160–166; Michael Clark, "The Meritorious and the Mandatory," *Proceedings of the Aristotelian Society* LXXIX (1978–1979):23–33. Joel Feinberg defends Urmson and takes his arguments still further in "Supererogation and Rules," *Ethics* 71 (1960–1961):276–288.

10. We recognize this in nonmedical situations as well. There are limits to the harms to which we allow employers to expose workers, even if the workers are aware of the harms and willing to risk them.

11. B. Brecher, "The Kidney Trade: Or, The Customer Is Always Wrong," *Journal of Medical Ethics* 16(1990):120–123.

12. Tom Murray, "Gifts of the Body and the Needs of Strangers," *Hastings Center Report* 17:4(1987):30–38.

13. Courtney Campbell, "Body, Self and the Property Paradigm," *Hastings Center Report* 22:5(1992):34–42.

CHAPTER 7

1. Among the most important narrative contributions to bioethics have been Kathryn Montgomery Hunter, *Doctors' Stories: The Narrative Structure of Medical Knowledge* (Princeton, NJ: Princeton University Press, 1991); Howard Brody, *Stories of Sickness* (New Haven, CT: Yale University Press, 1987); Anne Hunsaker Hawkins, *Reconstructing Illness: Studies in Pathography* (West Lafayette, IN: Purdue University Press, 1993); and Arthur Frank, *The Wounded Storyteller: Body, Illness and Ethics* (Chicago: University of Chicago Press, 1995). For an excellent recent collection of papers on narrative ethics, see Hilde Lindemann Nelson, ed. *Stories and Their Limits: Narrative Approaches to Bioethics* (New York: Routledge, 1997).

2. See, for example, Tod Chambers, "What to Expect from an Ethics Case (and What It Expects from You)," in Hilde Lindemann Nelson, ed., *Stories and Their Limits: Narrative Approaches to Bioethics* (New York: Routledge, 1997), pp. 171–184; "From the Ethicists' Point of View: The Literary Nature of Ethical Inquiry," *The Hasting Center Report* 21:3(1996):25–32; "Dax Redacted: The Economies of Truth in Bioethics," *Journal of Medicine and Philosophy* 21:3(1996):287–302; and especially "The Bioethicist as Author: The Medical Ethics Case as Rhetorical Device," *Literature and Medicine* 13:1(Spring 1994):60–78. The discussion which follows is taken from "The Bioethicist as Author."

3. Chambers, "The Bioethicist as Author," p. 61. See also Robert Veatch *A Theory of Medical Ethics* (New York: Basic Books, 1981).

4. Chambers, "The Bioethicist as Author," p. 76.

5. Chambers, "The Bioethicist as Author," p. 76.

6. Martha Nussbaum, *Love's Knowledge* (Oxford: Oxford University Press, 1990).

7. Sven Birkerts, *The Gutenberg Elegies: The Fate of Reading in an Electronic Age* (New York: Fawcett Columbine, 1994), p. 224.

8. Birkerts, *The Gutenberg Elegies*, p. 213.

9. Alasdair MacIntyre, *After Virtue* (Notre Dame, IN: University of Notre Dame Press, 1981.)

10. Or so MacIntyre argues. He ignores the fact that some descriptions, such as "boring my students," are in fact contrary to my intentions.

11. MacIntyre, *After Virtue*, p. 221.

12. James Lindemann Nelson, "Critical Interests and Sources of Familial Decision-Making for Incapacitated Patients," Journal of Law, Medicine and Ethics 23(1995):143–148.

13. Andrew Firlik, "Margo's Logo," *JAMA* 265(1991):201.

14. Nelson, "Critical Interests and Sources of Familial Decision-Making for Incapacitated Patients," p. 144.

15. Ronald Dworkin, *Life's Dominion* (New York: Alfred A. Knopf, 1993), pp. 201–202.

16. Rebecca Dresser, "Missing Persons: Legal Perceptions of Incompetent Patients," *Rutgers Law Review* 46:2(1994): 609–719.

17. MacIntyre, *After Virtue*, p. 217.

18. Nelson, "Critical Interests and Sources of Familial Decision-Making for Incapacitated Patients," p. 145. For Taylor's discussion of the punctual self, see Chapter 9 of Charles Taylor, *Sources of the Self: The Making of Modern Identity* (Cambridge, MA: Harvard University Press, 1989).

19. MacIntyre, *After Virtue*, p. 213.

20. MacIntyre, *After Virtue*, p. 217.

21. I can remember seeing a bumper sticker that said, "Life is just one damn thing after another." If we think of narrative in this way, then I suppose any life can be conceptualized as a narrative. But then we would lose any usefulness that the concept of life as a narrative provides.

22. Wittgenstein, *Philosophical Investigations,* §67. I am grateful to Hilde Lindemann Nelson for suggesting this to me and for pointing me towards the passage from Wittgenstein.

23. Oliver Sacks, *The Man Who Mistook His Wife for a Hat and Other Clinical Tales* (New York: Perennial Library, 1987). See the chapter titled "The Lost Mariner."

24. MacIntyre, *After Virtue*, p. 219.

25. Tom Tomlinson, "Perplexed About Narrative Ethics," in Hilde Lindemann Nelson, ed. *Stories and Their Limits: Narrative Approaches to Bioethics* (New York: Routledge, 1997), p. 130.

26. Tomlinson, "Perplexed About Narrative Ethics," pp. 129–132.

CHAPTER 8

1. Paul Auster, *New York Trilogy: City of Glass, Ghosts, The Locked Room* (New York: Viking Penguin, 1990).

2. The passage is from Chapter 6 of Lewis Carroll's *Through the Looking Glass*. For more on Humpty Dumpty and Wittgenstein, see Grant Gillett, "Humpty Dumpty and the Night of the Triffids: Individualism and Rule-Following," *Synthese* 105:2(November 1995):191–206; and George Pitcher, "Wittgenstein, Nonsense and Lewis Carroll," in K.T. Fann, ed., *Ludwig Wittgenstein: The Man and His Philosophy* (New York: Dell Publishing Company, 1967), pp. 315–335.

3. Nigel Barley, *Not a Hazardous Sport* (New York: Henry Holt and Company, 1988), p. 205.

4. Joan Didion, "The White Album," in *The White Album* (New York: Penguin, 1981), p. 11.

5. See, for example, Annette Baier, "Theory and Reflective Practices," in *Postures of the Mind* (Minneapolis: University of Minnesota Press, 1984), pp. 207–227; Robert L. Holmes, "The Limited Relevance of Analytical Ethics to the Problems of Bioethics," *Journal of Medicine and Philosophy* 15:2(1990): 143–159; and especially Stuart Hampshire, *Morality and Conflict* (London: Basil Blackwell, 1983).

6. See, for example, Grant Gillett's introductory bioethics textbook: Grant Gillett, *Reasonable Care* (Bristol: The Bristol Press, 1989).

7. I have in mind here not merely moral beliefs, which I think can be more easily changed, but the broader sense of values as structures of interpretation that James Edwards discusses in *The Plain Sense of Things: The Fate of Religion in an Age of Normal Nihilism* (University Park: The Pennsylvania State University Press, 1997).

8. For instance, see Alasdair MacIntyre, *After Virtue* (Notre Dame, IN: University of Notre Dame Press, 1981); John Hardwig, "What About the Family?" *The Hastings Center Report* 20:2(1990):5–10; Marion Danis and Larry Churchill, "Autonomy and the Common Weal," *The Hastings Center Report* 21:1(1991):25–31; Steven H. Miles and Kathryn Montgomery Hunter, "The Case: A Story Lost

and Found," "Commentary" and "Overview," *Second Opinion* 15(November):55–57.

9. MacIntyre, *After Virtue*, p. 2.

10. MacIntyre, *After Virtue*, p. 6.

11. See also the persuasive criticism of MacIntyre's account of moral language in Paul Johnston, *Wittgenstein and Moral Philosophy* (London: Routledge, 1989), p. 87–89.

12. See MacIntyre, *After Virtue*, pp. 1–5.

13. MacIntyre might disagree here; he makes some contentious distinctions between meaning and use in his discussion of emotivism. See *After Virtue*, Chapters 2 and 3.

14. For a more extended discussion of this broadly Wittgensteinian account of moral language, see Paul Johnston, *Wittgenstein and Moral Philosophy* (London: MacMillan, 1989); Grant Gillett, *Representation, Meaning and Thought* (Oxford: Oxford University Press, 1992) and Grant Gillett, "An Anti-Sceptical Fugue," *Philosophical Investigations* 13:4(1990):304–321.

15. Clifford Geertz, *Local Knowledge* (New York: Basic Books, 1983), p. 62.

16. Geertz, *Local Knowledge*, p. 63.

17. Geertz, *Local Knowledge*, p. 62.

18. Geertz, *Local Knowledge*, p. 64.

19. Geertz, *Local Knowledge*, p. 64.

20. See, for example, Joseph Fletcher, "The Cognitive Criterion of Personhood," *The Hastings Center Report* 4 (December 1975):4–7; H. Tristram Englehardt, "Ethical Issues in Aiding the Death of Young Children," in Ronald Munson, ed., *Intervention and Reflection: Basic Issues in Medical Ethics*, 4th edition (Belmont, CA: Wadsworth Publishing Company, 1992):119–126; Michael Tooley, "Abortion and Infanticide," *Philosophy and Public Affairs* 2:1(1975):29–65; John A. Robertson, "Involuntary Euthanasia of Defective Newborns," *Stanford Law Review* 27(1975):246–261.

21. Mary Anne Warren, "The Moral and Legal Status of Abortion," in Ronald Munson, ed., *Intervention and Reflection: Basic Issues in Medical Ethics*, 4th edition (Belmont, CA: Wadsworth, 1992), pp. 82–91.

22. I owe this way of putting this Wittgensteinian point to Cora Diamond. See especially her excellent essay, "Eating Meat and Eating People," in Cora Diamond, *The Realistic Spirit: Wittgenstein, Philosophy and the Mind* (Cambridge, MA: MIT Press, 1995), pp. 319–334.

23. Grant Gillett, "Is There Anything Wrong with Hitler These Days?" *Medical Humanities Review* 11:2(Fall 1997):14.

24. Gillett, "Is There Anything Wrong with Hitler These Days?" p. 13.

25. The best essay that I have read on this subject, and one which I have drawn on here, is Stuart Hampshire's superb "Morality and Conflict," in *Morality and Conflict* (London: Basil Blackwell, 1983).

Index

enhancement technologies 28–33;
and narrative, 136–140; and
pathology, 25–48; Balinese,
156–157; personal, 97–99,
133–136; sexual, 34–41
Imperato-McGinley, Julliane, 34
informed consent, 92
Institutional Review Boards, 12, 17, 92
integrity, xxviii, 18
intentional stance, 80–81
interpretation, xxvi–xxvii, 57–59, 72,
83, 123
intersexuality, 34–41
irony, xxxiv–xxxvi

Jehovah's Witness, 136
Jordan, King, 42

Kolakowski, Leszek, 141
Kramer, Peter: *Listening to Prozac*, 53,
29–39

Lane, Harlan, 43
Lantos, John, 4–6
Last Gentleman, 51–52
Lears, Jackson, 60
lek, 156–157
life-sustaining treatment, 133–136,
143–144, 158
Listening to Prozac, 53, 29–39
Little, Maggie, 28
Lord Jim, 115
Love in the Ruins, 54–56, 70, 73

MacIntyre, Alasdair, 6–8, 13, 22, 25;
After Virtue, 131–133, 139, 153–155
Martha's Vineyard, 47–48
McElwee, Ross: *Time Indefinite*,
121–122
meaning of life, xxxi–xxxvi; and
community, xxxiii; and consumer
culture, 59–62; and final justification, 136–140; and forms of life,

164; and narrative, 131–140; and
normal nihilism, 57–62; and psychiatry, 49–56; and solidarity, xxxiii
Medicaid, 2, 21
medical practice, 1–11; and postmodernism, 19–23; and technology,
63; ends of, 10–11, 22; specializa-
tion of, 5–6
Medical University of South Carolina,
1–2
memoir, xv–xvi
metaphysics, xxxiv–xxxvi
Moore, G.E., xxv
moral concepts, 155–164
moral disagreement, 153–156
Mother Night, 31–32

nadle, 35–36
narrative, 30, 122, 146–147; and
bioethics cases, 124–126; and identity, 139–140; and meaning of life,
131–140; and memory, 138; and
morality, 124–127, 133–136, 152
Navaho, 35–36, 40
Nelson, James Lindemann, 133–136
Nietzsche, Friedrich, 57
nihilism, 20, 57–62
Nussbaum, Martha, 126–127, 129

organ transplantation, 103–120, 158
organ sales, 116–119

Padden, Tom, 42
Pavona, Nick, 1
Percy, Walker: 62, 67, 68; *Love in the
Ruins*, 54–56, 66–68, 70, 72–73;
The Last Gentleman, 51–53
persistent vegetative state, 12, 157
personality disorder, 75–77, 82–86, 89
personhood, 158–161
placebo, 92, 102
Plain Sense of Things, 57–62
practical philosophy, xxi